BRITISH ELECT

AND

PARTIES YEARBOOK 1995

BRITISH ELECTIONS AND PARTIES YEARBOOK 1995

EDITED BY

Colin Rallings
David M. Farrell
David Denver
David Broughton

FRANK CASS
LONDON

First published in 1996 in Great Britain by
FRANK CASS & CO. LTD
Newbury House, 900 Eastern Avenue
London IG2 7HH

and in the United States by
FRANK CASS
c/o ISBS, 5804 N.E. Hassalo Street, Portland, Oregon 97213-3644

Printed in Great Britain by
Bookcraft (Bath) Ltd, Midsomer Norton, Avon

CONTENTS

PREFACE

This is the fifth volume of the British Elections and Parties Yearbook, the annual publication of the Elections, Public Opinion and Parties specialist group (EPOP) of the Political Studies Association.

Like its predecessors, this volume contains both original research articles and a comprehensive selection of reference material of interest to the group's members and others involved in the analysis of elections and political parties.

As this is the first edition of the Yearbook to go to press since the 1994 European Parliament elections, the analysis of that contest forms a central theme of half of the research articles included. We also include a comprehensive listing of the results of the elections for each constituency – a service which we are sure will be particularly welcomed given the regrettable demise of F.W.S. Craig's *Europe Votes* series.

The editors thank the authors for their patience and forbearance, and Cathy Jennings of Frank Cass Ltd. for her work in ensuring a smooth path to publication.

Further details about membership of EPOP and its other activities may be obtained from any of the editors.

Colin Rallings   David M. Farrell   David Denver   David Broughton

August 1995

NOTES ON CONTRIBUTORS

Simon Atkinson is a Senior Research Executive in MORI's political research unit. He joined MORI in 1990 and worked on the political team in the 1992 General Election. He and Simon Braunholtz were responsible for MORI's 1994 London Exit Poll.

David Baker is Senior Lecturer in British Politics, Nottingham Trent University. His main publications are on British Conservatism and fascism. He is co-director of the Members of Parliament Project.

Lynn Bennie is Lecturer in Politics at the University of Paisley. She is co-author of a number of academic articles on environmental activism and British political parties. She is currently completing a study of the Scottish Green Party and beginning a study of local protest activity against road building. She is co-author of two books to be published next year: with Wolfgang Rüdig and John Curtice on the Liberal Democrats and with Jack Brand and James Mitchell on the Scottish electorate in 1992.

Shaun Bowler is Associate Professor in Political Science at University of California, Riverside. He has published widely in the fields of rational choice, political parties, electoral behaviour and legislatures. He is co-editor (with David Farrell) of *Electoral Strategies and Political Marketing*.

Simon Braunholtz is a Director of MORI's Social Research Institute, having joined MORI in 1985. He has been involved in MORI's polling work in the last two general elections, as well as in regular polling for clients such as *The Times* and *The Sunday Times*.

David Broughton is Lecturer in Politics in the School of European Studies at the University of Wales. He is the author of *Public Opinion Polling and Politics in Britain* and of numerous articles on European politics and political systems.

Scott Clarke is a lecturer in Politics at London Guildhall University. He is currently completing a Ph.D at the University of Strathclyde on the European policies of the British and German Liberal Parties.

John Curtice is Senior Lecturer in Politics at Strathclyde University and Deputy Director of the ESRC Centre for Research into Elections and Social

Trends (CREST). He was a member of the MRS Working Party into the performance of the polls in the 1992 election but here is writing in a personal capacity.

David Denver is Senior Lecturer in Politics at Lancaster University. He is the author of *Elections and Voting Behaviour in Britain*, co-editor of the *Scottish Local Elections Results* series, and co-convenor of the PSA Elections, Public Opinion and Parties Group.

Cees van der Eijk is Professor of Political Science at the University of Amsterdam. He is past president of the Dutch Political Science Association and past Director of the Dutch National Election Studies. He is the author or co-author of various books in Dutch about political methodology and Dutch politics, and of *Political Change in the Netherlands* and *Choosing Europe? The European Electorate and National Politics in the Face of Union.*

Geoffrey Evans is a Fellow in the Centre for European Studies, Nuffield College, Oxford. He is a co-author of *Understanding Political Change* and has written numerous articles on social structure, political attitudes, and behaviour. Since 1992 he has been engaged in survey studies of political behaviour in Eastern Europe.

David M. Farrell is Jean Monnet lecturer in European politics at the University of Manchester. He is the co-editor of the journals *Party Politics* and *Representation*. His most recent book, *Comparing Electoral Systems* (Prentice Hall), will be published in 1996.

Imogen Fountain was Research Officer of the Members of Parliament Project at the University of Sheffield. Her research and publications are on the social composition of Conservative parliamentarians, and their attitudes to European integration.

Mark N. Franklin has been Professor of Political Science at the University of Houston since 1989, and Visiting Professor of Government at the University of Strathclyde where he taught from 1979 to 1989. He is a member of the Executive Committee of the British Politics Group of the American Political Science Association and Convenor of the European Union Politics Group of the same association. He is the author of *The Decline of Class Voting in Britain* and co-author of *Electoral Change: Responses to Evolving Social and Attitudinal Structures in Western Countries* and *Choosing Europe? The European Electorate and National Politics in the Face of Union.*

Andrew Gamble is Professor of Politics, University of Sheffield. He has published widely on political economy and British Conservatism. His published books include *The Conservative Nation*, *The Free Economy and the Strong State: The Politics of Thatcherism*, and *Britain in Decline*. He is co-director of the Members of Parliament Project.

Anthony Heath is a Fellow of Nuffield College and a co-director of the ESRC's Centre for Research into Elections and Social Trends (CREST). He was co-director of the 1983, 1987 and 1992 British Election Studies and is a co-author of *How Britain Votes*, *Understanding Political Change*, and *Labour's Last Chance*.

Steve Ludlam is Lecturer in Politics, University of Sheffield. His recent publications are on Conservatism, European integration, and the last Labour government, and include *Contemporary British Conservatism* (co-editor). He is co-director of the Members of Parliament Project.

James Mitchell is Director of the Territorial Politics Research Centre, University of Strathclyde. He is author of *Conservatives and the Union* and *Strategies for Self-Government* and co-directed the 1992 Scottish Election Study. With Jack Brand and Lynn Bennie, he is co-author of *How Scotland Votes: Scottish Parties and Elections* to be published in 1996.

Pippa Norris teaches at the Kennedy School of Government, Harvard University and is Associate Director (Research) of the Joan Shorenstein Center on the Press, Politics and Public Policy. She is author of *British By-elections: The Volatile Electorate* (Oxford University Press, 1990); *Politics and Sexual Equality: The Comparative Position of Women in Western Democracies* (Harvester Wheatsheaf, 1987); co-author of *Political Representation: Gender, Class and Race in the British Parliament* (Cambridge University Press, 1995); and co-editor of *Women and Politics: Different Voices, Different Lives* (Harper Collins, 1994); *Gender and Party Politics* (Sage, 1993); and the *British Elections and Parties Yearbook* (1991–93). She edits the *Harvard International Journal of Press/Politics*. She is currently developing books on *Comparative Political Recruitment* (Cambridge University Press), *Women, Politics and the Media* (funded by the Ford Foundation), and *British Voting Behaviour Since 1945* (Blackwells).

Erik Oppenhuis is a Ph.D. Candidate at the University of Amsterdam who is in the final stages of completing a dissertation on the subject of European elections. He was a Research Officer in charge of data management and analysis for the European Election Studies of 1989 and 1994.

Clive Payne is the Director of the Computing and Research Support Unit, Social Studies Faculty, University of Oxford and a Fellow of Nuffield College. He has written widely on both the methodology and substantive application of social science statistics.

Colin Rallings is Reader in Politics and co-Director of the Local Government Chronicle Elections Centre at the University of Plymouth. He is co-author of *The Media Guide to the New Parliamentary Constituencies* and writes widely on local elections and politics.

Dominic Wring is a doctoral student at Trinity Hall, Cambridge where he is researching the impact of marketing on electoral politics in Britain. He has taught politics at Anglia and Cambridge universities.

ABSTRACTS OF ARTICLES

Simon Braunholtz and Simon Atkinson

What Can We Learn from June 9? Voters in the 1994 European Parliament Elections

This article is based on the results of the London Exit Poll carried out on 9 June 1994 across London by MORI on behalf of the Electoral Reform Society. It addresses two questions. First, what are the characteristics of the one in three registered electors who actually voted? And second, what can we learn about the attitudes of those who did vote? The analysis indicates that the profile of voters in this election was older, more middle class and more pro-Europe than the population generally. The election is viewed as being primarily about the performance of the British Government. Labour leads across the main voter sub-groups, with many 1992 Conservatives having stayed at home. The vast majority of Labour's 1992 voters have remained loyal to the party, while many Conservatives and Liberal Democrats have changed allegiance. The Conservatives are viewed as a 'right-wing' party; even those remaining with the party perceive its political stance to be more right-wing than their own. Former (1992) Conservatives who switched their vote to Labour or the Liberal Democrats generally perceive the Tories to be far to their right.

Shaun Bowler and David M. Farrell

Voter Strategies under Preferential Electoral Systems: A Single Transferable Vote Mock Ballot Survey of London Voters

To properly explore the richness of the single transferable vote (STV) electoral system we need access to individual level data produced by mock ballot surveys. Very few such data sources are available. This article uses a mock ballot poll of London voters at the 1994 European parliament elections to examine (1) the issue of party attachment under STV, and ballot paper effects, across all voters in the sample; (2) asymmetry in transfer patterns, comparing voters for each of the parties; (3) different transfer trends, between those who plump for candidates in the order on the ballot and those who spread their preferences, within each party slate. The overall conclusion is that electoral and party systems combine to provide significant micro-level incentives for voters to respond to the ballot.

Mark N. Franklin, Cees van der Eijk and Erik Oppenhuis

The Motivational basis of Participation in European Elections, 1979–1994: The Case of Britain

Does British turnout in European elections reflect anything more than features of the British electoral system and other contextual factors which would lead any country in the same situation to have low turnout? The question is complicated by the fact that British turnout, though always low, has shown noticeable variations. The investigation proceeds by coding institutional and other contextual factors governing turnout in thirteen political systems that took part in European elections from 1979 to 1994, and using these factors as independent variables in analyses of turnout differentials. The variables include measures of the importance of each election and of the receptiveness of the electorates to group appeals – factors that can vary from election to election. The analysis succeeds in explaining by far the greater part of the differences in turnout from country to country and election to election, yielding expectations close to those observed in fact. British turnout is lower than expected, but not by much, and variations from election to election are explicable in terms of different political contexts. Britain's performance in comparative perspective emphasizes the importance of motivational factors in getting out the vote.

David Baker, Imogen Fountain, Andrew Gamble, Steve Ludlam

The Blue Map of Europe: Conservative Parliamentarians and European Integration

This article uses the results of the authors' 1994 ESRC survey of Conservative MPs, MEPs and candidates in the European Parliament election to measure the extent of Conservative divisions over European integration in relation to a range of policy issues. It discusses whether the party's European parliamentarians are becoming more Euro-sceptical, whether Thatcher's cohorts of new MPs are more sceptical than their predecessors, and how sceptical John Major's backbenchers really are. The problem of party management is demonstrated by the size of minorities on both wings of the European debate, and the centrality and divisiveness of the issue of national sovereignty is illustrated.

Scott D. Clarke

An Analysis of Britain's Party Manifestos for Europe, 1979–94

This article examines the nature and style of the European election manifestos of Britain's three major parties between 1979 and 1994. More specifically, content analysis is applied to the text of these twelve manifestos, in order to examine to what extent more rigorous techniques support the accounts of political commentators on trends in party positions and ideologies towards

Europe since the first direct elections to the European Parliament in 1979. In analysing the text of Britain's Euro election manifestos the article devotes particular attention to the thematic composition of each manifesto as well as to the balance between European and domestic oriented policy statements. The article is particularly concerned with the changing nature of the parties' European election manifestos since 1979 as well as with the growing convergence of European and domestic policy spheres as expressed within them.

James Mitchell and Lynn G. Bennie

Thatcherism and the Scottish Question

In her memoirs Margaret Thatcher acknowledged that the Conservatives under her leadership had problems in Scotland and that the Scots were unreceptive to Thatcherism. Drawing on the literature on Thatcherism and the Scottish Question, it is argued that it is important to distinguish between the different meanings of Thatcherism. It is wrong to conclude that it was Mrs Thatcher herself who was unpopular, as the party proved deeply unpopular even after it chose John Major who was fairly popular amongst Scottish voters. An interpretation of Thatcherism as a brand of British nationalism partly explains the party's misfortunes, and the perception that the Tories deliberately embarked on a 'two nation' strategy was also significant in explaining its weakness. Borrowing from Jessop's work, it is argued that an alternative 'chain of equivalencies' backing self-government in response to Thatcherism has emerged. A relationship between anti-Conservative attitudes, feelings of Scottishness, support for state intervention and demands for constitutional change is discussed.

Dominic Wring

From Mass Propaganda to Political Marketing: The Transformation of Labour Party Election Campaigning

In order to trace the historical transformation of electioneering in Britain it is useful to draw on an evolutionary model popular in marketing. Three different periods of campaigning can be identified, each comparable with what are known as the product, sales and market orientations in the development of a commercial strategy. With reference to electoral politics, the respective phases can be labelled as the propaganda, media and political marketing approaches to electioneering. Using this framework it is possible to understand the important if previously largely unrecognized part that basic marketing concepts have played throughout the campaigning life of the Labour Party in Britain. Contrary to popular perceptions, advertising and image consciousness have had a place in party strategists' considerations ever since the granting of near universal suffrage in 1918 ushered in an era of mass electoral propaganda. The realization of popular television in the 1950s exacerbated the need for image management and soon after Labour, under Harold Wilson, openly embraced media campaigning and the advice of professional publicists. With the embrace of the final stage in political marketing development during the Kinnock leadership it is possible to offer an understanding of the depth and scale of change that has taken place in Labour Party organization since the 1983 defeat.

Pippa Norris

Political Communications in British Election Campaigns: Reconsidering Media Effects

Like Sherlock Holmes' dog which did not bark, in Britain work on media effects has been remarkable mainly by its absence. This neglect needs to be overcome through theoretical and methodological innovations. To argue this case, the first section of this article sets out the theoretical framework and sketches the major literature on the impact of the media on British voting behaviour. The next section explores evidence from the 1992 British Election Study. Media influence is conceptualized as a sequential process from message through successive steps (information, agenda setting, framing, persuasion) to an attitudinal or behavioural response. The conclusion suggests we need to develop a more imaginative multi-method research design to unravel problems of reciprocal causality in political communications.

John Curtice

What Future for the Opinion Polls? The Lessons of the MRS Inquiry

The 1992 general election was a disaster for the opinion polls. Four polls published on polling day on average put Labour one point ahead of the Conservatives; in the event the Conservatives were seven and a half points ahead of Labour. Despite some important limitations in the evidence available to it, the Market Research Society's inquiry into what went wrong identified three main causes – a last minute change of opinion, inaccurate and inadequate quota controls and a greater propensity among Conservative voters to refuse to say how they would vote. Other possible causes, such as lying, the impact of the poll tax on electoral registration, or the votes cast by voters living abroad were of little or no importance. Its conclusions have already led the polling companies to make some changes to their application of the quota sampling methodology, but whether these will be sufficient is far from certain. The reliance on quota sampling in Britain is driven by the media's assumption that the best poll is the most recent one, but the experience of 1992 suggests that this and other media expectations of opinion polls require re-examination.

Geoffrey Evans, Anthony Heath and Clive Payne
Class and Party Revisited: A New Model for Estimating Changes in Levels of Class Voting

The supposed decline in the relationship between class and party in Britain has been the subject of heated debate over the last decade. Conclusions as to whether there has been a pronounced and gradual decline in the strength of association between class position and vote have tended to depend on the characteristics of the measures used to estimate the strength of the relationship and its change over time. This article extends this debate by articulating the limitations of techniques of trend estimation used in previous work on class voting. It then presents models that are more appropriate for testing whether there has been any convergence in voting behaviour between classes. Using data from all nine elections since 1964, the analysis confirms and strengthens previous arguments concerning the continued significance of the class basis of partisanship.

What Can We Learn From June 9?
Voters in the 1994 European Parliament Elections

Simon Braunholtz and Simon Atkinson

Introduction

On 9 June 1994, MORI conducted a large-scale exit poll of voters across London on behalf of the Electoral Reform Society. Interviews were conducted with a total of 3,893 voters outside 75 polling stations in the London region (full details of the methodology used are to be found at the end of this article). The main objective of the research was to undertake a full-scale field trial of the Single Transferable Vote system, by interviewing a large sample of voters as they left polling stations across the capital. This involved face-to-face interviewing and administering a self-completion STV ballot paper. The survey included a question on how respondents had just voted; and the actual result was within one percentage point of the share of the vote for each of the main parties – see Table 1.

TABLE 1
ACTUAL AND EXIT POLL SHARES OF THE VOTE, 9TH JUNE 1994

	Share of Vote %	Exit Poll %	Difference ±
Conservative	30	29	+1
Labour	50	51	-1
Liberal Democrat	12	13	-1
Green	4	4	0
Other	4	3	+1

We therefore have a data set that is both reliable and – given the size of the sample – robust, and this enables us to widen our analysis to other issues arising from the election. What are the characteristics of the people who actually voted? And, what can we learn about the motivations of voters? Was it merely a mid-term protest vote, or are there underlying currents that may have more serious implications for the Conservatives?[1]

Voting and Turnout

The 1994 European elections are widely seen as a triumph for the Labour Party. The party secured 44 per cent of the popular vote, winning 58 of the 81 British Euro-seats. The Conservatives avoided the meltdown predicted by some observers, but their 27.9 per cent share of the vote still represented the worst performance by a major party in a national election since 1918.

Labour took particular encouragement from a healthy increase in its share of the popular vote in southern and eastern England, taking seats in counties such as Hertfordshire, Essex, Kent and Norfolk. Reflecting on the party's success in the immediate aftermath of the election, Peter Kellner examined the electoral prospects of Tory ministers John MacGregor, Tony Newton, Michael Portillo and Gillian Shepherd, all of whom have majorities of 15,000 or more at Westminster. 'On the basis of local shifts in votes last Thursday, Labour would have captured all of these seats', he wrote.[2]

Our survey focused on London, and here too the results were encouraging for Labour, as indeed they had been at the local elections a month earlier. Labour secured half the votes cast, with the Conservatives on 30 per cent and the Liberal Democrats receiving 12 per cent. Two seats – London North West and London South East – were gained by Labour, leaving them in control of nine out of ten Euro-seats in the region. Indeed, Labour can claim to hold all the seats entirely within the boundaries of London – the only remaining Conservative seat is London South and Surrey East, which includes the Epsom & Ewell and Surrey East parliamentary constituencies – among the safest Conservative seats in the country.

Although the survey was conducted only in one region of the country, the voting patterns in London are broadly in line with those in the country as a whole, both in terms of share of the vote and change since the 1992 general election – see Table 2.

TABLE 2
VOTING PATTERNS IN LONDON AND GREAT BRITAIN – 1992 AND 1994 COMPARED

| | GB | | London | |
	1994 share	% Change 1992–94	1994 share	% Change 1992–94
Conservative	28	(-15)	30	(-15)
Labour	44	(+9)	50	(+13)
Liberal Democrat	17	(-2)	12	(-5)
Other	11	(+8)	8	(+7)

Of course, we do need to bear in mind the particular circumstances of London, in the context of this particular election. For example, the Liberal Democrats might expect to do relatively poorly in this region (it contains none of their target seats). That said, it seems reasonable to assume that many of the patterns observed in London in this election would also apply in the rest of the country. The sample interviewed in the Exit Poll provides us with the opportunity to look in more detail at the nature of Labour's victory. As Table 3 illustrates, Labour registers a substantial lead across almost all the main voter sub-groups. Even the Euro-sceptic voters who wish to leave the European Union were more likely to cast their vote for Labour than the Conservatives.

TABLE 3
PATTERNS OF VOTING BY SOCIO-ECONOMIC AND ATTITUDINAL CHARACTERISTICS

	Conservative	Labour	Lib Dem	Labour lead
Total %	29	51	13	+22
Age %				
18–34	20	58	13	+38
35–54	25	54	14	+29
55–64	33	47	15	+14
65+	42	43	11	+1
Social Class %				
AB	35	42	17	+7
C1	32	47	13	+15
C2	24	59	11	+35
DE	19	65	10	+46
Age left Full-time Education %				
Under 20	32	50	12	+18
20+	22	54	16	+32
Election about %				
Europe	42	41	11	-1
Government	25	54	14	+29
European Union %				
Continue	28	53	14	+25
Withdraw	33	42	11	+9

The European Parliament election is the only national election that reveals the voters' mood between general elections. However, we do need to bear in mind the fact that this is an election where participation was a minority pastime. Across Britain as a whole, 35.8 per cent of those registered actually voted, while in London the figure was 32.7 per cent. It is therefore important to look at the characteristics of the voters before drawing any conclusions about the implications of the result on 9 June.

Demographic Profile of Voters

The demographic and attitudinal variables collected in the Exit Poll provide an opportunity to look at the composition of the voters in some detail. Table 4 gives a breakdown of who voted in the election in London, compared with the profile of the Greater London population, according to the 1991 Census.

TABLE 4
EURO-ELECTION VOTERS AND THE GREATER LONDON POPULATION COMPARED

	Euro-election voters %	Gtr London population* %
Gender		
Men	50	48
Women	50	52
Age		
18–24	6	14
25–34	19	24
35–54	37	31
55+	38	31
Social Class		
AB	30	21
C1	32	31
C2	14	22
DE	24	26
Still in full-time education		
	3	n/a

* Greater London population profile includes Tandridge and Epsom & Ewell, which form part of the London South and Surrey East Euro-seat.

It is well documented that younger people are less likely both to register and to vote in elections,[3] and this pattern is clearly illustrated here. Some 14 per cent of the adult population of London is aged under 25, yet only six per cent of London's voters were under 25. On the other hand, people aged over 55 are over-represented; they comprise 31 per cent of the population, but 38 per cent of voters in the election. In addition to being older than the population at large, Table 4 shows our voters to be more middle class than the public generally (62 per cent are in social class ABC1 which compares with 52 per cent of adults in the London Euro-seat region). Looked at another way, seven in ten (73 per cent) of the adult population of London did not vote – either because they were not registered, or (in the majority of cases) they were registered but did not cast their vote. The election clearly left many voters unmoved and appears to have passed younger people by altogether; just one in nine Londoners aged under 25 voted – see Table 5.

TABLE 5
VOTING AND NON-VOTING BY AGE GROUP IN LONDON

	Population 18+ in London* (,000s)	Number of voters (est) (,000s)	Proportion voting (%)	Proportion not voting (%)
Total	5,337	1,433	27	73
Age				
18–24	757	86	11	89
25–34	1,280	272	21	79
35–54	1,669	530	32	68
55+	1,631	545	33	67

* Greater London population profile includes Tandridge and Epsom & Ewell, which form part of the London South and Surrey East Euro-seat

A picture thus emerges of a voting public whose demographic characteristics and background do differ markedly from those of the population as a whole. In an election where most of the electors stayed at home, this has significant implications. The few who do vote exercise disproportionate power in terms of how the parties fare.

Political Profile of Voters

Because we gathered information in the Exit Poll on respondent voting behaviour in the 1992 general election, we can also examine the characteristics of the voters by comparing their reported vote in the 1992 general election with the actual voting across London at that election – see Table 6.

TABLE 6
1992 GENERAL ELECTION RECALL VOTE OF 1994 SAMPLE

	1992 vote %	1992 recall %	Diff ±
Conservative	45	37	–8
Labour	37	45	+8
Liberal Democrat	15	16	+1

Voters' recollections of how they voted two years previously may not be totally accurate of course, and this 'spiral of silence' issue has been increasingly discussed by pollsters over the last few years.[4] However the eight point disparity between reported and actual Conservative vote is considerably higher than that recorded by MORI in the months leading up to the election (where an average three point discrepancy was observed). These figures therefore suggest that some 1992 Conservatives did indeed stay at home on 9 June, as some commentators (particularly at Conservative Central Office) suggested at the time. However, as we show later, many of those who voted Conservative in 1992 and turned out again to vote in 1994 did change their allegiance.

Election Issues

Arguably, the Conservatives tried harder than the other parties to focus the election campaign on European issues. This strategy seems to have failed. The Exit Poll reveals that seven in ten voters considered the campaign to have been about the record of the British government, while one in five (21 per cent) thought it was mainly about policies on Europe. Conservatives are most likely to see the campaign as primarily about Europe (30 per cent of Tory voters, rising to 36 per cent of those who say they identify strongly with their party).

But if the voters do not perceive the election to have been primarily about policies on Europe, they do display a commitment to the European Union. Almost three in four (72 per cent) want to see Britain remain in the European Union, four times as many as want to leave (19 per cent). These sentiments display a greater degree of Euro-enthusiasm than the public generally. When MORI previously asked a similar question in London (in October 1993), only half said they would like to see Britain continue in the EU. This commitment to a future within Europe is clear among voters of all three main parties. However, even within this Europhile voting population, there are some significant variations in outlook, with pro-Europe views most evident among younger people, graduates and ABC1s.

Changes in Party Support

Having established that London's voters in the European election differed in important respects from the population of the region as a whole, we can move on to look at the political attitudes and perceptions of voters in the election in a little more detail. In particular, what was it that motivated people to vote the way they did? By asking people to indicate how they had voted in the 1992 general election, and how they had just voted in the European election, we were able to assess the shift in voting behaviour at the *individual* level over the period. Of course one does need to be cautious in interpreting the findings because people's memories may not be entirely accurate. Any shift in their voting behaviour between the elections might also be due as much to the fact that they were voting in a different kind of election as to some shift in their essential political allegiance. For example, some may have voted tactically in the general election, but for their preferred party in the European election.

At its most simple, we can look to see what shift in voting behaviour people reported to us – see Table 7. Three-quarters of the Conservative vote remained loyal, compared with nine-tenths of the Labour vote, and just half of the Liberal Democrat vote. Each party benefited to some extent from voters deserting the party they supported in 1992. Labour gained 11 per cent of the Conservatives' 1992 vote, while the Liberal Democrats picked up 9 per cent. The haemorrhaging of Liberal Democrat support meanwhile benefited Labour over the Conservatives by around 3:1. On the other hand, Labour's 1992 vote in London remained generally loyal in 1994; only 3 per cent switched to the Liberal Democrats and 1 per cent switched to the Conservatives. To what extent does this movement indicate a decisive shift away from their previous party, and to what extent were there tactical, or Euro-specific motivations?

TABLE 7

TRANSITION OF VOTES, 1992 GENERAL ELECTION AND 1994 EUROPEAN ELECTION

1992 General Election vote

1994 Euro vote	Con %	Lab %	Lib Dem %
Conservative	74	1	11
Labour	11	92	30
Liberal Democrat	9	3	49
Other	6	4	10

We asked people whether they had cast their vote for the party that most represented their views, or for a different party because their preferred party stood no chance of winning locally. Just 7 per cent confessed (or at least comprehended) that they had voted tactically by this definition. Further analysis of the perspectives of these tactical voters was undertaken – using the Michigan party identification question followed by strength of identification with their party – and this reveals some interesting clues to people's motivations. First of all, and perhaps unsurprisingly, we find that those who say they identify with the Liberal Democrats are far more likely to say they voted tactically at the election than are those who identify with the other main parties. What is intriguing is that while *weakening* identification with the Conservatives and Labour tends to be accompanied by an *increasing* propensity to vote tactically, it is the strongest supporters of the Liberal Democrats who seem to be most willing to vote for another party if they feel their candidate stands no chance of winning.

What impact did this actually have on the way people voted in the European election? We can examine this by looking to see what proportions of each party's 'very strong', 'fairly strong' and 'not very strong' supporters actually voted for 'their' party in the election – see Table 8.

TABLE 8
VOTING AND PARTY IDENTIFICATION AT THE 1994 EUROPEAN ELECTION

	Strength of party identification		
1994 Euro vote	**Very** %	**Fairly** %	**Not very** %
Conservative	91	88	69
Labour	97	93	90
Liberal Democrat	73	63	54

Thus 91 per cent of the people who said they identified 'very strongly' with the Conservative Party actually voted for them, 88 per cent of those who said they identified 'fairly strongly' did so and just 69 per cent of those whose identification with the party was 'not very strong' went ahead and voted for the Conservatives. A similar pattern is evident for the Liberal Democrats, albeit at a lower level. Meanwhile, even among the people who said that their identification with the Labour Party was 'not very strong', as many as 90 per cent voted Labour.

Another way of examining the data is to look at the groups of people who indicated to us that they had actually switched their support between 1992 and 1994 (and those who had remained loyal) and see to what extent they say they voted tactically – see Table 9.

TABLE 9
LOYALTY, SWITCHING AND TACTICAL VOTING IN 1994

1992–1994 switch	Reported voting 'tactically' %
Con–Con	2
Con–Lab	12
Con–Lib Dem	16
Lab–Lab	5
Lab–Con	21
Lab–Lib Dem	23
Lib Dem–Lib Dem	9
Lib Dem–Con	15
Lib Dem–Lab	20

We would expect to find a low proportion of those who remained loyal to their 1992 general election party saying that their European election vote was tactical, and that indeed is what we find. Just 2 per cent of loyal Conservatives say that their vote in the European election was tactical, 5 per cent of loyal Labour voters, and 9 per cent of loyal Liberal Democrats. We have to wonder whether for these people a vote is always a tactical vote because of their party political sympathies and the nature of the constituency in which they live.

But looking beyond these 'loyalists' to those who confess to having switched their vote, it could be argued that the greater the proportion of the switching voters in each category, the greater the indication that their shift in voting behaviour was a temporary feature, likely to be reversed in future elections. If this is the case, then the Conservative Party's losses would appear to be the more serious (just 12 per cent of those who switched from Conservative to Labour say that their decision was a tactical one, and 16 per cent of the Conservatives who switched to the Liberal Democrats say the same). Meanwhile, as many as 21 per cent of those who switched from Labour to the Conservatives say that it was for tactical reasons, and 23 per cent of those who deserted Labour for the Liberal Democrats say the same.

Although one could argue about the extent to which the conventional left/right scale of political positioning is still appropriate in Britain, or even the degree to which some sections of the electorate ever actually understood how the labels were applied, it is interesting to examine the responses that people give when asked to place themselves on a left–right political scale, and then where they place each of the main parties. We have assigned values to each point on the scale – Left wing (+2), Somewhat to the left (+1), Middle of the road (0), Somewhat to the right (-1), Right wing (-2). By analysing the mean scores (x100) of the people who identify themselves with each of the three main parties according to whether they do so very strongly, fairly strongly or not very strongly, we produce the following fascinating picture – see Table 10.

TABLE 10
PARTY IDENTIFICATION AND THE ASSESSMENT OF PARTY/PERSONAL IDEOLOGY

	Left/right Party	assessment Self	Difference
Conservative			
Very strong	-93	-91	**-2**
Fairly strong	-84	-58	**-26**
Not very strong	-96	-39	**-57**
Liberal Democrat			
Very strong	+13	+26	**-13**
Fairly strong	+12	+20	**-8**
Not very strong	+10	+4	**+6**
Labour			
Very strong	+50	+72	**-22**
Fairly strong	+62	+59	**+3**
Not very strong	+55	+38	**+17**

Voters' self-assessments on the left–right scale provide an indication that strength of identification is clearly linked to political attitudes. Table 10 also indicates the party identifiers' perceptions of where their party stands on the left–right scale. For all three parties, there is relatively little difference between the perceptions of very, fairly and not very strong identifiers when it comes to evaluating the position of their party on a left–right scale. However, the column of figures marked 'difference' indicates the size of the disparity between the self-assessment of each party's 'identifiers', and their perception of their party. A highly positive figure means that the group assesses the party they identify with as much more 'left wing' than they consider themselves, and a highly negative figure represents an assessment that the party they identify with is much more 'right wing'.

This 'difference' column provides us with some interesting results. Strong Conservatives are much 'in tune' with their party, contrasting with weak Conservatives, who consider the party to be '57 points' more right wing than they are. In other words, groups whose identification with the Conservative Party is weaker are more likely to think that the party is more right wing than they are. As Table 10 indicates, Labour and Liberal Democrat identifiers tend to be more in line with their party on the left–right scale. However, this does vary somewhat according to strength of identification. Weak Lib Dems consider the party to be more left wing than they are (by 6 points), while strong Lib Dems perceive the party to be more right wing (by 13 points). Weak Labour identifiers perceive the party to be to their left (by 17 points), contrasting with strong supporters of the party, who view the party as on their right (by 22 points).

TABLE 11
PARTY/PERSONAL IDEOLOGY AND VOTE SWITCHING BETWEEN 1992 AND 1994

| | Left/right | assessment | |
	Party	Self	Difference
1992–1994 vote			
Con–Con	-89	-62	**-27**
Con–Lab	-88	-2	**-86**
Con–Lib Dem	-95	-28	**-67**
Lab–Lab	+55	+63	**-8**
Lab–Con	+63	-1	**+64**
Lab–Lib Dem	+77	+60	**+17**
Lib Dem–Lib Dem	+13	+15	**-2**
Lib Dem–Con	+12	-28	**+40**
Lib Dem–Lab	+9	+50	**-41**

What happens when we examine the self- and party-assessments of those who have stayed loyal or switched their vote between 1992 and 1994? In

Table 11 we use the same score allocation for each point on the left–right scale, and compare the assessment given to each party by the people who say they voted for that party in 1992 compared to their self assessment of their own political position. In the case of those who changed their vote, to what extent was this switch driven by a disparity between their own political outlook (based on self-appraisal) and their assessment of the party?

The overwhelming view of those who voted Conservative in 1992 is that it is a right-wing party. Conservative loyalists view it in a very similar way to ex-Conservatives who have now switched to Labour (-89 compared with -88). Former Conservatives switching to the Liberal Democrats, on the other hand, are slightly more likely to view the party as being right wing (-95). When it comes to people who voted Labour in 1992, those who remained loyal in 1994 view the Labour Party as least left wing (+55) and those who switched to the Liberal Democrats consider it is most left wing (+77).

We can then compare these party assessments with each group's self-assessment on the left–right scale. Even the 1992 Tories who remained loyal in 1994 regard the Conservatives as being more right wing than they consider themselves (by 27 points). On the other hand, the differences between the self-appraisal of Labour loyalists and their party (8 points) and Liberal Democrat loyalists and their party (2 points) are relatively slight. As far as the people who deserted the party they voted for in 1992 are concerned, the greatest political mismatch is with Conservatives who switched to the Labour Party (86 points), Conservatives who switched to the Liberal Democrats (67 points) and also Labour voters who switched to the Conservatives (who consider the Labour Party 64 points more to the left than they consider themselves). While Labour's 1992 voters who have switched to the Liberal Democrats consider the Labour Party 17 points more left wing than they are, 1992 Liberal Democrats who have switched the other way consider the Liberal Democrat Party to be 41 points more right wing than they would place themselves.

These findings suggest that the people who switched their votes between 1992 and 1994 were doing so, at least in part, on the basis of perceptions of significant mismatches between their own political stance and those of the parties that they had 'deserted'. It is interesting to note that the self-assessed left/right positioning of Conservatives who switched to Labour (-2), and of Labour voters who switched to the Conservatives (-1) is the same. Furthermore, the same pattern can be seen for Conservatives who switched to the Liberal Democrats (-28) and Liberal Democrats who switched to the Conservatives (-28). It would seem that their change in support is driven by the way these groups of voters perceive their previous party; their own self-assessment is the same, whether they are moving right to left or left to right.

If the size of the disparity between self-assessment and previous party assessment is taken as some kind of indicator of the 'decisiveness' of the switch, then it would appear that a large proportion of the 11 per cent of Conservative voters who switched directly to Labour did so on the basis of a fairly fundamental perception of conflict between their own politics and those of the Conservative Party. In this sense, the London Exit Poll reveals a political rationale behind the performance of the parties on 9 June that goes beyond differential turnout, voter apathy and protest voting.

Conclusions

In this article, we have sought to address two main issues. First the question of whether or not the minority who turned out to vote possess different characteristics from the population as a whole, to which the answer is certainly yes. As we have seen, voters in the election are disproportionately old, middle class and pro-Europe. There is also some evidence that Conservative supporters were more likely to stay at home on election day. All of this provides some encouragement for the Conservative Party.

On the other hand, when we turn to the issue of the attitudes and motivations of voters, including changes in their voting behaviour, the picture is less positive for the Tories. This suggests that the anti-Conservative vote may have been more than simply a protest. There are clear indications that there was a shift in the mood and behaviour of the electorate on 9 June. The Conservatives are seen as a right-wing party – out of tune with the self-assessed viewpoint of most voters, including all but their strongest supporters. The apparent gulf between former Conservatives and the party casts doubts on how easy the Tories will find it to persuade their lost voters to return to them at the 1996–97 general election.

APPENDIX

Polling Stations

The 760 wards in London were taken and ranked by the proportion of Conservative vote in the 1990 local elections. Seventy-three wards were then selected at random, with probability of selection proportional to the size of the electorate. In addition, one ward was sampled in Epsom & Ewell and one in Tandridge, which form part of the London South & Surrey East European constituency. Polling stations were then selected from these wards, with probability of selection proportionate to size. Each polling station was covered from 7am–10pm. Each interviewer was accompanied by a 'counter', who recorded the cumulative number of voters leaving the polling station, and identified the next respondent for interview.

Interviews

At each polling station, respondents were selected at random. Interviewers were provided with a fixed interval at which to approach voters as they left the polling station (for example every eighth). The interval set at each polling station was dependent on the size of its electorate and the estimated turnout. Interviewers were only permitted to interview outside this fixed interval in the event of refusal; where this occurred, interviewers were instructed to approach the next voter to leave the polling station. The characteristics of those 'fixed interval' voters who refused to take part were estimated and entered on an interlocking age/gender grid.

The interview process comprised two elements; a face-to-face questionnaire and a secret ballot paper. The ballot paper asked respondents to indicate how they voted in the election, as well as how they had voted (if at all) in the 1992 general election. In addition, respondents were asked to complete a ballot paper using a single transferable vote (STV) system of voting. For the purpose of this exercise, London was divided into two multi-member constituencies – North and South – comprising six of the current seats to the north and four to the south. The names of the candidates standing in the election were included on the ballot papers. Respondents were asked to place their completed ballot papers in a box, and then asked a number of questions relating to the STV system and the election generally, using a face-to-face method. The serial numbers of each questionnaire and ballot paper were linked, allowing for analysis of voting by demographic and attitudinal factors at the data processing stage.

Analysis

Of the 3893 interviews completed, 2600 were 'fixed interval' interviews, and 1200 were 'replacements'. There were 1894 refusals. At the analysis stage, the total sample was weighted to take into account differences in the fixed interview intervals allocated to polling stations and the total profile of voters (as defined by the profile of fixed interval respondents plus refusals in terms of age within gender).

NOTES

1. A more extensive consideration of the use of preferences in the 'mock' STV election can be found in the article by Bowler and Farrell which follows.
2. Peter Kellner, *The Times*, 14 June 1994.
3. Stephen Smith, *Electoral Registration in London* (London: OPCS, 1993).
4. Report to the Market Research Society, *The Opinion Polls and the 1992 General Election* (London: MRS, 1994).

Voter Strategies Under Preferential Electoral Systems: A Single Transferable Vote Mock Ballot Survey of London Voters

Shaun Bowler and David M. Farrell

Electoral systems have political consequences. The truth of this statement has been demonstrated on countless occasions in the burgeoning literature on electoral systems.[1] For instance, there is a clear relationship between electoral systems and proportionality (though this has not stopped an endless dispute on the hierarchy of disproportional systems and even on the definition and measurement of 'proportionality'). More indirectly there is the relationship between electoral and party systems; most prominent here are Duverger's 'laws' which, while disputed in the detail (and especially on the semantics of what is a 'law'), generally have been accepted in practice.[2] Finally, electoral systems have been shown to have effects on the nature of party competition and on modes of political representation.[3]

For the most part, these discussions are focused either on the macro level of the systemic effects of electoral systems, or on the meso level of their effects on parties and politicians. The mainstream literature has tended to ignore the micro level of the effects of electoral systems on voters. About the only exceptions have been theoretical discussions on the 'psychological' effects of electoral systems,[4] and several studies on electoral systems and tactical voting.[5] The general lack of attention to individual voters is understandable given the non-availability of sufficient individual-level data. For instance, the studies on tactical voting have all relied on the high levels of information which can be garnered at an aggregate level from second ballot, two-vote and preferential electoral systems.

In recent years, there have been several micro level studies which have been able to make use of mock ballot data – that is, data produced from surveys where voters were required to complete ballots as if in a real election. In an Irish survey, where voters completed a mock single transferable vote (STV) ballot paper around the time of a European Parliament election, an analysis revealed important findings on the effects of STV on levels of party attachment, ballot position effects, and the nature of party competition.[6] A more ambitious project, set to coincide with the 1992 British general election, tested a range of different electoral systems on a sample of British voters, providing fascinating information not only on how the results might have varied, but also, among other things, on potential coalitional tendencies among certain categories of voters.[7]

Following in this tradition, this article is based on a special exit poll by Market and Opinion Research International (MORI) of 3,893 London voters during the 1994 European Parliament elections, which was commissioned by the Electoral Reform Society. For the purposes of this experiment, the ten London constituencies were aggregated into two multi-seat STV constituencies, London North with six seats and London South with four seats. The STV ballots (see appendix A) included the names of the Euro candidates for all the parties (apart from Others).[8]

The focus of this paper is on the strategic implications of STV, explored at three levels. We begin with an examination of all voters in the sample, considering the issues of party attachment under STV and of ballot paper effects. The sample is then broken down by party affiliation to explore the patterns of vote transfers and what they reveal about the nature of British party competition (at least in this election). Finally the sample is disaggregated still further as we explore transfer trends within party, analysing the pattern of transfers among the respective slates of party candidates.

STV and Party Identification

The central building block of voting studies research for over a generation has been party identification. Underlying this notion are several presumptions which are relevant to the case of STV. First, party identification is likely to be unique rather than multiple. Thus we should expect voters to mark preferences only for one party rather than several. Second, strongly identifying voters should mark a preference for all of the candidates from that party slate (though this cannot tell us much about the rank ordering of those candidates).[9]

A simple measure of 'party loyalty' is the number of voters who voted for just one party, choosing not to transfer lower preferences to candidates from other parties. In South London more than half of the sample (54 per cent) voted for just one party; in North London (where there were more seats and more candidates) that proportion rose to 61 per cent. Whether the size of the ballot paper had anything to do with these tendencies cannot be explored here.[10] For a more elaborate assessment of party loyalty we need to look at the preference schedule. In previous research on Ireland we examined consistency in pairs of preferences: that is, the extent to which the first preference matches the second preference, the second the third and so on.[11] The data in this London poll reveal a clear pattern of voting in blocks of party candidates (six in North London, four in South London) that dampens just as does the numbers of preferences expressed as we move down the ballot, showing that, as in Ireland, the role of party in structuring the vote occurs predominantly among the higher preferences expressed by voters. In short, therefore, London voters seem to be behaving in ways markedly similar to those of Irish voters. The impact of parties in expressing ideologically consistent choices is felt largely in the first few preferences, but this consistency begins to unravel fairly rapidly as we move down the preference ranking while, at the same time, we see a marked drop-off in the numbers of preferences marked and in the active participation of voters.

TABLE 1
THE IMPACT OF STRENGTH OF PARTY IDENTIFICATION (ID) UPON THE EXPRESSION OF
PREFERENCES

	Conservative			Labour			Liberal Democrat	
Very strong ID	Fairly strong ID	Not very strong ID	Very strong ID	Fairly strong ID	Not very strong ID	Very strong ID	Fairly strong ID	Not very strong ID
LONDON NORTH (N=)								
162	256	109	450	388	126	30	131	77

Average values (expressed as percentages)

Very strong ID	Fairly strong ID	Not very strong ID	Very strong ID	Fairly strong ID	Not very strong ID	Very strong ID	Fairly strong ID	Not very strong ID
Labour total								
0.21	0.20	0.45	3.79	3.71	2.79	0.53	0.84	0.69
Conservative total								
3.90	3.25	2.39	0.06	0.10	0.22	0.27	0.36	0.55
Liberal Democrat total								
0.16	0.41	0.52	0.38	0.53	0.62	3.67	2.56	2.53
Green total								
0.12	0.21	0.33	0.36	0.67	0.52	0.33	0.60	0.84
Party vote								
1.33	1.57	1.78	1.45	1.62	1.71	1.53	2.01	1.92
Total preferences								
4.64	4.27	3.89	4.67	5.07	4.18	4.87	4.50	4.70
Average pairs								
3.27	2.59	1.94	3.06	3.23	2.15	3.33	2.22	2.55

	Conservative			Labour			Liberal Democrat	
Very strong ID	**Fairly strong ID**	**Not very strong ID**	**Very strong ID**	**Fairly strong ID**	**Not very strong ID**	**Very strong ID**	**Fairly strong ID**	**Not very strong ID**
LONDON SOUTH (N=)								
93	207	104	240	243	75	42	121	74
			Average values (expressed as percentages)					
Labour total								
0.06	0.18	0.44	3.27	2.70	2.69	0.74	0.78	0.73
Conservative total								
2.89	2.66	1.63	0.08	0.21	0.31	0.07	0.32	0.80
Liberal Democrat total								
0.31	0.47	0.85	0.36	0.63	0.76	3.21	2.31	2.20
Green total								
0.22	0.30	0.50	0.45	0.52	0.39	0.62	0.68	0.82
Party vote								
1.37	1.65	2.33	1.42	1.77	1.79	1.69	2.06	2.19
Total preferences								
3.55	3.76	3.62	4.22	4.15	4.25	4.74	4.14	4.69
Average pairs								
2.15	2.04	1.13	2.75	2.25	2.37	2.88	1.85	2.20

Note: The sample is all those who expressed a preference
Source: ERS/MORI survey

The effect of party on voting behaviour may vary at different stages in the preferences schedule; it also varies across different types of voters. The principal point at issue here is the effect of varying levels of party attachment on the tendency of voters to vote for more than one party. Table 1 provides pretty conclusive evidence that those voters with weak identification vote for more parties, and vote for fewer candidates from their 'own' party, than do voters with strong identification. Indeed, the staunch partisans simply do not vote for any candidates from other parties. Furthermore, stronger partisans tend to complete more of the ballot than do weaker partisans.

While party clearly shapes the way in which voters approach the ballot, the strict version of party identification (voters who vote for all the candidates of one party only) applies to under one-third of voters from the two constituencies combined. And, while a majority of voters may only express a preference for one party, at least one-third and for South London almost one-half of voters express a preference for two or more parties.[12] This provides a very rough upper boundary for the applicability of even a slightly more relaxed version of party identification, which would allow voters to pass over candidates from 'their' party (but would still disallow voting for multiple identifications on the grounds that the concept is one of 'party' identification in the singular).

A number of interrelated questions follow on from this. For instance, attention should be paid to isolating factors which, in addition to weaker party attachments, help promote cross-party voting. One of the obvious factors we should consider in this regard is the importance of localism, or a personal vote of some kind; another is the question of ballot paper effects, particularly in the form of alphabetical voting. These issues are dealt with in the remainder of this section. An alternative tack, which we follow in the next two sections, is to disaggregate the sample – first, across party, and, second, within party – to try and get a clearer impression of the strategic choices being made by sub-samples of British voters in an STV election. But first we should deal with the evidence of candidate and ballot paper effects.

So far we have been able to demonstrate some evidence of party influence on the vote, specifically at the higher end of the preference schedule and with regard to partisan voters in particular. The fact that there are plenty of other voters who do not follow these trends indicates that other factors are influencing the vote. Prominent among these, and to be expected with STV, is the influence of the candidates themselves.[13] In the Irish context it is usual to examine this under the theme of localism, or the 'friends and neighbours' effect, where the personal vote of the candidate is seen to be influenced by his/her geographic location within the constituency.[14] Therefore if there are candidate effects, and assuming they follow a pattern similar to the Irish case, we should see evidence of voters ranking candidates from their parts of the constituency above others.

There is at least one other possible effect on why voters vote the way they do, and this has nothing to do with candidates. One of the drawbacks of STV and a factor much focused on by critics of the system is the tendency for ballot papers to be longer than under most other electoral systems. This requires more effort of the voters who have to work their way through long lists of names to find their preferred candidate(s). A consequence of this is for voters to take shortcuts, the most usual of these being to vote in order of sequence rather than in order of preference. This phenomenon has attracted some rather colourful names such as 'donkey' or 'bullet' voting, but the graphically most clear title for it is 'alphabetical' voting, where candidates whose surnames start with letters high (or low) in the alphabet tend to benefit from a larger number of early voter preferences.[15] In short, we have two possible expectations. Either we find evidence of the rank ordering of candidates being determined by localist concerns in which case we can talk of candidate effects on voting, or else we find evidence that candidates are elected pretty much in terms of their ranking on the ballot paper in which case we can talk of ballot effects on voting.

TABLE 2
BALLOT POSITION EFFECTS: OLS ESTIMATES

Constant	121
Position on party list	-80 **
	(25)
Position on party list squared	8 **
	(4)
Gender	-7
	(22)
North/South	-0.6
	(21)
Major Party	120 **
	(20)
Position on ballot paper	4 **
	(1.7)
adj R^2	0.56
N=	40

** = significant at .05 level or better (2-tailed)

Source: ERS/MORI survey

The data reveal a distinct tendency for voters to vote for candidates in the order in which they appear on the ballot, and this is particularly the case for candidates from the two larger parties. This tendency is evident from a regression analysis. If we take the number of first preferences received by each candidate and use this as a dependent variable in a simple equation where the number of first preferences received is predicted by: whether or not the candidate was from one of the two major parties (1=Conservative or Labour candidate, 0=not); whether the candidate was a woman (1=woman, 0=man); whether the candidate was from north or south of the Thames (1=North, 0=South); the position on the ballot within the party list; that position squared; and the position on the ballot paper. As can be seen in Table 2, this very basic model does show a significant impact of position on the party list and on the ballot paper. Candidates at the top of the party list generally receive more votes than those below them. Candidates at the bottom of the list, and those at the bottom of the ballot, do, however, also receive a boost.

There is therefore clear evidence of ballot effects, which helps account for a large share of the variation in the number of first preferences received by candidates: a large number of the voters can be said to see candidates as mere substitutes for each other. Having said that, we must note some exceptions: there are cases of deviation from this general pattern in that some candidates low on the party list receive more first preferences than candidates listed above them. At least some of this is due to candidate effects.

We tested for possible 'friends and neighbours' effects by running a series of simple regressions which took, as their dependent variable, the preference ranking of the candidates from each of the three major parties. To assess possible geographic effects, we included a dummy variable for the real (that is, first past the post) Euro-constituency of the voters if that matched the candidate. We also included various demographic controls on age, gender, race, education and class. Out of the 30 equations involved in this analysis, 17 were statistically significant. Of these, 13 supported the hypothesis of candidate effects (based on geographic location), while four rejected the hypothesis. In short, therefore, the 'friends and neighbours' effect worked to the advantage of some candidates, but not to others. The fact that we are dealing with two urban constituencies may have something to do with this weak relationship; after all, the bulk of Irish research on this has tended to focus on rural constituencies where localism is bound to be more prominent. And, of course, there are bound to be other factors relating to candidates which may affect the vote, such as fame or ideological location.

Overall, clearly there is no single vote model which captures the processes at work. A model grounded in party identification theory captures some of the patterns in sensible ways. And when this is supplemented by a concern for the costs of completing a ballot, it helps to explain some of the ways in which voters choose between candidates. Having said that, there is also evidence to suggest that voters find no difficulty in supporting multiple parties, choosing on the basis of candidates rather than parties. One obvious interpretation to advance is that as party identification weakens, other factors such as individual candidacies become relatively more important. Where party identification does not 'work', we can expect to see other factors become more prominent. This suggests that the electorate is comprised of sub-groups of voters; many behaving as Michigan would suggest, many others behaving as though party identification was not meaningful.

Table 3 provides confirmation for the most likely hypotheses at this point. First, those with weaker party identification are more likely to express preferences, transferring their vote to any other party. Second, as policy distance increases (defined as the absolute value between voters' own left/right self-placement and that of the named party) voters become less willing to transfer preferences. Third, the two big parties are less reluctant to transfer to the Liberal Democrats than to each other. This last point, on the nature of inter-party transfers, is explored next.

TABLE 3
WILLINGNESS TO TRANSFER: LOGIT ESTIMATES

	to Labour		to Conservatives		to Liberal Democrats	
	North	South	North	SoutH	North	South
Constant	-4.7	-4.1	-6.3	-5.9	-4.0	5.6
Age	-.10**	-.10+	.02	-.07	-.002	.05
	(.05)	(.06)	(.06)	(.07)	(.04)	(.04)
Gender	-.12	-.16	-.04	-.16	-.001	-.15
	(.17)	(.18)	(.19)	(.21)	(.12)	(.14)
Education	.08	.05	.07	.07	.07*	.10**
	(.05)	(.06)	(.07)	(.07)	(.04)	(.05)
Conservative ID	2.6**	2.6**	–	–	2.0**	3.3**
	(.29)	(.36)			(.30)	(.43)
LibDem ID	3.5**	3.6**	3.9**	4.5**	–	–
	(.28)	(.34)	(.60)	(.73)		
Labour ID	–	–	2.9**	3.8**	2.1**	3.2**
			(.60)	(.73)	(.29)	(.43)
Strength of ID	.59**	.49**	.38**	.60**	.40**	.72**
	(.12)	(.13)	(.14)	(.15)	(.08)	(.10)
Policy distance	-.33**	-.43**	-.14+	-.37**	-.24**	-.22**
	(.09)	(.10)	(.08)	(.10)	(.05)	(.05)
N=	1753	1217	1751	1209	1751	1215
% correct	89	86	93	91	80	77

** = significant at .05 level or better (2-tailed);
* = significant at .10 level or better (2-tailed);
+ = significant at .10 level or better (1-tailed)

Source: ERS/MORI survey

Asymmetry in Inter-Party Preferences

What do voters do when their preferred party's candidates have all been either elected or eliminated from the count? Or, indeed, what of the case of a voter who likes a particular candidate but knows full well that they do not stand a chance of being elected? These questions draw attention to the strategic concerns faced by what are referred to as 'non-exclusive' voters, or voters who are prepared to vote for more than one party.

This relates to the debate about the 'psychology' of voting, for instance where a voter has a sympathy for a party (or candidate) but knows that it (or the candidate) has little chance of winning. Under most electoral systems the crucial concern then becomes one of isolating the conditions in which voters believe their vote might make sufficient difference to warrant giving the party or candidate in question a chance. Under some systems the scenario can take the form of 'split-ticket' voting. Under preferential systems like STV, there is the fact that voters may actually give a first or high preference to their preferred candidate without fearing a wasted vote, because they can also give lower preferences to other candidates who stand more realistic chances of being elected.[16]

All this leads to the expectation that supporters of smaller parties, which by definition tend to stand little chance of having many of their candidates elected, are more likely to vote for more parties than large party voters.[17] There is plenty of evidence to support this expectation from studies of Irish voters over the years. In his seminal research on Irish transfer patterns from the 1920s to the 1970s, Michael Gallagher found clear evidence of variations in the transfer patterns between the three established parties in the system – Fianna Fáil, Fine Gael and Labour – variations which have remained prominent in Irish electoral behaviour to this day.[18]

First, Gallagher noted higher degrees of voter 'loyalty' (or 'solidarity') among the supporters of the largest party, Fianna Fáil, and less among the smaller parties, Fine Gael and especially Labour. Fianna Fáil voters are more likely to vote for all the party's candidates, rather than chopping and changing between candidates of other parties. This has important implications for vote management strategies, because a party needs to maximize the efficiency of its vote. Candidate chances are threatened whenever the party cannot rely on the consistency of the transfers between its candidates.

Gallagher also found that Fianna Fáil supporters tend to be more 'exclusive' than the supporters of the other parties: that is, they are more likely to plump only for Fianna Fáil candidates, not declaring any preferences for other candidates. On the one hand, plumping is actually potentially damaging for the party involved because its supporters are not making maximum use of the possibility to influence the election outcome; the best way to 'use' STV is to declare as many preferences as possible. On the other hand, as Sinnott notes: 'from a party point of view... it is possible to argue that any losses involved in failing to affect the outcome by not transferring beyond the party are more than compensated for by encouraging the party supporters to think exclusively of the party and not to contemplate the possibility of giving even lower order preferences to another party. The presumed effect of this would be to strengthen the voters' loyalty to the party and minimize leakage or defection in future elections'.[19]

Gallagher has examined the transfer patterns in the most recent Irish 1992 election, finding that there was a marked drop in the levels of voter 'loyalty' or 'solidarity' among Fianna Fáil supporters, dropping from 83 per cent in the 1980s to 70 per cent in 1992 –the party's worst result since 1927.[20] This reflects the fact that Fianna Fáil had been going through an unusually difficult period of internal indiscipline and faction fighting. Fine Gael's solidarity figure was even lower at just 65 per cent, its lowest since 1944.

TABLE 4
TRANSFER PATTERNS IN TWO LONDON (MOCK) EURO-CONSTITUENCIES, 1994

	No. of Counts	Con	Transfers to (%) Lab	LD	Green	Other	Non-Trans
IntermediateTransfers from							
Conservatives	7	51.33	7.98	4.97	0.41	0.00	35.31
Labour	4	1.47	66.13	7.03	1.64	0.06	23.67
LibDem	8	12.48	14.70	43.92	1.23	na	27.67
Green*	7	2.95	28.86	17.68	33.29	0.90	16.32
Terminal Transfers from							
Labour	1	7.39	na	9.84	na	na	82.77
LibDem	1	1.40	11.92	na	na	na	86.68
Green	2	4.36	27.07	25.24	na	na	43.33
Others**	3	29.25	7.27	13.23	6.59	2.76	40.91

* In certain cases, Green transfers are based on a smaller number of counts. For the most part, this does not significantly affect the percentage transfers. One exception is Labour transfers to the Greens (based on two counts) where the revised figure is 4.27 per cent (instead of 1.64).

** Others include National Front and UK Independence.

Source: ERS/MORI survey

Table 4 provides indications of how the British trends compare with the Irish ones. The first point to note is generally how much lower the figure of voter 'loyalty' is for all the British parties. The intermediate transfer patterns –

when not all a party's candidates have been elected or eliminated – reveal a significant proportion of 'disloyal' supporters (voters switching preferences to candidates from other parties) among each of the parties. In no case does a party enjoy the sort of 'solidarity' of the Fianna Fáil party, more than 70 per cent. Only (British) Labour, with 66 per cent, comes close to Fine Gael at its low point! In general the larger parties (Conservative and Labour) have higher degrees of voter loyalty than the smaller parties. The most interesting case, in this regard, is the Green party, where only 33 per cent of its supporters were 'loyal'.

The other side of the equation is party 'exclusivity', or the extent to which voters are prepared to vote for candidates from other parties once the first choice party has no more candidates left in the field. The trends are revealed in the terminal transfers. In this election there were no cases of terminal transfers for the Conservatives; however, the non-transferable column suggests that the Conservatives may be the most 'exclusive' of the parties. Labour (83 per cent) and the Liberal Democrat (87 per cent) supporters were clearly highly exclusive. Once again it was the Green supporters who had a greater tendency to switch between the parties. Finally, the trends in inter-party transfers are relatively unsurprising, certainly in the case of the two main parties. The Liberal Democrats tended to split fairly evenly between the two main parties, with a slight bias in favour of Labour; the Greens split fairly evenly between Labour and the Liberal Democrats, again with a slight Labour bias.

'Plumping' and 'Spreading' Intra-Party Vote Transfers

We have seen how the pattern of preferences across parties can reveal something about the psychology of party voters and the potential for certain coalition formations. It is also of interest to explore the pattern of preferences within the different party blocks.[21] Research on the Australian and Irish cases reveals very different patterns in the transfer of voter preferences by party voters. In a system where voters have to contend with a variety of difficulties – regulations on compulsory turnout, an array of different electoral systems depending on the level of election, very large ballot papers, rules requiring them to vote for every candidate on the ballot paper (or face having their vote declared invalid) – it is to be expected that the transfer patterns of the voters will be heavily patterned by the parties. This is exactly what we find in the Australian case which has the added feature of high proportions of foreign born voters requiring party guidance – where, in effect, the transfer patterns are determined by the party elites. This produces a pattern of vote transfers which is somewhat akin to 'program trading' on stock exchanges, where thousands (in Senate races, millions) of vote preferences switch down the line from one candidate to the next in instant avalanches. Another way of characterizing this pattern of vote transfers is to refer to it as a 'Plump for One' (PFO) strategy: that is, where the first preferences are concentrated on the candidate at the top of the party list, and the subsequent preferences are transferred down the line, in order, to the remaining candidates.

Contrast this with the Irish case, renowned for its localist, clientelist politics, characterized by an emphasis on 'friends-and-neighbours' voting. In this case we find the constituencies carved up between the different party candidates, with each candidate looking for top preferences in their particular bailiwick. This produces a very different tendency in voter preferences, which can be termed 'Spread the Preferences' (STP), where there is no clear pattern of vote transfers because the voters are following different practices depending on their preferred party candidates. In the past decade or so the Irish parties have adopted STP as a central feature of their vote management strategies, as shown by the greater role of the party headquarters in head-hunting high profile candidates, in the amending (or greater use) of party statutes to allow the centre more influence over candidate selection, and in the use of candidate cards and sophisticated canvassing strategies (buttressed by constituency polling) to encourage suitable variations in the spread of transfers and thereby (at least in theory) to increase the efficiency of the party vote.[22]

There is some division of opinion over which of the two strategies is more effective; on balance, the bulk of expert opinion (though clearly not supported by the practitioners) favours STP over PFO. Michael Gallagher puts it most succinctly: 'Under the assumption that no votes transfer across party lines, a party's ideal strategy under STV is to ensure that all of its candidates have exactly the same number of votes at every stage of the count, and that when any one is eliminated, his or her votes transfer evenly among all the party's other candidates.'[23] However, STP is not easy to produce, particularly in a scenario where there have not been any party vote management strategies. Furthermore, given the lack of any strong evidence of localist voting tendencies, we have good reason to expect voters not to exhibit evidence of voting strategically across the range of candidates. There are at least three other reasons why we should expect the voters in this London experiment to be PFO rather than STP in their preference voting. First, as the appendix shows, the ballot paper design was modelled on the Australian form rather than the Irish form: that is, party labels were grouped across the top of the ballot paper (from left to right) and candidates names were grouped under each party, as opposed to simply listing the candidates in one vertical alphabetical list (with a mixing of party labels throughout). Therefore, we should expect the voters to make use of information shortcuts, selecting one party list and voting for the slate in straight alphabetical order. Second, inevitably there were high levels of voter ignorance about the candidates, given the fact that the constituency boundaries had been artificially changed so that, in most cases, the candidates were even more unfamiliar than normal. We would expect voters, therefore, to take a shortcut in the transfer of preferences and, much like in the case of alphabetical voting (which relates usually to first preferences), vote in order of sequence for the candidates on the party slate, thereby producing a PFO pattern. Finally, given the high levels of voter disinterest in this election there is little reason to expect voters to be prepared to pick and choose carefully between the different party candidates.

To date it has not been possible to test categorically for STP and PFO voting patterns because we have only had access to aggregate data, making it impossible to strip out vote-switchers, to get a true picture of the transfer patterns of the party 'loyalists'. This mock ballot survey provides a first real insight to the tendencies of one set of voters (albeit in an experimental scenario). The evidence is easy to summarize, as the hypothetical example in Table 5 shows.

TABLE 5
A HYPOTHETICAL REPRESENTATION OF PFO VERSUS STP VOTING

| Candidates | Preferences | | | | |
	1	2	3	4	5
1	x	o	o	o	o
2	o	x	o	o	o
3	o	o	x	o	o
4	o	o	o	x	o
5	o	o	o	o	x

If the voters are stacking up preferences in a PFO strategy we should see the bulk of voters lying along the diagonal (among the 'X's, where the first candidate gets the first preferences, the second receives second preferences, and so on). By contrast if the voters are spreading their preferences then we should see a much wider variation in the patterns of preferences among the various '0's in the columns. In short, then, 'diagonal voting' can be seen as evidence of PFO tendencies, while 'off-diagonal voting' would suggest STP tendencies. Rather than reproducing the full run of figures across the two constituencies for each of the parties, the results are summarized in Table 6 by a comparison between diagonal and off-diagonal voting.

TABLE 6
PROPORTIONS OF PFO AND STP VOTERS AMONG LONDON PARTY LOYALISTS

	Conservative	Labour	Lib Dem	Green
LONDON NORTH				
diagonal	1075	1777	363	215
off-diagonal	903	2234	829	481
diagonal as % of off-diagonal	54	44	30	31
LONDON SOUTH				
diagonal	595	959	388	141
off-diagonal	599	957	957	228
diagonal as % of off-diagonal	49	50	29	38

Source: ERS/MORI survey

There are two interesting points which emerge from Table 6. First, against our expectations, the evidence of PFO voting tendencies is by no means distinct. At most (in the case of the two larger parties) a bare plurality of the voters are voting along the diagonal – hardly conclusive evidence of Australian-style 'program trading' in transfers! Second, the smaller parties, if anything, are showing quite clear STP voting tendencies. Once again this shows the strategic nature of voting for smaller parties: voters feel the need to choose their preferred candidates carefully so as to maximize the effectiveness of their vote; the support for smaller parties (reflecting their campaigns) is more individualistic, focused on specific candidates rather than blindly following pre-set party slates.

In general, the higher than expected levels of STP voting indicates that we need to pay more attention to candidate effects on voting. As we have shown, we had difficulties in trying to demonstrate candidate effects in terms of localist voting: therefore we need to give attention to other possible factors influencing the levels of support for particular candidates, such as the fame and importance of the candidate, or their ideological placement.

Finally, it is worth noting that the unexpectedly high levels of STP voting may simply be an artefact of an unusually high number of party candidates (especially for the smaller parties) caused by our artificial merger of London constituencies in this STV experiment. There has been much discussion in the STV literature about the problems of nominating too many candidates. Arguably the STP tendencies we are witnessing have been produced by having too many candidates on the ballot paper.[24]

Conclusion

An analysis of voting practices under preferential systems can reveal a lot of interesting features. This study of a set of voters in London during the last European Parliament elections suggests a number of important implications of the STV electoral system on voting behaviour, and not just for this London sample. First, as the voting literature has argued, party does shape the preference schedule of voters in predictable ways. However there is also significant evidence of both candidate and ballot effects on voting behaviour, suggesting that the standard Michigan model of how party shapes the vote does not provide a complete guide to the behaviour on display here. At the same time, however, an account of voter behaviour grounded in alternative conceptions, such as one which focuses on the importance of candidate effects, clearly also has limited applicability. In short, the Michigan model may have some utility here, but, given the complexity of STV and particularly the greater freedom to choose which it allows the voters, there is clearly a lot more to the voting behaviour of these London voters than can easily be explained by one model.

Second, we saw how the pattern of transfers between the parties tends to vary between the larger and smaller parties. The larger parties benefit from greater degrees of voter 'loyalty' and 'exclusivity' than the smaller parties; smaller party supporters (especially Green Party voters) have a tendency to 'leak' across to other parties in greater numbers. Third, an examination of the transfer patterns within each of the party slates of candidates revealed a higher than expected tendency for voters to spread their preferences across candidates, rather than piling them up against the candidates in the order they appeared on the ballot paper. To an extent this higher than expected STP tendency (especially noted among the supporters of smaller parties) was probably an artefact of the artificial role voters were being asked to play in this survey. But to some extent at least, it does suggest that there is some role for candidate effects, requiring more attention to teasing out its precise nature.

Finally, in our reference to the Australian and Irish cases, we were comparing two actual systems with the case of this hypothetical London election. In some ways our results are comparable, suggesting that even though the survey concerns a hypothetical race our findings are nonetheless of interest, and certainly of more than local interest to this specific London case. But in some ways too the patterns revealed in this survey offer an intriguing mid-point between the Irish and Australian patterns, particularly in relation to the vote transfers. This raises some interesting questions: if STV were to be adopted would the British voters stay at this mid-point? Would they become more 'Irish' or 'Australian' in orientation with regard to their vote transfers? An important part of any answer to such questions relates to the role of the parties. It is the ability of the Australian parties to shape preferences which give them such great control over the expression of preferences. Clearly in this UK survey the British parties were in no position to organize the voters. In this respect, the survey provides a useful benchmark of how UK voters would express their preferences if left to their own devices. But this is not necessarily how voters would behave if the parties had been able to mobilize. In conclusion, the electoral and party systems provide significant micro-level incentives for voters to respond to the ballot; it is important to take account of these incentives in any account of voter decision-making.

APPENDIX

Election of Six Members for London North by Single Transferable Vote

Number in order of preference. Write a "1" beside the name of your first choice candidate, a "2" beside your second choice, a "3" by you third and so on (until you are unable to express a preference for any remaining candidates). Do not mark your ballot paper with an "X

Name of Candidate and Description	Name of Candidate and Description	Name of Candidate and Description	Name of Candidate and Description	Name of Candidate and Description
BETHELL, Lord Conservative Party	BAGULEY, John Green Party	ELLIOTT, Michael Labour Party	APPIAH, Koll Liberal Democrats	BINDING, William National Front
ELLIOTT, Andrew Conservative Party	BRADLEY, John Green Party	EVANS, Robert Labour Party	LEIGHTER, Hilary Liberal Democrats	BATTEN, Gerard UK Independence
GORDON, Simon Conservative Party	JAGO, Hilary Green Party	GREEN, Pauline Labour Party	LUDFORD, Sarah Liberal Democrats	BOOTH, Ian, UK Independence
GUY, Robert Conservative Party	JOHNSON, Darren Green Party	LOMAS, Alf Labour Party	MANN, Ian Liberal Democrats	COMPOBASSI, Peter UK Independence
KEEGAN, Michael Conservative Party	KORTVELYESSY, Niki Green Party	NEWENS, Cian Labour Party	MALLINSON, Bill Liberal Democrats	LE FANU, Hugh UK Independence
TAYLOR, Virginia Conservative Party	LAMBERT, Jean Green Party	TONGUE, Carole Labour Party	MONTGOMERY, Ken Liberal Democrats	ROBERTS, Gerald UK Independence
16-27	28-39	40-51	52-63	64-75

Election of Four Members for London South by Single Transferable Vote

Number in order of preference. Write a "1" beside the name of your first choice candidate, a "2" beside your second choice, a "3" by your third and so on (until you are unable to express a preference for any remaining candidates). Do not mark your ballot paper with an "X".

Name of Candidate and Description	Name of Candidate and Description	Name of Candidate and Description	Name of Candidate and Description	Name of Candidate and Description
BOFF, Andrew Conservative Party	COLLINS, Shane Green Party	BALFE, Richard Labour Party	BLANCHARD, Gerry Liberal Democrats	LOWNE, Kevin National Front
MOORHOUSE, James Conservative Party	CORNFORD, John Green Party	POLLACK, Anita Labour Party	REINISCH, Mark Liberal Democrats	SCHOLEFIELD Anthony UK Independence
PRICE, Peter Conservative Party	MOULAND, Ian Green Party	ROLLES, Gillian Labour Party	FRYER, Jonathan Liberal Democrats	
TRELEAVEN, Philip Conservative Party	WALSH, Tom Green Party	SPIERS, Shaun Labour Party	GRAVES, Adrian Liberal Democrats	
16-23	24-31	32-39	40-47	48-51

ACKNOWLEDGEMENTS

Earlier versions of this article were presented to the annual EPOP conference, Cardiff 27–29 September 1994, and to the 'Party Politics in the Year 2000' conference, Manchester, 13–15 January 1995. We are grateful to the participants and especially to Paul Wilder for their comments, to Simon Osborn of the Electoral Reform Society for having approached us to carry out this research, and to Simon Atkinson of MORI for having responded to our numerous queries; the usual disclaimer applies. We wish to acknowledge the generous financial support of the Arthur McDougall Fund, EPOP, and the Senate of UC Riverside.

NOTES

1. For prominent examples, see Douglas Rae, *The Political Consequences of Electoral Laws* (New Haven: Yale University Press, 1967); Rein Taagepera and M.S. Shugart, *Seats and Votes: The Effects and Determinants of Electoral Systems* (New Haven: Yale University Press, 1989); Arend Lijphart *et al.*, *Electoral Systems and Party Systems: A Study of Twenty-Seven Democracies, 1945–1990* (Oxford: Oxford University Press,1994); Giovanni Sartori, *Comparative Constitutional Engineering: An Inquiry into Structures, Incentives and Outcomes* (Houndmills: Macmillan, 1994).

2. Maurice Duverger, *Political Parties*, (London: Methuen, 1954); W. H. Riker, 'The Two-Party System and Duverger's Law: An Essay on the History of Political Science', *American Political Science Review*, 76 (1982), pp.753–66; Giovanni Sartori, 'The Influence of Electoral Systems: Faulty Law or Faulty Method?', in B. Grofman and A. Lijphart (eds), *Electoral Laws and Their Political Consequences*, (New York: Agathon Press, 1986); Taagepera and Shugart, *Seats and Votes*.

3. Richard S Katz, *A Theory of Parties and Electoral Systems* Baltimore, MD: Johns Hopkins University Press, 1980; Shaun Bowler and David M. Farrell, 'Legislator Shirking and Voter Monitoring: Impacts of European Parliament Electoral Systems upon Legislator–Voter Relationships', *Journal of Common Market Studies* 31 (1993), pp.45–69.

4. See, for instance, Sartori, 'The Influence of Electoral Systems'.

5. For an example, see Shaun Bowler and David Denemark, 'Split Ticket Voting in Australia: Dealignment and Inconsistent Votes Reconsidered', *Australian Journal of Political Science*, 28 (1993), pp.19–37.

6. Shaun Bowler and David M. Farrell, 'Party Loyalties in Complex Settings: STV and Party Identification', *Political Studies* 39 (1991), pp.350–62; Shaun Bowler and David M. Farrell, 'Voter Behavior under STV-PR: Solving the Puzzle of the Irish Party System', *Political Behavior* 13 (1991), pp.303–20.

7. Patrick Dunleavy, Helen Margetts, Stuart Weir, *Replaying the 1992 General Election: How Britain Would Have Voted Under Alternative Electoral Systems,* LSE Public Paper No.3, 1992; Patrick Dunleavy, Helen Margetts, Stuart Weir, 'The 1992 Election and the Legitimacy of British Democracy', in David Denver, Pippa Norris, David Broughton, Colin Rallings (eds), *British Elections and Parties Yearbook 1993* (Hemel Hempstead, Herts.: Harvester Wheatsheaf, 1993).

8. For detailed analysis of the representativeness of the ERS/MORI survey, see the article by Braunholtz and Atkinson in this volume.

9. The requirement that they should mark all preferences might seem somewhat strict, and perhaps a looser requirement of voting for 'most' candidates might seem reasonable if vaguer. However, the stricter requirement is more in keeping with the idea of party identification and, moreover, it gives us some benchmark expectation against which to assess the importance of party. If a voter in North London marks only four candidates from the six their party has on offer that voter passes up the chance to cast a vote in favour of what is supposed to be their party. Voting for only some candidates from a party slate suggests that some factor other than party is operating upon vote choice. If this kind of behaviour is to be expected of those who more strongly identify with a given party then we can expect weaker identifiers to be more ready to cross party lines and vote for more than one party. Moreover, weaker identifiers may be likely to vote for fewer of 'their' candidates.

10. What indications are there of how fully the voters understood what they were supposed to do? One relevant bit of information is the level of informal (or invalid, or spoiled) voting. If voters do not mark a complete sequence of preferences (for example, mark a ballot 1, 2, 3, 6 and skip 4 and 5) this gives some indication of how well voters understand what they are supposed to do. For North London the rate was 3.3 per cent (N=64), for South London 2.8 per cent (N=39), suggesting that Londoners on the whole did understand the process of voting in an STV election. The printed instructions on the ballot papers made it very clear that voters could write down a large number of preferences. They were told to indicate 1, 2, 3 'and so on (until you are unable to express a preference for any remaining candidates)'. The fact that a number of respondents marked more than six preferences shows that voters did generally get the idea of what they were supposed to do.
11. Bowler and Farrell, 'Party Loyalties'; Bowler and Farrell, 'Voter Behavior'.
12. This is consistent with the findings of Dunleavy and his colleagues in their 1994 poll. See Dunleavy et al., Replaying, p.11.
13. See Katz, A Theory of Parties.
14. See, for example, R.K. Carty, Electoral Politics in Ireland: Party and Parish Pump (Dingle: Brandon, 1983); A. Parker, 'The Friends and Neighbours Voting Effect in the Galway West Constituency', Political Georgaphy Quarterly, 1 (1982)
15. Robert Darcy and Ian McAllister, 'Ballot Position Effects', Electoral Studies, 9 (1990), pp.5–17.
16. See especially A. Cohan, R. McKinlay, A. Mughan, 'The Used Vote and Electoral Outcomes: The Irish General Election of 1973', British Journal of Political Science, 5 (1975) pp.363–83. Dunleavy and his colleagues have also noted an asymmetry in transfer patterns in their UK survey. They provide one other interesting rationale for this: 'British voters receive much more political information about the Conservative and Labour parties than about rival parties. Hence it is inherently easier for 'minor' party voters to form multiple preferences about the 'major' parties, than for 'major' party voters to rank the 'minor' parties'. See, Dunleavy et al., 'The 1992 Election', p.184.
17. In this context, it is worth noting the interesting Ph.D. research being carried out by Neil Jesse at UCLA.
18. Michael Gallagher, 'Party Solidarity, Exclusivity and Inter-Party Relationship in Ireland 1922–1977: The Evidence of Transfers', Economic and Social Review, 10 (1978) pp.1–22; Richard Sinnott, Irish Voters Decide: Voting Behaviour in Elections and Referendums in Ireland 1918–92 (Manchester: Manchester University Press, 1995).
19. Sinnott, Irish Voters Decide, p.212.
20. Michael Gallagher, 'The Election of the 27th Dail', in Michael Gallagher and Richard Sinnott (eds), How Ireland Voted 1992 (Dublin: Folens/PSAI Press, 1993).
21. See Robert Darcy and Michael Marsh, 'Decision Heuristics: Ticket-Splitting and the Irish Voter', Electoral Studies, 13 (1994), pp.38–49; David Farrell, Malcolm Mackerras and Ian McAllister, 'Designing Electoral Institutions: STV Systems and their Consequences', Political Studies (in press); Shaun Bowler, David Farrell and Ian McAllister, 'Constituency Campaigning in Parliamentary Systems with Preferential Voting: Is There a Paradox?' (mimeo).
22. David Farrell, 'Ireland: Centralization, Professionalization and Campaign Pressures', in Richard Katz and Peter Mair (eds), How Parties Organize: Adaptation and Change in Party Organizations in Western Democracies (London: Sage, 1994).
23. Michael Gallagher, 'Comparing Proportional Representation Electoral Systems: Quotas, Thresholds, Paradoxes and Majorities', British Journal of Political Science, 22 (1992) p.482.
24. A. Cohan et al., 'The Used Vote'; Richard Katz, 'But How Many Candidates Should We Have in Donegal?', British Journal of Political Science, 11 (1981) pp.117–22.

The Motivational Basis of Participation in European Elections, 1979–1994: The Case of Britain

Mark N. Franklin, Cees van der Eijk and Erik Oppenhuis

Until the European elections of 1994, Britain had regularly displayed the lowest turnout in European elections of any member country of the European Union; and while in 1994 Britain's low turnout was matched for the first time by equally low turnout in two other countries, British turnout was lower in 1994 than in 1989. Some have seen this as a manifestation of the Euroscepticism routinely associated with the British, yet this interpretation is hard to reconcile with the generally pro-European sentiment in Britain as measured by regular Eurobarometer surveys.

In this article we will try to explain British turnout in European elections on the basis of systemic and contextual features of the European electoral process in Britain that make low turnout all but inevitable there. Some of these features have to do with Britain, and would apply even in General Elections, others have to do with European elections and apply only in such contexts (though it is possible that some features of European elections may be found to apply in other elections of low salience, such as British local government elections and perhaps some by-elections). Indeed, the British performance in European elections, by diverging so sharply from performance in General Elections, has helped to unravel the puzzle of why people vote.

The Turnout Puzzle

After more than half a century of careful research, it was still possible for Brody in 1978 to refer to turnout as a 'puzzle';[1] and fifteen years later that puzzle is only just starting to be resolved. In particular, though we knew much about why some people voted while others did not,[2] and why certain countries or regions saw higher turnout than others,[3] we had almost no way of explaining the decline in turnout that has occurred in the United States and Europe in recent decades.[4]

The major problem with most of these past studies is that they have not incorporated predictors that can change very much between one election and the next. Turnout, after all, can change quite dramatically from election to election, yet most of the variables employed to explain turnout in past research have been variables that change seldom or slowly, if at all. Variables like the proportionality of the electoral system or the presence of compulsory voting can generally only change as a consequence of constitutional amendment which in most countries is a rare occurrence, while variables like educational attainment can only change with the maturing of a new generation of better-educated individuals. In general it seems clear that what Milbrath and Goel call 'facilitative' factors, which would include many of the variables listed above,[5] do not vary enough over time to account for observed changes in electoral participation. We are thus driven to focus on the other class of factors identified by these authors – what they call 'motivational' factors – though of course in any actual analysis of motivational factors, facilitative factors need to be controlled for.

It might be tempting to suppose that, when considering turnout at elections, facilitative factors would in general be institutional in nature (the rules of the game) or contextual (the civic culture), whereas motivational factors would reside at the individual level. In fact both facilitative and motivational factors operate on individuals, but the factors themselves can arise at any level. In particular, one motivational characteristic that has been neglected in past research is the nature of the electoral contest – clearly a contextual phenomenon. Some elections are quite simply more important than others, and in important elections it is reasonable to expect more people to be motivated to cast their vote than in unimportant elections. Of course, what is important is partly a matter of interpretation, and people may disagree about whether a particular election is important; nevertheless it is possible to characterize different contests in such a way as to highlight differences that will be perceived in the same way by most if not all voters. Thus US Presidential elections are generally seen as more important than Congressional elections, and turnout in Presidential races is indeed higher.

In the next section we will abstract a general principle from this observation which can be applied to countries other than the US and to differences that occur between one election and the next. We will then design a critical test that demonstrates the importance of motivational factors in determining differences in turnout, both between countries and over time. We do so by studying electoral participation across the entire string of European elections conducted since 1979 – including those of 1994.

European elections might at first sight appear to be poor venues for studying turnout. Such elections are generally regarded as 'second-order' national elections which, just like many local and regional elections, lack salience.[6] However, exactly this low-key character of EU elections yields a number of important advantages. Turnout is expected to be low, maximizing the variance of the variable of prime interest. Moreover, since at each election some countries hold national (first-order) elections on the same day as the European elections (two in elections for the Parliament of 1979–84, one in 1984, three in 1989 and one in 1994), the difference between the two types of election becomes a matter for empirical investigation rather than an impediment to research. Above all, the fact that European elections are held at the same time in twelve countries minimizes the risk of contaminating influences that might occur with elections held at different times.[7] Though the European Union (formerly the European Community) had twelve members at the time of the 1989 and 1994 European elections, we in fact distinguish thirteen different political systems: treating Great Britain and Northern Ireland separately since they employ different electoral systems for European elections (and show very different levels of turnout).

TABLE 1

TURNOUT IN EUROPEAN ELECTIONS BY COUNTRY, 1979–1994

	Election year				Average
	79	84	89	94	79–94
Belgium	90.4	91.2	89.7	90.2	93.2
Denmark	47.8	52.4	47.4	52.9	50.1
France	60.7	56.7	48.8	52.7	54.7
Germany	65.7	56.8	62.3	60.0	61.2
Great Britain	32.3	32.6	36.6	36.1	34.3
Greece	91.6*	90.2	93.1	84.2	89.8
Ireland	63.6	47.6	65.9	44.0	55.3
Italy	84.9	83.4	81.4	74.8	81.1
Luxembourg	88.9	88.8	96.2	88.5	90.6
Netherlands	58.1	50.6	48.8	35.6	48.3
Northern Ireland	64.4	54.4	47.5	49.8	40.3
Portugal	–	72.4**	51.1	35.5	53.0
Spain	–	68.9**	54.7	59.6	61.1
EC-Wide	68.0	65.0	63.4	58.6	63.6
N	11	13	13	13	50

*   Greece's first election was held in 1981. Because it is generally recognized that turnout in Greece is underestimated, 13 per cent was added to each of the figures for turnout in that country on the basis of analysis conducted in Chapter 19 of Van der Eijk, Franklin, *et al.*, *Choosing Europe?*
**   The first elections for Portugal and Spain were held in 1987.

Average turnout in these countries did vary considerably in all four of the elections that have been held for the European Parliament. Table 1 shows it ranging from 96 per cent in Luxembourg in 1989 to a mere 32 per cent in Britain in 1979. The variability of turnout in European elections over time is not to be dismissed either. Portugal has seen an astonishing decline in turnout at such elections from 72 per cent at their first European elections in 1987 to 35 per cent in 1994, and even in Britain, turnout has varied between 32 and

37 per cent.

Our purpose in what follows is to investigate the over time and country-level variance between countries, explaining as much of it as we can on the basis of factors that are general to all countries. In the process we will see to what extent, when country names are replaced by these more theoretically interesting concepts, we can account for the effects of country differences. In the analysis of individual variations this orientation has become rather commonplace. When we take a random sample we are not interested in Mary, Heinz or Charles, but in people who can be characterized in terms of gender, education, attitudes, and so on. Adequate specificity in terms of variables of this kind removes the need for us to know respondents' proper names so as to be able to make meaningful statements about them. The same reasoning applies to countries or, in the words of Przeworski and Teune, 'the basic assumption is that names of nations ... are treated as residua of variables that influence the phenomenon being explained...'[8] To the extent that we are successful in this enterprise, the result will be a set of concepts that explain the level of (and changes in) British turnout at European elections without requiring us to bring any specifically British considerations to bear.

The Motivational Basis of Electoral Participation

Our focus in this article on predictors of turnout that can change quite radically from election to election leads us to look, as already explained, particularly at motivational factors. With given institutional arrangements governing the costs of voting, individuals will be differentially motivated to go to the polls mainly by the benefits. These benefits are of two kinds: affective and instrumental. Affective benefits clearly accrue to people who are motivated by a sense of duty or habit. Such things are difficult to measure empirically, and will be treated by us as residual – part of the variance we are unable to explain by more directly measured factors. This is no great loss, since habitual voting will by definition tend to persist over time, dampening the variations in turnout that might have occurred had there been no one motivated to vote for these reasons; and our interest lies primarily in factors that can change. Some of these are indeed affective in nature, as we shall see; but more interesting to us are those instrumental benefits that depend on the nature of the specific contest being fought at a specific election. Such benefits evidently depend on voters being able to identify electoral outcomes that differ in ways that are significant to them, and also on voters feeling that their vote might make a difference to the outcome. Thus it will be relevant whether parties and candidates have different programmes, whether the programmes have realistic goals, whether candidates put forward their programmes in a credible fashion and whether voters have a preference for one programme over another. Above all it will matter whether, by voting one way or another, individuals feel that they can affect the outcome of the election and so help to determine what government policies will be put into effect.

Of course it is true that no individual vote is ever likely to be decisive in nationwide elections. Indeed voting has often been characterized as an irrational act from the point of view of the individual voter, who could easily take a free ride on the civic-mindedness of others.[9] Nevertheless it is clear that people behave as though each vote is important. Indeed, what we might call the 'illusion of individual empowerment' goes far beyond the decision to vote. It also affects the choice that is made between parties and candidates. The fact that in suitable circumstances up to half of all voters vote other than for the party they 'really prefer' makes it clear that they are not simply treating elections as popularity contests.[10] If they care about the outcome they often adjust their behaviour in the light of expected outcomes, just as though they regard their vote as potentially decisive.

The fact that voters can perform so very rationally when engaging in what is, seen from a strictly individual viewpoint, irrational behaviour, suggests that we should not regard voting as an individual act but rather as a collective act in which people cast their vote so as to benefit the group interests or causes with which they identify.[11] Voting thus becomes an affirmation of solidarity with such groups. Following this line of argument, one of the factors that will determine whether people vote or not will be the nature and extent of their group affiliations. It is true that the group basis of voting choice has declined in recent decades but all countries see a residual group basis of voting that shows no sign of ultimately disappearing;[12] and, although 'class solidarity' is nowhere any longer invoked as a slogan to get working class individuals to the polls, the fact is that class and group affiliations are still likely to be strong influences on the decision to vote. Indeed, the extent of group-party linkage was one of the variables found by Powell to be a powerful predictor of the level of turnout when comparing one country with another.[13]

We hypothesize that people are more likely to vote when their vote might affect the allocation of power in an election whose outcome will decide the nature of government policies important to them or to the groups with which they identify. When a large number of people view an election in this light the election will be seen to be an important one which (we hypothesize) will generate a high level of turnout. Indeed, commentators often employ the level of turnout as an indicator of the importance of an election; but how can we know whether a particular election is important other than by the level of turnout? Alternative indicators, for example of the differences between policy proposals and the credibility of candidates, are difficult to operationalize. European elections provide us with a critical test of the potency of such factors without requiring that they be specifically measured. This is because

European elections are not in themselves elections that determine the allocation of power or the nature of government policies. However, some European elections occur in tandem with national elections where real political power is at stake and whose outcome will indeed help to determine the policies pursued by national governments. In such countries turnout in the European election is very close to turnout in the national election because people who are motivated to vote in one contest in fact generally cast their votes in both. By comparing turnout in countries that have concurrent national elections with turnout in other countries we can estimate the generic importance of this factor.

A second way in which European elections differ from each other is even more variable as between countries: they occur at different times in the national electoral calendar.[14] Elsewhere we have argued that European elections, while never very important in their own right, will differ in the extent to which they gain importance from their role as 'markers' of national party standing.[15] If a national election is expected in the near future, this role will be more pronounced than if a national election is not expected for some months or years. And if a national election has occurred only recently, European elections will be 'throw away' elections to which no one will pay much attention because a better marker of the relative standing of political parties already exists in the shape of the recent national election. In the research referred to, our concern was to relate 'time elapsed since the previous national election' to the different vote choices made in different political contexts. We argued that in the aftermath of a national election, voters will tend to 'vote with the heart' free of any need to think in terms of the effect their vote might have on the political situation in their country. In such elections we argued that we could expect to see more sincere voting than at any other time. By contrast, in the national election itself voters would tend to 'vote with the head' to produce an outcome maximally favourable to their concerns, bearing in mind the inability of small parties to achieve policy goals. A quite different type of voting would occur during the run-up to a national election. At such times real outcomes are not at issue; but commentators and party leaders, by paying attention to the outcome, provide an incentive to voters to send any messages of discontent that they may have, free of any fears of practical repercussions. These are thus elections in which protest voting is likely to be most prevalent – what we called 'voting with the boot', borrowing a phrase from the lexicon of British football hooliganism.

In this article we take a different view of the effects of the electoral timetable, arguing that not only party choice but also turnout will be affected by the extent to which politicians and commentators seem inclined to pay attention to the results. In 'throw-away elections' held immediately after a national election there will tend to be much lower turnout than in national elections or in elections held shortly before national elections. Moreover, turnout in a European election will tend to be higher the further the country is along the path from one national election to the next. Time to the next national election may have effects additional to those of concurrent national elections, or the former variable may turn out to incorporate the effects of the latter. This is a question for empirical investigation. Either way these data will provide us with variation in the importance of elections that we expect to be related to variations in turnout from country to country.

European elections in Britain have never occurred in conjunction with a national election, but they have occurred at very different times in the national election cycle. In 1979 they occurred only a month after the Conservatives were returned to office for Margaret Thatcher's first term as Prime Minister – in precisely the circumstances in which we suppose that a 'throw-away' election will engender little interest. Much the same was true in 1984, when the European elections occurred within a year of Thatcher's second General Election victory. In 1989, on the other hand, the European elections fell two years after the most recent General Election in circumstances in which the 'marker' set by 1987 was no longer current, and the European election outcome was looked to by commentators and some politicians as a pointer to what might happen in a national election. These are circumstances in which we expect turnout in a European election to be higher, as indeed it was. The same was also true in 1994, though in that election British turnout was slightly lower than in 1989 (but still much higher than in 1979 or 1984).

Whether we can use these facts to 'explain' the broad trends in British turnout at European elections cannot be established with reference to Britain alone. In one country over four elections, variations in turnout might appear to correspond to differences in the timing of elections for reasons that were quite different from those that we suppose. Only if the same forces were found to operate elsewhere in Europe, so that British turnout could be shown to be reflecting a general pattern of responsiveness to electoral timing, would we be justified in concluding that this factor was decisive in Britain as well.

Not only the importance of the choice between parties but also the efforts of the parties to get themselves chosen will affect the motivations of individuals – a distinction corresponding to what Rosenstone and Hansen have termed 'push' and 'pull' effects.[16] The effectiveness of parties at mobilizing their followers will depend, we suppose, on the strength of links between these parties and the social groups that traditionally support them. Parties that have a clear constituency in social terms will find it easier to get out the votes of loyal supporters. The extent of voter loyalty has been measured in the past by the variance explained in party choice by social structural variables,[17] but we know from other work that this measure differs not only between countries but also over time.[18] The strength of such links can vary for a variety of reasons, from global trends affecting the importance of cleavage politics to specific 'local difficulties' that may temporarily affect the importance of group-party links.

In Britain in the 1970s the rise of new parties and the seeming irrelevance of Labour Party programmes to current social and economic problems had reduced to a very low point the class-based nature of British voting choice.[19] Labour supporters were demoralized after the 'Winter of Discontent' and the long period of ineffective minority Labour government, and they were unlikely to be very responsive to appeals to party loyalty. At the other side of the class divide, the 1979 Tory victory was won with the support of many who had voted for Labour or minor parties in 1974, and who had not had time to become 'established' Tory voters. Appeals to this group to turn out for the sake of party solidarity might have fallen on partially deaf ears. So in the European elections of 1979 the ability of parties to appeal for support from their traditional supporters would have been low, perhaps explaining the low turnout in that election. By the time of the second Europe-wide elections of 1984, this situation would have been little improved, and perhaps even worsened following the creation of the Social Democratic Party and the reduction of the Labour vote in 1983 to its lowest level in fifty years. By 1989, however, a revival in Labour's fortunes had taken place, and some even talked of a Labour victory at the next national elections that had to be held by 1992. Moreover, Tory voters who had been new in 1979, had by 1989 enjoyed the possibility of repeated reaffirmation of their Tory identity, making them perhaps more receptive to party appeals than ten years earlier. In this atmosphere, parties should have been able for the first time in a European election to appeal with some success to established loyalties. The same would have been true in 1994. So variations in the strength of links with social groups, just like variations in the timing of these elections relative to national elections, show signs of being able to account for some part at least of the variations we observe in British turnout at European elections. But as in the case of timing, we can only assess the actual importance of group-party links in comparative perspective. We would have to show that the same factors influence turnout in other countries in the same way before concluding that these variations are the important ones in driving variations in British turnout.

The importance of elections, as indicated in our data by their timing, and the responsiveness of individuals to party appeals, might well account for the variations we observe in British turnout at European elections, but what of the generally lower level of British turnout in European elections compared to other countries? This cannot be a function of timing, since European elections in other countries fall at all points in their national political calenders, and is unlikely to be a function of party links to social groups, since other research has shown British group-party links to be unexceptional in comparative perspective.[20] But these two sets of motivational factors are not the only ones determining turnout. Other research has shown that turnout responds to variations in the institutional settings within which elections take place.[21] In particular, compulsory voting has a strong effect in establishing a social norm buttressed by legal sanctions (even if these are rarely applied). This is evidently a facilitative factor that might be expected to operate in a similar fashion regardless of the importance of an election or the effectiveness of mobilization efforts. Also important is the nature of the electoral system, with proportional representation widening the attractions of voting by reducing the number of individuals who might consider it a waste of time to vote in a constituency or district where the outcome was a foregone conclusion. Another facilitative factor often suggested is whether polling takes place on a weekday or at the weekend, since many people might find it harder to find the time to vote on a working day.[22]

European countries provide us with extensive variations in those institutional factors. Some countries have compulsory voting while others do not; some have elections at the weekend and some on working days; and these countries employ a wide range of electoral systems that vary greatly in proportionality. All of these are factors that directly or indirectly facilitate turnout, by making it easier to get to the polls (Sunday voting), providing penalties for non-voting, or by trying to reduce the incidence of wasted votes (proportional representation). In Britain, voting is not compulsory and takes place on a Thursday, and Britain, moreover, falls at the low extreme of variations in proportionality, being the only country in which European elections are conducted by means of a plurality voting system in which the winner takes all in each of a large number of constituencies. For all these reasons low British turnout in European elections is perhaps only to be expected – though again this conclusion can only be reached after making sure that in other countries turnout also responds to variations in these factors.

Many other factors have been proposed as being responsible in part for turnout. Many of these relate to the characteristics of individuals, and while perhaps accounting for which particular individuals vote and which do not, cannot account for the overall level of turnout that concerns us in this article. However, some individual characteristics, seen as contextual phenomena, might account for variations in levels of turnout from country to country. In particular, high levels of education have often been suggested as being likely to generate high levels of turnout. In other work we have investigated this and many other contextual phenomena created by aggregating the characteristics of individuals to the level of the country and coding European countries according to their level of education, unionization, class composition, and many other features that might have affected turnout.[23] None of these factors proved important in the European elections of 1989 in determining differences in the level of turnout from country to country, once institutional variations had been taken into account. In the present article, therefore, we feel able to ignore variations in the social environment of voters in different countries, while focussing on the institutional and political forces that appear to condition turnout levels in Europe.[24]

Methods and Measures

In this article we employ a pooled cross-sectional research design that investigates differences between countries and over time, taking our data from the aggregate characteristics (turnout together with systemic and political context) of all elections that have ever been conducted in the countries of the (now) European Union. Our procedure is to first establish a statistical model describing the effects on turnout of the various factors we have identified as being potentially important, and then to determine to what extent turnout in individual countries conforms to the expectations that flow from this model. It would in principle be possible to create a model that explained a high proportion of the variance but which did not predict the British case very well. In statistical parlance, Britain might constitute an 'outlier' whose turnout differed significantly from what we would expect on the basis of its characteristics. For this reason, after establishing a model that explains turnout variations as well as possible, we need to analyse the residual variance that remains unexplained.

The theory of electoral participation upon which we focus in this research points to the importance of a small number of concepts in determining changes in turnout. These concepts, however, can be implemented in a number of ways. Rather than blindly adopting a formulation taken at random (or on the basis of previous research) we followed a strategy that would enable us to choose between different formulations. The relatively small number of data points available for analysis (50) made it important for us to keep to a minimum the number of variables employed in conjunction, to avoid capitalizing upon chance. Nevertheless this is a far larger N than generally available in the analysis of turnout variations and is sufficient to permit us to decide empirically which version of each variable seemed most potent.[25]

The variables from which our choices were made are as follows:

1. *Institutional context:* What are the rules of the game? Two aspects are generally deemed particularly important, the first one in terms of the extent to which voters are likely to feel that their votes may turn out to be wasted, and the second in terms of other incentives for voting. The first aspect is the nature of the electoral system – most obviously whether it employs plurality voting (Britain), Single Transferable Vote (Ireland and Northern Ireland) or List

System proportional representation (elsewhere) – but with many other differences, such as thresholds for representation (caused either by the number of seats to be filled, or by imposed restrictions) and possibilities for apparentement, all of which translate themselves into the proportionality of outcomes (votes/seats ratio) which turned out to perform significantly better than an alternative formulation in terms of electoral system types.[26] The second aspect of the institutional context that we considered important is whether compulsory voting was in effect (as in Flanders, Wallonia, Greece, Luxembourg and Italy) or not (elsewhere). The third aspect took account of whether the election was held on a Thursday (Denmark, Great Britain, Ireland, Northern Ireland, the Netherlands and Spain) or on the following Sunday (elsewhere).

2. *Political context*: Domestic political events and processes in the member countries of the European Union determine in large part the political context within which European elections are fought. Overriding and encapsulating all others is the position in the national electoral calendar occupied by the European election, which determines how much attention is paid to it by politicians and commentators, as already explained. This variable turned out to perform better than one which simply identified European elections that occurred in conjunction with concurrent national elections, evidently because it incorporated the latter variable into a more general concept.[27] In the case of elections conducted in 1994, many countries had not yet at the time of writing held or announced the timing of subsequent national elections. We handle this problem by assuming that countries that had not held or announced national elections at the time of writing (March 1995) would hold national elections after a delay equivalent to the average found following past European elections.[28] It made no difference to the findings reported in Table 2 if these cases were treated as 'missing' (indeed, doing so considerably increased the variance explained). However treating these cases as missing when we were also having to treat as missing cases for which we had no measures of the links between parties and social groups (see below) had too big a cost in terms of sample size for this to be a viable procedure in the present context. Turning to these links between parties and the social groups normally supporting them, for 1979 and 1984 the variable is taken from the variance explained in left voting by social structure in national elections, as reported in the country chapters of *Electoral Change*.[29] In 1989 and 1994 the variable is taken from an identical analysis of the determinants of (national) voting choice in the European election studies conducted in those two years.[30] The 'splicing' of these two series of measures was not totally straightforward. Several of the country chapters in *Electoral Change* did not employ the full set of social structural variables in their analysis of the group basis of party choice in particular countries, either because of lack of data or for more idiosyncratic reasons. Two different means could be adopted to circumvent this problem.

The first would be to treat as missing any elections for which *Electoral Change* data was non-comparable; the second would be to 'correct' the findings from *Electoral Change* to reflect the difference found in 1989 and 1994 when the links were calculated from the same subset of variables as employed in *Electoral Change*. Because we could not afford the loss of cases involved in treating all anomalous cases as missing, we adopted the second procedure.[31] Though not strictly concerned with any theory of turnout, we also felt it necessary to control for whether the European election concerned was the first one ever conducted in each country, on the basis that such an election would be held in a context of unusual publicity.[32]

Findings

The first step in our investigation is to see to what extent differences in turnout from country to country can be explained by the systemic, social and political settings that characterize the different countries at each election, and to discover which systemic and other characteristics matter in this regard. In Table 2 we display our findings, which show that with only five variables we explain almost 87 per cent of the variance in turnout. No other systemic variable is significant at even the .01 level.

TABLE 2

REGRESSION OF ELECTORAL PARTICIPATION ON SYSTEMIC CHARACTERISTICS IN AN EC-WIDE ANALYSIS FOR ALL ELECTIONS 1979–94 (N = 50)

VARIABLE	B	BETA	SIGF
Compulsory voting	29.954	0.737	.000
Time until next national election	-0.226	-0.180	.003
First European election for country	7.542	0.175	.003
Proportionality of electoral system	0.452	0.137	.019
Sunday voting	5.365	0.141	.050
(CONSTANT)	12.539		.473
Variance explained			0.867

Our principal findings are quite interpretable. Compulsory voting, a short time until the next national election, proportionality of the electoral system and the excitement surrounding the first European elections ever held in each country all contribute significantly to higher electoral participation. Sunday voting just barely does the same. These results enable us to calculate what level of turnout is to be expected under various combinations of systemic and political characteristics.[33] Strikingly, the possible values encompass virtually the whole range of turnout rates up to a maximum of 99.8 per cent which one would expect in a system with perfect proportionality, compulsory voting, and Sunday voting with no time before the next national election. Scholarly caution limits the range over which we can realistically model our findings to little more than the range actually seen in the countries we investigate, but this range runs from 32 to 96 per cent.

TABLE 3
REGRESSION OF ELECTORAL PARTICIPATION ON SYSTEMIC CHARACTERISTICS IN AN EC-
WIDE ANALYSIS AT ELECTIONS FOR WHICH A CODING OF SOCIAL LINKS TO PARTIES WAS
AVAILABLE, 1979–94 (N = 39)

VARIABLE	B	BETA	SIGF
Compulsory voting	31.246	0.744	.000
Time until next national election	-0.339	-0.250	.000
Links to social groups	0.468	0.157	.006
Sunday voting	7.205	0.181	.012
(CONSTANT)	47.815		.000
Variance explained			0.910

What of the links to social groups, the importance of which seemed so self-evident on theoretical grounds and on the basis of past research? This variable has too much missing data to add significantly to an analysis that includes all 50 cases. When we restrict the universe to those cases for which we have data for Social Links, the effects of this variable become significant, but First Election and Proportionality fail to reach significance (see Table 3). This is not because these variables are collinear with Social links. Even without including Social Links, First Election and Proportionality fail to reach significance at the 0.05 level in this universe. The major difference between the two data sets, of course, is the small number of 1979 cases with valid data when the social linkage variable is included. This one difference easily accounts for the failure of First Election to reach significance in the smaller dataset. The failure of Proportionality to figure significantly is harder to explain, but must be due to happenstance features of the cases which could not be coded on the Social Links variable.[34]

Residual Country Effects

We saw in Table 2 that the variance we could explain in turnout by means of systemic and contextual effects was was 86.7 per cent. With an N of 50, this is an impressive result. Nevertheless, there might be room within the variance left unexplained for residual country effects to prove significant.

TABLE 4
DEVIATIONS OF RESIDUAL BY COUNTRY

VARIABLES	DEV	SIG
Spain	+11.8	.05
Great Britain	-8.5	.05

(Data: All European Elections to date; N=50)

If the explanatory variables identified in Table 2 had failed to capture all of the relevant differences between our fourteen systems then the systemic characteristics omitted would cause the residuals from the analyses to differ on average when we compare them across nations. Such differences would, in the absence of specified variables, only be 'explained' by proper names which can be introduced into a one-way analysis by country of the residual remaining after the independent variables in Table 2 have explained all they can. To the extent that country differences prove significant, the possibility of finding additional systemic or contextual influences will remain open.

Given the N=50 findings, it will come as no surprise to discover that the residual effects of country in such an analysis are small. The details are given in Table 4. Two countries showed deviations from predicted turnout that were significant at the .05 level (no other residual effect was even significant at the 0.1 level). Spain's turnout is some 12 per cent higher on average than would have been expected from its characteristics in terms of the systemic and political variables identified at the country level; Britain sees turnout that is a little more than half that distance from what would have been expected, though the deviations are still significant. The same countries stand out when we analyse the residuals from the other equation (summarized in Table 3).

So British participation in European elections cannot be entirely explained on the basis of systemic and political factors common to all European countries. Even when we take account of factors that appear generally responsible for turnout differences between countries, British turnout is lower than would have been expected. We will return to this point below. Meanwhile, rather than emphasizing the extent to which two systems diverge from expectations, we should stress the converse implications of our findings: eleven political systems show no significant deviations from what we would expect on the basis of their systemic and compositional characteristics, and have turnout levels that are within five per cent of what would be expected on the basis of the systemic and political contexts within which these elections were held.

Accounting for the Decision to Vote

In the analyses reported above we have looked at electoral participation in the member states of the European Union at the aggregate level over the course of all four elections held for the European Parliament. The findings presented in Tables 2 and 3 were impressive in terms of explanatory power, with some 90 per cent of variance explained. The explanatory variables account for the quite different levels of turnout found in the different countries of the European Union (which can be modelled from the b coefficients shown in each table).[35] We saw in Tables 2 and 3 that compulsory voting, for example, makes a difference of some 30 per cent to average turnout, even without strict efforts to enforce this norm in systems characterized by it. Sunday voting adds between 5 and 7 per cent to turnout. Other effects are less certain, since they differ somewhat between the two tables, but time to the next national election is worth between a quarter and a third of one per cent per month prior to a national election that the European election occurs. This could easily account for a ten point difference in turnout between a European election occurring early in the election cycle and one occurring in the shadow of an imminent national election. The effect of social links is particularly impressive in Table 3, amounting to half of one per cent in turnout for each percentage point difference in variance in left voting explained by social structure. Since the extent of these links range from near 30 per cent (in Belgium, Italy and the Netherlands in the late 1970s) to a mere 4 per cent (in Greece, Ireland and Portugal in the latest election) we are talking about a 25 point span that translates into differences of up to 12 per cent in turnout. Proportionality appears to have effects of about the same order, but its failure to prove significant in the analysis of the subset of countries for which we have social linkage data leads us to treat that finding with more caution.

Assessment

A less banal setting than EC-wide elections, by introducing additional sources of variation arising from political events, or from additional institutional differences not present in the countries of the European Union, might well yield additional variance not explicable with the variables we employ here. How far we could go towards explaining such additional variance would depend on how well we could characterize the additional complexities that such a setting might introduce. Any such study would, however, have the advantage of being able to build on the benchmark findings reported here.

In elections to the European Parliament, turnout can be characterized virtually completely with just three systemic variables and two contextual phenomena (three when 'first EC election' can be taken into account) which are entirely motivational in character. This confirms the findings of other studies that focussed on systemic effects,[36] but adds evidence that contextual effects, generally omitted in previous studies, can also be of importance. The characteristics we have identified account for virtually all the differences in turnout observed between countries and over time in European elections. This permits us to assert that electoral participation is subject to political control, even in a country with free and democratic elections. A political system in which relevant variables had been so manipulated as to produce perfect turnout might have other deficiencies that would lead us to eschew it, but we need to recognize the primacy of electoral institutions. Such a realization may be particularly important when we are faced with political systems such as those in the United States and Switzerland where electoral participation is often thought to be undesirably low. While it is unlikely that the systemic and contextual characteristics we have isolated would be the only ones determining turnout in countries not included in our study, the very fact that country differences can account for such large turnout differentials suggests that this level is the first one that should be addressed when attempting to manipulate the level of electoral participation. Our findings also imply that this should be the level we first turn to when we try to understand the puzzle of declining European turnout.

In particular, our findings contribute towards solving this puzzle in Europe. Powell's analysis found effects from group links that are confirmed in our findings.[37] Other work has shown that the strength of such links has declined throughout Europe in the past 30 years.[38] This is confirmed in our own data, which show the strength of this linkage (as measured by variance in left voting explained by social structure) declining from 23.4 per cent on average in 1979 to 10.2 per cent on average in 1994. With each percentage point in variance explained worth almost 0.5 of one per cent in turnout (Table 3) the decline in turnout associated with this change would be some 6 per cent – two thirds of the 9 per cent decline in turnout that has occurred in European elections over this period.[39]

Returning to the specific case of Britain, we have already shown that turnout is significantly less in that country than would have been expected on the basis of its systemic and contextual characteristics; but only by 8.5 per cent on average over four elections. Adding this amount to measured turnout would still leave Britain with by far the lowest turnout in European elections of any EU country. Most of its distinctiveness is well explained by its electoral system (the least proportional of any), its Thursday elections, and the fact that it does not make voting compulsory. Its variations in turnout from election to election correspond with differences in the position that European elections occupy in the national election cycle (much later in 1989 and 1994 than in 1979 and 1984), and with a small increase in the strength of links to social groups that also occurred after 1984. Indeed, the British case, by providing critical variation on at least two of our independent variables, has greatly aided us in unravelling the puzzle of declining electoral participation in Europe.

ACKNOWLEDGEMENTS

The authors would like to thank Raymond Duch, Christopher Wlezien and Colin Rallings for helpful comments on an earlier draft.

NOTES

1. Richard A. Brody 'The Puzzle of Political Participation in America' in Anthony King (ed.) *The New American Political System* (Washington DC: American Enterprise Institute, 1987).
2. Angus Campbell, Philip Converse, Warren Miller and Donald Stokes, *The American Voter* (New York: Wiley, 1960); Sidney Verba and Norman Nie, *Participation in America: Political Democracy and Social Equality* (New York: Harper and Row, 1972); Jae Kim, John Petrocik and S. Enokson,'Voter Turnout among the American States: Systemic and Individual Components', *American Political Science Review* 69, 1975, pp.107–123; Raymond Wolfinger and Steven Rosenstone, *Who Votes?* (New Haven: Yale University Press, 1980); Ivor Crewe, 'Electoral Participation' in David Butler and Howard Penniman (eds.) *Democracy at the Polls: A Comparative Study of Competitive National Elections* (Washington DC: American Enterprise Institute, 1981).
3. Charles Merriam and Howard Gosnell, *Non-Voting: Causes and Methods of Control* (Chicago: University of Chicago Press, 1924); Herbert Tingsten, *Political Behavior* (London: King, 1937); Donald Matthews and James Prothro, 'Political Factors and Negro Voter Registration in the South', *American Political Science Review* 57, 1963, pp.355– 67; Kim, Petrocik and Enokson, 'Voter Turnout among the American States'; Wolfinger and Rosenstone, *Who Votes?*; Bingham Powell, 'Voter Turnout in Thirty Democracies: Partisan, Legal and Socio-Economic Influences' in R. Rose (ed.) *Electoral Participation: A Comparative Analysis* (Beverly Hills: Sage, 1980); Bingham Powell, 'American Voter Turnout in Comparative Perspective', *American Political Science Review* 80, 1986, pp.17–43; Robert Jackman, 'Political Institutions and Voter Turnout in the Industrial Democracies', *American Political Science Review* 81, 1987, pp.405–23.
4. Ruy Teixeira, *The Disappearing American Voter* (Washington, DC: Brookings, 1992) p.39; R. Flickinger, and D. Studlar (1992), 'Exploring Declining Turnout in Western European Elections', *West European Politics* 15, 1992, p.1.
5. Lester Milbrath and M. Goel, *Political Participation: How and Why Do People Get Involved in Politics?* (Chicago: Rand McNally, 1977); see also Sidney Verba and Norman Nie, *Participation in America* (New York: Harper and Row, 1972).
6. Karlheinz Reif, 'Ten Second-Order National Elections' in Karlheinz Reif (ed.) *Ten European Elections* (Aldershott: Gower, 1985); Karlheinz Reif and Hermann Schmitt, 'Nine Second-Order National Elections – A Conceptual Framework for the Analysis of European Elections Results', *European Journal of Political Research* 8, 1980, pp.3–44.
7. The timing of national elections in Europe is seldom set by a fixed electoral calendar but more often by domestic political circumstances which, because of the very fact that they differ from country to country, may disguise the effects of institutional factors. The election was not necessarily held on the same day in all countries (see below), but polling was completed in all countries during the same week.
8. Adam Przeworski and Henry Teune, *The Logic of Comparative Social Inquiry* (New York: Wiley, 1970) p.29.
9. Anthony Downs, *An Economic Theory of Democracy* (New York: Harper and Row, 1957).
10. Richard Niemi, Guy Whitton and Mark Franklin, 'Constituency Characteristics, Individual Characteristics and Tactical Voting in the 1987 British General Election', *British Journal of Political Science* 22, 1992, pp.229–240; Mark Franklin, Richard Niemi and Guy Whitton, 'Two Faces of Tactical Voting', *British Journal of Political Science* 24, 1994, pp.549–557.
11. Cf. Wolfgang Hirczy, Electoral Participation (Ann Arbor: University Microfilms, 1992) University of Houston PhD Dissertation, p.204.
12. Mark Franklin, Tom Mackie, Henry Valen *et al.*, *Electoral Change* (Cambridge: Cambridge University Press, 1992), Chapter 19.
13. Powell, 'Voter Turnout in Thirty Democracies'.
14. Reif and Schmitt, 'Nine Second-Order National Elections'; Reif, 'Ten Second Order National Elections'.
15. Cees van der Eij, Erik Oppenhuis and Mark Franklin, 'Consulting the Oracle: The Consequences of Treating European Elections as Markers of Domestic Political Developments' (Madrid: European Consortium for Political Research) 1994.

16. Steven Rosenstone and John Hansen, *Mobilization, Participation, and Democracy in America* (New York: Macmillan, 1994).
17. Powell, 'Voter Turnout in Thirty Democracies', 'American Voter Turnout in Comparative Perspective'.
18. Mark Franklin, *The Decline of Class Voting in Britain* (Oxford: Oxford University Press, 1985); Franklin, *et al.*, *Electoral Change*.
19. Franklin, *Decline of Class Voting*, Chapters 5 and 7.
20. Franklin, *et al.*, *Electoral Change*, Chapters 5 and 19.
21. See especially Powell, 'Voter Turnout in Thirty Democracies', 'American Voter Turnout in Comparative Perspective', and Jackman, 'Political Institutions and Voter Turnout'.
22. See, for example, Crewe, 'Electoral Participation'.
23. Mark Franklin, Cees van der Eijk and Erik Oppenhuis, 'Why People Vote: The Influence of Systemic, Contextual and Individual Characteristics on Electoral Participation in Europe' (Washington DC: American Political Science Association) 1993; Cees van der Eijk, Mark Franklin *et al.*, *Choosing Europe? The European Electorate and National Politics in the Face of Union* (Ann Arbor: The University of Michigan Press, 1995) Ch.19.
24. These findings should not be taken as suggesting that social context is never important in conditioning levels of turnout and differences between countries in these terms. Over a wider universe of countries social factors might well be found to be important. European countries, however, are sufficiently alike in social terms for such factors to play no role in differentiating these countries from each other on the basis of turnout.
25. Powell and Jackman based their analyses on less than twenty cases each. See Powell, 'American Voter Turnout in Comparative Perspective', and Jackman, 'Political Institutions and Voter Turnout'.
26. This measure has been operationalized not in terms of the European elections themselves, but in terms of the most recent national election: the systemic context in which voters were socialized and to which they have become accustomed.
27. Concurrent national elections are coded as occurring at no temporal distance from the European election.
28. On the basis of findings reported in van der Eijk, Franklin *et al.*, *Choosing Europe?* we also treated the Spanish election of 1987 as a concurrent election, though the elections that were held concurrently were regional rather than national elections. Regional elections in this instance were conducted throughout Spain, and their concurrance with the European elections is the normal explanation given in the literature for the unexpectedly high turnout that occurred in Spain at that European election. See, for example, Pilar del Castillo, 'Spain: A Dress Rehearsal' in van der Eijk, Franklin *et al.*, *Choosing Europe?* Making an exception of this kind for Spanish regional elections is plausible because Spain has allocated so much real power to its regions. Indeed, when people are asked about the importance of various institutions, regional councils rank with the national parliament in Spain, in contrast to all other EU countries (even Germany, where, despite the very real importance of the Länder, state elections rank much lower in popular assessment than parliamentary elections).
29. See Franklin *et al.*, *Electoral Change*, Part II.
30. Van der Eijk, Franklin, *et al.*, *Choosing Europe?* The dependent variable was derived from the party that would have been preferred had the European election been a national election, by contrasting parties of the left with other parties. Though this is precisely the procedure employed in *Electoral Change*, there remains a question as to whether the resulting coefficients are comparable, since European elections are such different contests than national elections. However, it has always been argued that European elections should be regarded as 'second-order' national elections (see Reif and Schmitt, 'Nine Second-Order National Elections', and Reif, 'Ten Second-Order National Elections'). In other research we have shown that the extent of linkage between social groups and political party support is the same in European as in national elections. See van der Eijk, Franklin, *et al.*, *Choosing Europe?* Ch.20.
31. There still remained a number of countries for which links to social groups could not be estimated for elections prior to 1989. Portugal and Luxembourg were not included in *Electoral Change*, and it proved impossible to replicate the German findings reported there

(see *Electoral Change*, p.288). Spain and Greece were included, but the recency of democratic elections in those countries meant that the findings reported in *Electoral Change* did not extend back before the mid-1980s. Even the extrapolated data are thus missing for Germany, Greece, Luxembourg, Spain and Portugal in 1979 (Portugal and Spain are in any case missing for this election) and for Germany, Luxembourg and Portugal in 1984 (Spain's election to the European Parliament of 1984–89 was conducted not in 1984 but in 1987).

32. See Hermann Schmitt, 'Germany: A Bored Electorate' in van der Eijk, Franklin, *et al*, *Choosing Europe?*

33. This can be done by taking all the characteristics of an actual or hypothetical political system and multiplying the value taken on by each of them by the appropriate regression effect (B) in Table 2, and then adding up the results of these multiplications, together with the constant term, much as a telephone bill can be totalled from the time used at each of a number of rates together with a connection charge. Except for proportionality, independent variables are all dichotomies measuring the presence (1) or absence (0) of some characteristic. When multiplied by the appropriate coefficients, such variables yield either the value of the coefficient or 0. The measure of proportionality ranges from 0 to 100 with a maximum (in our data) of 99.

34. When brought into the equation in Table 3, Proportionality adds less than half of one per cent to variance explained, and is not quite significant at the 0.2 level. When added to an equation that excludes Social Links but is computed for the universe of countries included in Table 3, it adds almost one per cent to variance explained and is significant at almost the 0.08 level. But when that equation is taken as a starting point to which Social Links are added, the latter variable is significant at the 0.015 level and adds almost two per cent to variance explained. So it is clear that if we have to choose between these variables, it is Social Links that is the winner. Presumably in a larger dataset Proportionality would regain significance, though with a weaker effect than when Social Links are not included in the equation. The effect of Social Links is hardly affected by whether Proportionality is included or not.

35. See footnote 33 for an explanation of how to do this.

36. Especially Powell, 'Voter Turnout in Thirty Democracies' and 'American Voter Turnout in Comparative Perspective', and Jackman, 'Political Institutions and Voter Turnout'.

37. See Powell, 'Voter Turnout in Thirty Democracies' and 'American Voter Turnout in Comparative Perspective'.

38. Franklin, *et al.*, *Electoral Change*.

39. Of course, this conclusion rests on analyses that have not specifically investigated differences over time. We make the customary assumption that differences across space are equivalent to differences across time – an assumption that it is beyond the scope of the present article to evaluate.

The Blue Map of Europe: Conservative Parliamentarians and European Integration

David Baker, Imogen Fountain, Andrew Gamble and Steve Ludlam

John Major leads a party divided from top to bottom over Europe. European integration has stimulated by far the most serious rebellions in the Conservative Party's postwar history. In the early 1970s it made Edward Heath's backbenchers more rebellious than those of his postwar predecessors. But the havoc wreaked over Europe since the mid-1980s is unprecedented in scale, scope, and impact.[1] In the early 1980s, the Conservatives enjoyed watching Labour divide and split over Europe. Yet within a few years Tory divisions over Europe had contributed crucially to the damaging removals of six senior Cabinet ministers including, most spectacularly, Thatcher herself. On 22 July 1993 the prolonged Maastricht rebellion resulted in the most serious defeat sustained in parliament by any Conservative government in the twentieth century, which Major was only able to survive by resorting to a vote of confidence, threatening his backbenchers with electoral annihilation.[2] Then in March 1994, his U-turn over reform of the Qualified Majority Voting (QMV) procedure was received with contempt throughout his party.[3] He managed to survive the subsequent electoral catastrophe in the European Parliament (EP) elections because party unity had been maintained – since rebels did not want to be blamed for the expected losses – and because the losses were less severe than had been predicted, and because he then blocked the appointment of the Franco-German candidate to succeed Jacques Delors as EU Commission President.

But divisions once again dominated parliament from November 1994 when Major took the unprecedented step of making his government a minority administration by withdrawing the party Whip from eight Euro-sceptics who rebelled against increased EU budget contributions. He was almost immediately humiliated as a result when a Finance Bill to impose a higher rate of VAT on domestic fuel was lost. The early months of 1995 saw open divisions within the Cabinet over Economic and Monetary Union (EMU) and the government's approach to the 1996 Intergovernmental Conference (IGC), and tortuous manoeuvring to avoid parliamentary defeats by the 'whipless' rebels. Major's successful defeat of Labour's motion on his European policy in March 1995 – in spite of the collapse of his July 1993 Maastricht pact with the Ulster Unionist Party – suggested a respite. The 'whipless' rebels split, and although three other Tory MPs rebelled, Major held on by five votes, avoiding the necessity of another embarrassing confidence vote.

Academic debate of the Euro-rebellion has been hampered by the failure of most models of Tory ideology to integrate division over national sovereignty and foreign policy into the accounts of the dimensions of Tory thinking.[4] This article is based on an attempt to provide quantitative evidence of that dimension. It considers a number of questions that the rebellion raises about the extent and ideological content of the party's divisions, using the results of a survey of Conservative parliamentarians conducted during the 1994 EP election campaign.[5]

The Euro-rebellion has been widely portrayed as a last gasp revolt of Thatcherites unable to come to terms with her removal.[6] It has been demonstrated that the ideological impact of Thatcherism on the Conservative Party has been more limited than the heroic myth of the 'Thatcher Revolution' implies.[7] The survey allows us to test this in relation to the disputes over European integration in two ways: by comparing the responses of sitting MEPs before the 1994 EP election who were for the most part selected by the party before 1979, with those of the EP Candidates (EPCs) selected to contest the 1994 EP election; and by comparing the responses of cohorts of MPs who entered parliament before and after Thatcher took over the leadership.

The fact that a relatively small number of irreconcileable Euro-sceptics tend to dominate media interviews on Europe has given some credence to their prominence. Unsubstantiated claims and counter-claims have characterized estimates of how far Euro-scepticism actually extends on Major's backbenches beyond the core of intransigents, and how far his 'British Agenda' has support.[8] In spite of the significance of the question for party and state, it remained unanswerable during and after the Maastricht rebellion.[9] The reaction to Major's QMV U-turn in March 1994 suggested that it extended quite a distance, as the rebels often claimed, but the focus on the 'whipless' rebels after November 1994 emphasized the apparent isolation of diehard Euro-rebels. The state of backbench opinion is demonstrated here across a range of key policy issues, raising some implications for party management.

Europe is a divisive issue for several reasons. It is a grand issue that raises the place of Britain in the world economy, like the historic disputes over Corn Law repeal and tariff reform that actually split the party.[10] It tests the soul of British Conservatism, because unlike these earlier disputes, it also threatens the sovereign status of the nation and state whose defence has been crucial to the Tories' extraordinary electoral appeal since the mid-nineteenth century as the party of the Union, the Constitution, and the Empire. Insofar as it is also in part a dispute over economic intervention and monetary policy, it also follows the other main fault-line of historic Tory divisions over economic policy. It is one of the most explosive features of the European issue that it combines such ingredients in ways that cut across the familiar left–right, 'wet'–'dry', ideological wings of the party.[11] In previous work on Conservative divisions over European integration we have argued that a sovereignty/interdependence dimension, that cuts across the more familiar limited state/extended state dimension, is crucial to understanding recent divisions within the PCP.[12] In this article, we use our survey results to test this argument.

Conservative Euro-parliamentarians: Residue of Heathism or Thatcherite Expeditionary Force?

Thatcher's dismissal of her MEPs as a 'residue of Heathism'[13] was based partly on her ideological disagreements with them, and partly on the simple fact that most of them had been selected to sit in the original unelected European Assembly before she had control of the selection process and at a time when she was in any case still regarded as representing mainstream party opinion.[14] Only eight new Tory MEPs had been elected between the first EP election in 1979 and the 1994 election. Opinion differs as to whether Tory MEPs 'go native' once embraced by Community life, or whether – as most of those we interviewed before our survey agreed – they chose to be MEPs because of their Europeanism or because of family or business links with Europe. Major's 1994 cohort of new MEPs make up more than a third of sitting Tory MEPs. We are unable to test the 'going native' hypothesis here as our survey was anonymous: we cannot distinguish which of our EPC respondents was elected in 1994. But the survey does suggest that if a large group of Major's EPCs had been elected, and not succumbed to continental vices, they would have formed a substantially more 'sceptical' group than the 'residue of Heathism'. Tables 1 and 2 present survey results for MEPs and EPCs with the figures for MPs provided as a benchmark.[15]

TABLE 1

ATTITUDES OF MPs, MEPs, AND EPCs TO EUROPEAN INTEGRATION AND THE 'BRITISH AGENDA'

Statement	Status	Strongly Agree or Agree (%)	Neither (%)	Disagree or Strongly Disagree (%)
1.1 The disadvantages of EU membership have been outweighed by the benefits	MP	60	8	32
	MEP	77	0	23
	EPC	77	0	23
1.2 People who believe in free trade cannot support the EU as it has turned out	MP	32	10	58
	MEP	4	0	96
	EPC	5	18	77
1.3 Sovereignty cannot be pooled	MP	62	7	31
	MEP	27	9	64
	EPC	57	10	33
1.4 An Act of Parliament should be passed to establish explicitly the ultimate supremacy of Parliament over EU legislation	MP	50	17	33
	MEP	5	10	85
	EPC	32	14	54
1.5 The UK should incorporate the European Convention on Human Rights into law	MP	23	12	65
	MEP	73	23	4
	EPC	28	27	45
1.6 Agriculture should be handled under subsidiarity at the national level	MP	68	6	26
	MEP	24	9	67
	EPC	54	14	32
1.7 Immigration should be handled under subsidiarity at the national level	MP	81	4	15
	MEP	25	10	65
	EPC	80	8	12
1.8 Britain should join a single currency if it is created because of the economic consequences of remaining outside	MP	27	7	66
	MEP	86	5	9
	EPC	33	10	57
1.9 The establishment of a single EU currency would signal the end of the UK as a sovereign nation	MP	48	11	41
	MEP	9	5	86
	EPC	41	8	51
1.10 There should be a national referendum before the UK enters a single currency	MP	50	5	45
	MEP	23	14	63
	EPC	45	13	42
1.11 Britain should adopt the Social Protocol	MP	5	3	92
	MEP	5	14	81
	EPC	0	5	95
1.12 The extension of 'social dialogue' through the institution of works councils is a necessary component of economic progress in the EU	MP	2	3	95
	MEP	18	18	64
	EPC	2	5	93
1.13 The Conservative Party's association with the EPP is more of a political liability than an asset	MP	36	20	44
	MEP	5	0	95
	EPC	10	13	77

Note: MEP at time of EP elections in 1994; EPC means EP election candidate. Not all respondents answered every question. The overall samples were: MEPs 22 (69%), EPCs 41 (70%), MPs 110 (33%). See Appendix.

Source: Conservative Parliamentarians and European Integration Survey, ESRC/University of Sheffield 1994.

With the exception of ratification of the social protocol of the Maastricht Treaty, where all Tory parliamentarians are broadly in agreement with Major's opt-out (statement 1.11), MEPs were clearly out of line with Major and the PCP. With two further exceptions – the impact of the EU on the principle of free trade (statement 1.2) and the value of the party's link with the mainly Christian Democratic, pro-single currency, pro-social protocol European Peoples Party (statement 1.13) – the MEPs were also out of line with majority opinion among EPCs in 1994. If the gap in opinions between MEPs and EPCs on issues of European integration is a measure of the legacy and impact of Thatcherism, then the survey suggests a considerable legacy and a striking impact. On key questions on the sovereignty of the Westminster Parliament and related subsidiarity questions, the EPCs line up with the PCP with majorities taking opposite positions from MEPs (statements 1.3 to 1.7). A significant minority of MEPs favour the quintessential 'social partnership' institution of works councils (statement 1.12). On Major's other triumphant opt-out from the third, single currency stage of EMU, the EPCs are as sceptical as MPs and a long way from MEPs' attitudes (statements 1.8 to 1.10). Even when it comes to the relative powers of the institutions of the EU in which they aspire to become political actors, the EPCs largely share the suspicion and hostility of MPs.

TABLE 2
ATTITUDES OF MPs, MEPs, AND EPCs TO CONSTITUTIONAL ISSUES AT THE IGC

Statement		Status	Strongly Agree or Agree (%)	Neither (%)	Disagree or Strongly Disagree (%)
2.1	The 1996 IGC should not	MP	87	5	8
	increase the supranational	MEP	32	14	54
	powers of EU institutions	EPC	78	12	10
2.2	The key to closing the	MP	79	11	10
	'democratic deficit' is	MEP	41	9	50
	strengthening the scrutiny	EPC	73	17	10
	by national parliaments of				
	the EU legislative process				
2.3	The European parliament	MP	31	6	63
	should be given the right	MEP	82	0	18
	to initiate EU legislation	EPC	78	2	20
2.4	The Commission should	MP	60	6	34
	lose the right to initiate	MEP	18	9	73
	legislation	EPC	50	10	40
2.5	Britain should block the	MP	85	9	6
	use of QMV in the areas of	MEP	73	9	18
	foreign and defence policy	EPC	84	8	8
2.6	A Single European Army	MP	73	12	15
	would undermine rather	MEP	29	19	52
	than underpin the security	EPC	60	23	17
	of the UK				

Note: See Table 1.

Source: Conservative Parliamentarians and European Integration Survey, ESRC/University of Sheffield 1994.

Like MEPs, Major's EPCs favour the EP gaining the right to initiate legislation (statement 2.3). But beyond that they take the sceptical – and, indeed, government – line that national parliamentary scrutiny of the EU's semi-feudal legislative process is the key to endowing the EU with democratic legitimacy (statement 2.2). A bare majority agree with the rebel demand that the Commission lose its right to initiate new laws (statement 2.4). And EPCs are closer to MPs on preserving the UK veto in foreign policy, and take the opposing view to MEPs on the desirability of a single European Army (statements 2.5 to 2.6).

These findings suggest several conclusions. Apart from hostility to the labour movement, Conservative MEPs in office before the 1994 EP election were clearly out of line with the Westminster party on most issues. By contrast, the EPCs selected under Major were far closer in their opinions to the PCP than to their MEP colleagues on most key issues. If, as we must assume, the views of EPCs were known and congenial to the party bodies that selected them as candidates, then on European integration it seems clear that the legacy of the Thatcher years in the party and among its aspiring Euro-parliamentarians is both real and considerable.

A Thatcherite Cohort Effect?

Euro-rebels have frequently claimed that the more recent cohorts of new Tory MPs, like the 1983 entrants who formed the No Turning Back Group in 1985, are generally more sceptical than older MPs from the Macmillan and Heath eras. The survey permits us to compare views on Europe among Westminster MPs selected by the party and elected under Thatcher's leadership, and MPs already in the Commons in 1975 (see Appendix). The results for MPs as a whole conceal some interesting cohort effects.

In almost every case in Table 3, the Thatcher cohort appears most sceptical. Of the survey questions reported here, there are just two where majorities of the two groups of cohorts take opposing views: these are on the crucial issue of Westminster's sovereignty in relation to the supremacy of EU legislation and in relation to the impact of joining a single currency (statements 3.3 and 3.4). On the other issues the majorities of both groupings coincide, but the differences between the two groups of cohorts are marked. Pre-Thatcher MPs are more convinced of the benefits of EU membership, and less concerned with the implications for free trade (statements 3.1 and 3.2). The Thatcher cohort is more hostile to the social chapter, to industrial intervention, and to the Common Agricultural Policy (statements 3.5 to 3.7). On questions facing the 1996 IGC, it is generally among the Thatcher cohort that the strongest support is to be found for Major's 'British Agenda' (statements 3.8, 3.9, 3.11, 3.12) and indeed for Euro-rebel positions

TABLE 3

ATTITUDES OF CONSERVATIVE MPs TO EUROPEAN INTEGRATION:
PRE-THATCHER AND THATCHER COHORTS

	Statement	Status	Strongly Agree or Agree (%)	Neither (%)	Disagree or Strongly Disagree (%)
3.1	The disadvantages of EC membership have been outweighed by the benefits	1959–74	73	7	20
		1979–92	58	8	34
3.2	People who believe in free trade cannot support the EU as it has turned out	1959–74	20	7	73
		1979–92	37	11	52
3.3	An Act of Parliament should be passed to establish explicitly the ultimate supremacy of Parliament over EU legislation	1959–74	27	13	60
		1979–92	61	18	21
3.4	The establishment of a single EU currency would signal the end of the UK as a sovereign nation	1959–74	37	7	56
		1979–92	55	9	36
3.5	Britain should adopt the Social Protocol	1959–74	10	10	80
		1979–92	4	0	96
3.6	In principle there should be a Union strategy on industrial investment	1959–74	23	7	70
		1979–92	11	14	75
3.7	Agriculture should be handled over subsidiarity at the national level	1959–74	60	10	30
		1979–92	71	4	25
3.8	The 1996 IGC should not increase the supranational powers of EU institutions	1959–74	77	7	16
		1979–92	92	4	4
3.9	The key to closing the 'democratic deficit' is strengthening the scrutiny by national parliaments of the EU legislative process	1959–74	69	21	10
		1979–92	84	7	9
3.10	The Commission should lose the right to initiate legislation	1959–74	50	7	43
		1979–92	64	7	29
3.11	Britain should block the use of QMV in the areas of foreign and defence policy	1959–74	80	13	7
		1979–92	88	7	5
3.12	A single European Army would undermine rather than underpin the security of the UK	1959–74	60	13	27
		1979–92	78	11	11

Note: An MP's cohort is defined as the general election at which s/he entered parliament, or the general election following the by-election at which s/he entered. Not all respondents answered every question. The average N was 110 (33% of MPs).

Source: Conservative Parliamentarians and European Integration Survey, ESRC/University of Sheffield 1994 (statement 3.10).[16] As well as among the party's Euro-parliamentarians, then, there appears to be solid evidence of a Thatcher effect among her cohort of MPs. This suggests that while in the long run Major may be politically dead, he (or his successor) can at least look forward to the prospect of a PCP in which the passage of time will disproportionately remove the Euro-enthusiasts.

Backbench Conservative MPs: Obedient Sceptics?

The actual extent of Euro-scepticism and Euro-enthusiam on the Conservative backbenches has been a matter of partisan speculation. The small number of 'whipless' rebels in 1994–45, and the public differences between rebels, have helped divert attention from the existence of broader scepticism in the PCP. Similarly, the isolation of the small numbers of committed Conservative Euro-federalists, and the quiescence of the broader group of Euro-enthusiasts who have been used to support Conservative leaders, have distracted pundits from the strength of feeling among such MPs. The survey provides plentiful evidence that the backbenches are overwhelmingly sceptical, but also populated by considerable minorities of enthusiasts. Party discipline has suppressed much of this sentiment. This section considers their responses to a range of policy statements.

EU Membership and UK Sovereignty: Backbench Attitudes

Responses to statements 4.1–4.3 in Table 4 suggest continuing widespread belief in the advantages of EU membership on the benches of the traditional 'party of Europe'. Trends in the world economy are seen as strengthening the need for membership, and in spite of the revolt of the Thatcherite ultras, backbenchers do not regard the Union as an enemy of free trade.

Backbench Tories have considerable reservations about membership. Two-thirds reject the notion that sovereignty can be shared (statement 4.4) and are not prepared to concede the judicial interference of the European Convention on Human Rights (statement 4.8). Indeed, more than half see the 'interpretative' tendency of the European Court of Justice (ECJ) as a threat to liberty (statement 4.6). One startling consequence of such reservations is that Major's backbenchers would like to see a new 'Act of Supremacy' that would in effect overturn the Treaty of Rome's insistence on EU legislative precedence over Westminster law (statement 4.5). Paradoxically, but consistent with several other such anomalies, they welcome the ECJ's new Maastricht powers to police the single market (statement 4.7).

As Major found in March 1994, QMV – which will be on the 1996 IGC agenda – is a constitutional question capable of provoking considerable backbench anger. The QMV procedure for overriding national vetoes was

TABLE 4

EU MEMBERSHIP AND UK SOVEREIGNTY: BACKBENCH CONSERVATIVE ATTITUDES

	Statement	Strongly Agree or Agree (%)	Neither (%)	Disagree or Strongly Disagree (%)
4.1	The disadvantages of EC membership have been outweighed by the benefits.	59	9	32
4.2	The globalisation of economic activity makes European Union (EU) membership more, rather than less necessary for the UK.	62	8	30
4.3	People who believe in free trade cannot support the EU as it has turned out.	32	11	57
4.4	Sovereignty cannot be pooled.	64	6	30
4.5	An Act of Parliament should be passed to establish explicitly the ultimate supremacy of Parliament over EU legislation.	56	16	28
4.6	The continental system of jurisprudence as practiced by the European Court of Justice is a threat to liberty in Britain.	55	19	26
4.7	The increased powers of the European Court to enforce the Single Market are welcome.	67	15	18
4.8	The UK should incorporate the European Convention on Human Rights into law.	24	8	68
4.9	The 1996 IGC should abolish QMV.	20	14	66
4.10	Britain should block the use of QMV in the areas of foreign and defence policy.	87	6	7
4.11	QMV should be used to advance EU policy against terrorism and drug trafficking.	59	22	19

Note: Not all respondents answered every question. Average N of 90 backbenchers.

Source: Conservative Parliamentarians and European Integration Survey, ESRC/University of Sheffield 1994

invoked by Thatcher to brush aside opposition to the single market programme but was subsequently extended by the Maastricht Treaty to more policy areas. Because it is such a direct abrogation of national sovereignty, it has enormous potential for igniting rebellion. Backbenchers are nevertheless ambivalent. Only a fifth want the procedure to be abolished at the IGC (statement 4.9), and a clear majority favour the use of the mechanism to stiffen EU anti-terrorism and anti-drug trafficking activity (statement 4.11). The demand by 87 per cent of backbenchers that Britain should prevent QMV being extended to the EU's Foreign and Security intergovernmental pillar, as presaged in the Maastricht Treaty[17] (statement 4.10), is in line with the party's stance in the EP election but may complicate the 'softly softly' attempts of the Foreign Office to further develop European military integration.[18]

'Variable Geometry', Community Competence, and Subsidiarity: Backbench Attitudes

Major's perception that future enlargement of the EU will bolster his intergovernmentalist line also has backing. A majority see 'widening' as the best defence against 'deepening' and are happy to see enlargement proceed along 'multi-track' lines without the precondition of full legislative obligations, *acquis communitaire* (statements 5.1 and 5.2). More worrying for Major is the two-thirds of his backbenchers who agree with the rebel demand to abolish the 'cohesion funds'[19] (statement 5.3), a vital EU mechanism for compensating poorer areas – including all the current candidates for enlargement – likely to be stricken by the economic effects of the single market and EMU.

Hostility to fiscal interventionism from the EU extends over a range of taxation issues, embracing both the push towards an EU energy tax that Britain has blocked, and the harmonization of VAT, two combustible issues that ignited in the VAT on fuel revolt in December 1994 (statements 5.4 and 5.5). Only one statement proposing central economic strategies secured the support of more than half of backbench Tories. This was a call for a deregulation strategy (statement 5.6), a key plank in Major's 'British Agenda' platform. There was 70 per cent opposition to a Community industrial investment strategy (statement 5.8), and corresponding opposition (statement 5.9) to the 'Union Bond' mechanism proposed to ensure funding of the Trans-European Networks programme that was blocked by Kenneth Clarke at the December 1993 summit.[20] Tory MPs clearly do not trust the Commission to pursue a privatization strategy, particularly after it derailed 'contracting out' in the public services by enforcing continuity of workers' contracts (statement 5.7).

The emphasis in the Maastricht Treaty on subsidiarity and its subsequent elaboration has been a key feature of Major's 'British Agenda'. The survey suggests that Tory MPs approve of it and even look forward to repatriating some policy agendas already ceded to the EU's competence. Over 70 per cent of respondents apparently want to regain national control over the health and safety legislative process conceded under the Single European Act, and furthermore would welcome the abolition of the Common Agricultural Policy (statements 5.11 and 5.12). Even larger majorities want to retain control of policy areas sensitive to Tory backbenchers such as border controls and immigration, both subject to provisions of the Maastricht Treaty[21] (statements 5.13 and 5.14).

TABLE 5
'VARIABLE GEOMETRY', EU COMPETENCE, AND SUBSIDIARITY: BACKBENCH
CONSERVATIVE ATTITUDES

Statement		Strongly Agree or Agree (%)	Neither (%)	Disagree or Strongly Disagree (%)
5.1	Acceptance of the *acquis communitaire* must be a condition of entry of new states into the Union.	36	14	50
5.2	Enlargement is the best means to arrest the centralization of political power in the EU.	56	24	20
5.3	Cohesion funds should be phased out.	66	18	16
5.4	Environmental taxation should be harmonised within the EU.	26	5	69
5.5	VAT should be harmonised within the EU	20	4	76
5.6	In principle there should be an EU strategy on deregulation	54	9	37
5.7	In principle there should be an EU strategy on privatisation	26	15	59
5.8	In principle there should be an EU strategy on industrial investment	16	14	70
5.9	If necessary, major EU projects should be funded by the issue of 'Union Bonds' by the EU	24	24	52
5.10	Environmental protection should be handled under subsidiarity at the national level	48	8	44
5.11	Health and safety should be handled under subsidiarity at the national level	71	6	23
5.12	Agriculture should be handled under subsidiarity at the national level	72	5	23
5.13	Border controls should be handled under subsidiarity at the national level	74	7	19
5.14	Immigration should be handled under subsidiarity at the national level	81	4	15
5.15	Trade union rights should be handled under subsidiarity at the national level	86	5	9
5.16	Subsidiarity reinforces the federalist tendency in the EU.	31	12	57

Note: See Table 4.

Source: Conservative Parliamentarians and European Integration Survey, ESRC/University of Sheffield 1994.

There is ambivalence on control of environmental protection (statement 5.10), which did not extend to harmonizing environmental taxation (statement 5.4). There is no ambivalence, as might be expected, on trade union rights (statement 5.15). A surprisingly large minority of one-third of backbenchers adopt the subtly hardline rebel attitude[22] that subsidiarity is merely a cloak for a federal regime dispensing subsidiary powers to nation states (statement 5.16).

Major's Maastricht Opt-outs: Backbench Attitudes

In the Maastricht Treaty the key elements of Major's multi-tracking agenda were the opt-outs from the treaty's social protocol and from the third, single currency stage of EMU. Not surprisingly, the social chapter opt-out that produced such drama during the ratification of the treaty has almost unanimous support on the backbenches (statement 6.1). The statement (6.2) on social costs, ironically reflecting the stance of Delors's white paper on growth, produced a large majority on a key 'social dimension' issue, as did one of the core assumptions of the Commission's social policy white paper (statement 6.3).[23] On two specific social policy developments, the 48-hour working week and the introduction of works councils in multinational companies – which the British Government has resisted in the European Court and by invoking the Social Chapter opt-out respectively – Major can count on overwhelming backbench support (statements 6.4 and 6.5).

Both the Cabinet and the Conservative parliamentary ranks are divided over the third stage of EMU. The programme of the third stage will be discussed at the 1996 IGC, and the prospect of a single currency has formed the focal point of Euro-dissidence as well as of demands for a referendum. The survey revealed backbench hostility far beyond the official Cabinet agnosticism. Considering the humiliation of government and party in September 1992, a suprisingly narrow majority took the view that Britain should never rejoin the Exchange Rate Mechanism (statements 6.6). Barely a third of backbenchers saw EMU as desirable (statement 6.7). Backbench attitudes to a single currency were uncompromisingly hostile, by large majorities. The single currency was not seen as essential to the operation of a single market,[24] and only a quarter of backbench Tories thought the UK should join a single currency, rather than risk the economic consequences of staying out, or allow a European Central Bank to set UK monetary policy (statements 6.8 to 6.10). A bare majority believed (with Thatcher)[25] that a single currency would bring about the end of the UK as a sovereign nation, and over half agreed with the Euro-rebel demand that a referendum should precede entry into such a currency (statements 6.11 and 6.12). Since the survey, support for a referendum has spread among MPs who see it more as a device to prevent the Conservative Party splitting than as a strategy for derailing EMU, and as such it has become an ace up Major's sleeve. His refusals to rule out a referendum have become increasingly positive as pressure has mounted on him, and he is confident in any case that no vote on EMU will be necessary in this parliament, nor is the IGC likely to produce any recommendations with serious constitutional consequences before the next general election.

TABLE 6
MAJOR'S MAASTRICHT OPT-OUTS: BACKBENCH CONSERVATIVE ATTITUDES

Statement	Strongly Agree or Agree (%)	Neither (%)	Disagree or Strongly Disagree (%)
6.1 Britain should adopt the Social Protocol	5	2	93
6.2 Reduction of the burden of social costs placed on employers is essential to job creation in the EU.	88	2	10
6.3 Convergence of working standards should be a key objective of EU integration.	11	10	79
6.4 The UK should use the 'Luxembourg Compromise' to prevent imposition of a maximum 48 hour week in Britain.	84	5	11
6.5 The extension of 'social dialogue' through the institution of works councils is a necessary component of economic progress in the EU.	2	2	96
6.6 Britain should never rejoin the ERM.	52	15	33
6.7 EMU is not desirable	61	9	30
6.8 You will not be able to maintain a Single Market unless you have a single currency.	14	9	77
6.9 Britain should join a single currency if it is created because of the economic consequences of remaining outside.	26	6	68
6.10 Britain should never permit its monetary policy to be determined by an independent European Central Bank.	64	9	27
6.11 The establishment of a single EU currency would signal the end of the UK as a sovereign nation.	51	11	38
6.12 There should be a national referendum before the UK enters a single currency.	55	4	41

Note: See Table 4.

Source: Conservative Parliamentarians and European Integration Survey, ESRC/University of Sheffield 1994.

The 1996 IGC and the EU Constitution: Backbench Attitudes

On the range of constitutional reform issues facing the IGC in 1996, a majority of Major's backbenchers revealed themselves to be closely aligned with his open rebels, many of whom shifted their focus to constitutional issues after the collapse of ERM in August 1993. The strong opposition to further supranationalism should encourage the Government in its approach to the

IGC but may unsettle it, given that some compromises are virtually inevitable (statement 7.1). The neo-Gaullism of the Tory benches is further illustrated by attitudes to the main EU institutions. The Council of Ministers, in which ministers of nation states adopt legislation, is strongly preferred as the supreme institution (statement 7.2). The pattern of ambivalence in respect to the single market is revealed again in relation to the European Commission (statement 7.3). Over 60 per cent of backbench Conservatives nevertheless adopt the Euro-rebel view that the Commission should lose control of the initiation of the legislative process,[26] and a similar percentage oppose the proposition that the EP should acquire the right of legislative initiative (statements 7.4 and 7.5). Four-fifths endorse the position common to many rebels, and to Major and his allies, that the best means of restoring popular legitimacy to the EU is by enhancing the role of national parliaments in scrutinizing legislation (statement 7.6). The misery of Bosnia as well as the development of the Common Foreign and Security pillar will ensure that military amalgamation climbs the agenda of European integration. Opposition to a Euro-army incidentally formed the subject of one of the party's central slogans directed in vain against the opposition parties in the EP election campaign. On this matter, three-quarters of the party's backbench MPs take a view that may eventually turn out to be more difficult for the party leadership than many other opinions revealed in the survey (statement 7.7).

TABLE 7
THE 1996 IGC AND THE EU CONSTITUTION: BACKBENCH CONSERVATIVE ATTITUDES

	Statement	Strongly agree or Agree (%)	Neither (%)	Disagree or Strongly disagree (%)
7.1	The 1996 IGS should not increase the supranational powers of EU institutions.	88	5	7
7.2	The Council of Ministers should be the supreme institution in the EU.	80	4	16
7.3	A strong Commission is vital for the success of the Single Market programme.	47	9	44
7.4	The Commission should lose the right to initiate legislation.	61	4	35
7.5	The European Parliament should be given the right to initiate EU legislation.	34	4	62
7.6	The key to closing the 'democratic deficit' is strengthening the scrutiny by national parliaments of the EU legislative process.	82	9	9
7.7	A single European Army would undermine rather than underpin the security of the UK.	73	12	15

Note: See Table 4.
Source: Conservative Parliamentarians and European Integration Survey, ESRC/University of Sheffield 1994.

Problematic Minorities

Major's general problem of party management over European integration can be illustrated by identifying issues where backbench opinion is so divided that it could overwhelm his tiny Commons majority, and particularly on EU issues where he has to contend with a significant hard-core minority of backbench MPs who may translate discontent into rebellious voting behaviour. On certain issues more than 40 per cent of backbenchers can be found on *both* sides of an argument. Such is the case in responses to the propositions that 'A strong Commission is vital for the success of the Single Market programme', that 'There should be a national referendum before the UK enters a single currency', and that 'Environmental protection should be handled under subsidiarity at the national level'. This places over 100 backbenchers on opposing sides of the argument. Table 8 identifies significant minorities of both Euro-sceptics and Euro-enthusiasts across a range of policy issues.

Such a degree of division over such a range of key positions, including some that must become prominent during the debates about the 1996 IGC, suggests that in spite of the quiescence that characterized the EP election campaign, and indeed in spite of the support that Major enjoys for much of his Conservative agenda for Europe, he is nevertheless confronted by a monumental party management task. He faces such considerable bodies of opinion on both wings of the European argument that he seems to have little room for manoeuvre, even if he could set the parameters for debate in the run up to 1996. By early 1995 it was clear that Euro-enthusiasts had decided they could no longer rely on the tacit support of the Cabinet. The 'Positive Europe' group of MPs delivered to Major a strongly worded petition bearing 52 signatures demanding that ministers 'counter the relentlessly negative attitudes of the media and the Eurosceptics'. The newly-formed ginger group Action Centre for Europe (ACE) amassed considerable funds and heavyweight backing to launch a campaign against the 'wave of anti-European sentiment' and an 'unrelenting stream of misleading propaganda'.[27]

A New Dimension of Conservative Ideology?

We have argued elsewhere that the traditonal left–right dimension of Conservative ideology has cut across a sovereignty versus interdependence axis. This divides Tory MPs who regard national sovereignty as a policy resource, to be exchanged for prosperity or security, from MPs who regard the sovereignty of the British state – and above all that of the House of Commons – as sacrosanct and as the essential feature of British democracy legitimizing the rule of law.[28] The extension of QMV, the pursuit of a single currency and a European Central Bank, and the fear of a Maastricht Mark Two emerging from the 1996 IGC have all threatened Conservative unity because of fears over sovereignty.

TABLE 8
SIGNIFICANT BACKBENCH CONSERVATIVE MINORITIES

Statements on which minorities between 30% and 40% adopt a 'Euro-sceptic' stance:
• The disadvantages of EC membership have been outweighed by the benefits.
• People who believe in free trade cannot support the EU as it has turned out.
• The globalisation of economic activity makes EU membership more, rather than less, necessary for the UK.

Statements on which minorities between 15% and 30% adopt a 'Euro-sceptic' stance:
• Sovereignty cannot be pooled.
• Intergovernmentalism is an effort to diminish the power of the central EU institutions.
• The increased powers of the European Court to enforce the Single Market are welcome.
• The 1996 IGC should abolish QMV.
• QMV should be used to advance EU policy against terrorism and drug trafficking

Statements on which minorities between 30% and 40% adopt 'Euro-enthusiast' stance:
• Acceptance of the *acquis communitaire* must be a condition of entry of new states into the EU.
• The establishment of a single EU currency would signal the end of the UK as a sovereign nation.
• Britain should never rejoin the ERM.
• EMU is not desirable.
• An Act of Parliament should be passed to establish explicitly the ultimate supremacy of Parliament over EU legislation.
• The Commission should lose the right to initiate legislation.
• The European Parliament should be given the right to initiate EU legislation.

Statements on which minorities between 15% and 30% adopt a 'Euro-enthusiast' stance:
• A single European Army would undermine rather than underpin the security of the UK.
• The UK should incorporate the European Convention on Human Rights into law.
• Britain should never permit its monetary policy to be determined by an independent European Central Bank.
• Britain should join a single currency if it is created because of the economic consequences of remaining outside.
• In principle there should be Union strategies on industrial investment.
• If necessary, major EU projects should be funded by the issue of 'Union Bonds' by the EU.
• Agriculture policy should be handled under subsidiarity at the national level.
• Health and safety should be handled under subsidiarity at the national level.

Note: See Table 4. 15% is the approximate equivalent of 38 backbenchers, 30% of around 75, 40% of around 100.

Source: Conservative Parliamentarians and European Integration Survey, ESRC/University of Sheffield 1994

Defence of sovereignty is rarely absolute. Membership of the Union always meant subordination of Westminster law to EU law, and very few sceptics favour withdrawal. Ambivalence is displayed by rebels who defend the use of QMV to create the single market – pooling sovereignty in pursuit of economic liberalism – but who attack the new uses of QMV in the Maastricht Treaty as undermining national sovereignty. On currency control and independent central banking, older divisions over state intervention are criss-crossed by new disputes within the 'monetarist' camp of the early 1980s over whether discretion in monetary policy should be retained by the British government or whether it should be 'privatized' at a European level. 'Fixers v Floaters', the title of a chapter in Thatcher's memoirs, reflects neo-liberal antagonism to all fixed exchange rate mechanisms. [29]

We can identify the location of backbench MPs along the left–right and sovereignty–interdependence axes using responses to statements on the social chapter and on EMU, arguably the most controversial 'pooling' sovereignty issue in the party. Figure 1 plots backbench MPs' responses to the following statements:

- Britain should adopt the Social Protocol.
- Reduction of the burden of social costs placed on employers is essential to job creation in the EU.
- Inflexibility in European labour markets is the principal cause of unemployment.
- Convergence of working standards should be a key objective of EU integration.
- The UK should use the 'Luxembourg Compromise' to prevent imposition of a maximum 48-hour week in Britain.
- The extension of 'social dialogue' through the institution of works councils is a necessary component of economic progress in the EU.
- EMU is not realizable.
- EMU is not desirable.
- Britain should never rejoin the ERM
- The operation of the European Monetary Institute will improve UK macroeconomic policy.
- You will not be able to maintain a Single Market unless you have a single currency.
- Britain should join a single currency if it is created because of the economic consequences of remaining outside.
- Britain should never permit its monetary policy to be determined by an independent European Central Bank.
- The establishment of a single EU currency would signal the end of the UK as a sovereign nation.
- There should be a national referendum before the UK enters a single currency.

Responses – the standard scale of 'strongly agree' through to 'strongly disagree' – were coded 1 to 5 and then aggregated. A score of 1 or 2 on the EMU sovereignty-interdependence X axis indicates agreement with the sceptical, sovereignty stance; whereas scores of 4 or 5 indicate agreement with the integrationist, Europeanist stance. Similarly, on the social dimension Y axis, scores of 1 or 2 indicate support for the neo-liberal limited state stance; and 4 or 5 support for the 'progressive' Conservative extended state stance. Scores of 3 indicate neither agreement nor disagreement. The most nationalistic and neo-liberal position is thus 1 on both scales, while the most integrationist and 'progressive' position is 5.

FIGURE 1

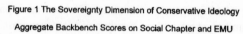

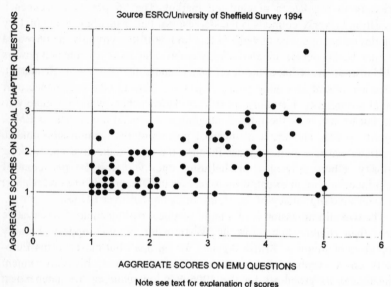

AGGREGATE SCORES ON EMU QUESTIONS

Note see text for explanation of scores

Apart from the concentration of opinion in the neo-liberal and pro-sovereignty corner of the graph, what is striking about it is that while there are just two cases with scores placing them at the pro-social chapter end of that dimension, backbenchers are divided from end to end of the sovereignty (EMU) dimension. This is very powerful quantitative evidence endorsing the argument we have made in the past, that the party's ideological composition is now best analysed in terms of a sovereignty–interdependence axis as well as traditional left–right dimensions.[30]

Conclusions

Our findings demonstrate that whatever else may be said about the impact of Thatcherism, the period of her leadership witnessed a marked shift of attitudes among both potential new MEPs and new cohorts of MPs. Conservative candidates for the EP are not seeking a career insulated from a sceptical Westminster party; they are, on most questions, indistinguishable from their Commons colleagues. In the Commons, the MPs elected under Thatcher are significantly more sceptical than their predecessors, and are opposed to them on some key issues bearing on Westminster's sovereignty.

The survey reveals the impact of the political shifts of the Thatcher years in terms of the hostility of the parliamentary Conservative party to social and labour policy and to most forms of economic intervention, other than those necessary to regulate a deregulated market. The 96 per cent backbench opposition to works councils is the starkest symbol of this dimension of Tory attitudes on Europe. The obverse of this finding is that virtually the only area in which backbenchers are consistently ambivalent about the role and powers of EU institutions is that of the development and policing of the single market, where neo-liberal economic policy objectives seem to take precedence over formal sovereignty. Certainly most Tory backbenchers want not merely to halt, but to turn back the tide of integration in crucial areas such as EMU, majority voting, and the constitutional powers of the Commission, and to repatriate sensitive policy areas. Perhaps the most indicative and striking majority, albeit not an overwhelming one, was the 56 per cent of backbenchers who, in effect, want to tear up the Treaty of Rome and reassert the legislative supremacy of the House of Commons over EU law.

The overall impression is of a more sceptical parliamentary Conservative Party than visible behaviour at Westminster would suggest, broadly supportive of Major's 'British Agenda for Europe', but closer to his Euro-rebels on a number of key issues. If, as expected, his Government concentrates its proposals for the 1996 IGC on reducing the independent power of the Commission and strengthening the intergovernmental wing of the EU and the scrutiny function of national parliaments, it would appear to have the backing of the majority of its backbenchers, though again there is majority support for Euro-rebel demands. Almost any acceleration of integration at the 1996 IGC will generate even more dissent and potential rebellion by Euro-sceptics who remain the principal source of active dissent. If Major faces widespread sceptical discontent, in the final analysis disaster will be prevented, not by MPs' attitudes to European integration, but rather by fear of electoral annihilation and the absence of an alternative right-wing parliamentary party for the Euro-rebels to join. Whether Major calls the next general election before or after the conclusion of IGC may even depend as much on such calculations as on the state of the economy.

In terms of party management, the size of the minorities of Euro-enthusiasts or Euro-sceptics on most contentious issues is arguably as serious a sign for party leaders as is the evident sympathy for rebel positions that have become increasingly mainstream. Coverage of the party's Euro-travails frequently underestimates the anger of its Euro-enthusiasts, which may become much more significant if Major approaches the IGC in an overwhelmingly obstructive mood. There is a considerable group of backbenchers committed to deeper European integration and for whom the recent and probable future direction of Conservative policy on Europe is likely to be very unwelcome. There may come a time when, like Labour's Europeanists in the early 1980s, some decide that there is no longer any point in remaining in the party.

Again and again, responses to our survey reveal not only overall hostility to ceding sovereignty, but also the existence of very strong divisions over such issues. For many MPs, sceptics included, whether to 'pool' sovereignty is a pragmatic matter about how best to bargain with sovereignty as a policy resource. The support for strong intervention to regulate the single market by the Commission and the ECJ – the two EU institutions which Tory backbenchers see as most threatening to Westminster's sovereignty – is the clearest evidence of this. But on a wide range of policy issues, solid majorities of Major's MPs – and, as far as we can tell, his ministers – are keen not just to resist further political integration, but to dismantle many existing Community competences. They want to restore national control of agricultural, and health and safety policy, and proposals at the IGC to weaken national control of foreign and defence policy or border and immigration controls would provoke fury on his backbenches. The sovereignty-interdependence dimension is now the crucial dividing line among Conservatives. Figure 1 is the starkest empirical evidence of this development, upon which future research will need to focus.

John Major has made party unity his highest priority over Europe. He has manoeuvred skillfully to avoid confrontation but has not hesitated to confront his rebels with the threat of a ruinous general election when he has been forced to hold a vote of confidence. So far he has succeeded where it is hard to see other potential leaders managing, not least Thatcher. But the fact that he is the least objectionable leader available merely highlights the degree of irreconcilable division revealed in our survey. In spite of all its leaders' warnings, the Conservative Party may yet find itself re-enacting the calamitous historic splits over Corn Law Repeal and Tariff Reform that kept it out of office for a generation.

APPENDIX

The survey contained 65 questions on European integration framed to reflect a variety of standpoints on the main issues. In four mailings, between 21 April and 15 June 1994, the questionnaire was sent to all Conservative MPs, MEPs and candidates in the EP election. Excluding non-respondents to identification questions, the response rate was as follows: 69 per cent of sitting MEPs (N=22); 70 per cent of EPCs (N=41; of those who were not already sitting MEPs or MPs); 38 per cent of backbench MPs, and 19 per cent of ministers, giving an overall response rate of 33 per cent for MPs. The resulting sample of MPs was tested for ideological bias because of the controversial nature of the issues covered and the high level of tendential activity. Questionnaires were anonymous, but three-quarters of respondents also returned a separate identity-coded postcard, enabling such tests. We used Norton's typology of Conservative MPs, whose merits we have discussed elsewhere,[31] with the following results:

TABLE 9
DISTRIBUTION OF IDENTIFIED MP RESPONDENTS, INCLUDING MINISTERS,
BY NORTON CATEGORY

	% 1989 PCP	% Identified Respondents
'Thatcherites'	19	15
'Loyalists'	63	66
'Damps/Wets'	18	18

Note: excludes MPs elected in 1992 who are not classified by Norton.

We also analysed respondents in terms of their cohort, that is, which general election brought them into parliament or followed their entry in a by-election:

TABLE 10
REPRESENTATIVENESS IN TERMS OF COHORTS

	% PCP	% respondents		% PCP	% respondents
1950	0	0	1979	17	18
1959	1	2	1983	20	18
1964/66	6	8	1987	15	19
1970	10	10	1992	17	16
1974 I/II	14	10			

We further tested our known respondents by two measures of *backbench* parliamentary behaviour over Europe. In rounded figures, our *known* respondents include 31 per cent of all Tory backbenchers, 30 per cent of the Maastricht Bill Third Reading rebels, and 33 per cent of the wider 'sceptical' group of signers of the two 'fresh start' Early Day Motions presented in 1992 after the first Danish referendum and after Black Wednesday.

Overall, the tests establish a very high degree of representativeness in the sample in terms of cohort representation, of ideological typology, and of measurable backbench behaviour over Europe.

NOTES

1. See Nigel Ashford, 'The European Economic Community' in Zig Layton-Henry (ed.), *Conservative Party Politics* (London: Macmillan, 1980); Philip Norton, *Conservative Dissidents: Dissent within the Parliamentary Conservative Party 1970–74* (London: Maurice Temple Smith, 1978).
2. See David Baker, Andrew Gamble and Steve Ludlam, 'The Parliamentary Siege of

Maastricht 1993: Conservative Divisions and British Ratification of the Treaty on European Union', *Parliamentary Affairs* Vol 47, No.1 (1994).

3. See Steve Ludlam, 'Britain and the European Union' in Peter Catterall and Virginia Preston (eds), *Contemporary Britain: An Annual Review 1995* (Aldershot: Dartmouth, 1995).

4. David Baker, Andrew Gamble and Steve Ludlam, 'Mapping Conservative Fault Lines: Problems of Typology', in Patrick Dunleavy and Jeffery Stanyer (eds), *Contemporary Political Studies 1994* (Exeter: University of Exeter Press, 1994).

5. The survey was funded as part of ESRC Award No.R000231298, and was carried out by the Parliament Project in the Department of Politics at the University of Sheffield. See the appendix for details. The survey dataset is available from the ESRC Data Archive; other enquiries should be addressed to Steve Ludlam.

6. For a general discussion of this argument, see Steve Ludlam 'Backbench Rebellions: Europe, the Spectre Haunting Conservatism' in Steve Ludlam and Martin J. Smith *Contemporary British Conservatism* (Basingstoke: Macmillan, 1996).

7. For evidence see Ivor Crewe and Donald Searing 'Ideological Change in the British Conservative Party', *American Political Science Review* Vol.82 No.2. (1988); Philip Norton 'The Lady's not for Turning' But What about the Rest? Margaret Thatcher and the Conservative Party 1979–89' *Parliamentary Affairs* Vol.43 No.1. (1990); Paul Whiteley, Patrick Seyd and Jeremy Richardson *True Blues: the Politics of Conservative Party Membership* (Oxford: Oxford University Press, 1994).

8. The 'British Agenda' contains a number of core elements: enlargement to bring in 'net contributor' states supposedly more congenial to UK policy; greater flexibility in labour markets and reduced social costs; development of intergovernmentalism and subsidiarity to secure a Community of nation states; economic liberalization including global free trade and deregulation within the Community; fiscal restraint; and, most famously the 'flexible co-operation' of a 'multi-track' Europe exemplified by Britain's Maastricht opt-outs. Major set out his perspective in 'Raise your eyes, there is a land beyond' *The Economist* 25/09/93, re-iterated during the EP election campaign in the 'Ellesmere Port Declaration' of the 'Speech by the Rt Hon John Major MP, Prime Minister and Leader of the Conservative Party, to a European Rally at the Civic Centre, Ellesmere Port, 31/05/94' and at Leiden in 'Europe: a Future that Works. William and Mary Lecture given by the Prime Minister the Rt Hon John Major MP at the University, Leiden, 7 September 1994'. The manifesto version is in Conservative Party *A Strong Britain in a Strong Europe: the Conservative Manifesto for Europe 1994* (London: Conservative Central Office, 1994).

9. The difference between the proportions of the PCP taking a sceptical view on European integration issues and the proportions actively rebelling is discussed in David Baker, Andrew Gamble, Steve Ludlam and David Seawright, 'Backbenchers with Attitude: the Gap between British Conservative MPs' Private Opinions and Parliamentary Behaviour during the Passage of the Maastricht Bill 1993', European Consortium for Political Research Joint Sessions, Bordeaux 1995.

10. See David Baker, Andrew Gamble and Steve Ludlam, '1846 ... 1906 ... 1996? Conservative Splits and European Integration', *Political Quarterly* Vol.64 No.4 (1993).

11. Arthur Aughey, *Conservative Party Attitudes Towards The Common Market: Hull Papers in Politics No.2* (Hull: University of Hull, 1978) p.14. Hugh Berrington, *Backbench Opinion in the House of Commons 1945–55* (Oxford: Pergamon, 1973) p.167. Samuel Finer, Hugh Berrington and D.J. Bartholomew, *Backbench Opinion in the House of Commons, 1955–59*, (Oxford: Permagon, 1961), pp.87ff. Patrick Seyd, 'Factionalism within the Conservative Party: the Monday Club', *Government and Opposition* Autumn 1972, p.478.

12. Baker *et al.*, '1846', 'Mapping'.

13. Margaret Thatcher, *The Downing Street Years* (London: HarperCollins, 1993), p.749.

14. Ashford, 'The European Economic Community'.

15. Figures given here are for all MPs. A fifth of serving ministers completed questionnaires, insufficient to make sound generalizations. On most issues, there was little significant difference between minsters' and backbenchers' responses. Ministers were usually marginally less sceptical than backbenchers, but sometimes markedly less so in contentious areas of policy.

THE BLUE MAP OF EUROPE 73

16. See No Turning Back Group *A Conservative Europe: 1994 and Beyond* (London: European Foundation/No Turning Back Group, 1994); European Research Group *A Europe of Nations: Report of the European Research Group* (London: European Research Group, 1995).
17. In the Maastricht *Treaty on European Union* 'Declaration on Voting in the Field of the Common Foreign and Security Policy'.
18. For pro-European views on CFSP see Ian Taylor, *The Positive Europe*, (London: The Conservative Group for Europe, 1993) pp.4–13; Conservative Political Centre, *The Common Foreign and Security Policy of the European Union: a Report to the Foreign Secretary from a CPC National Policy Group*, (London: Conservative Political Centre, 1994).
19. No Turning Back Group, *A Conservative Europe*, p.12.
20. Commission of the European Communities, *European Council in Brussels 10 and 11 December 1993, Presidency Conclusions. SN 373/93*, (London: Office of the Commission of the European Communities, 1993).
21. Article K1 of the Maastricht *Treaty on European Union.*
22. See Michael Spicer MP, *A Treaty too Far: a New Policy for Europe* (London: Fourth Estate, 1992), p.115.
23. Commission of the European Communities, *Com(93) 700 Final. Brussels, 5 December 1993. Growth, Competitiveness, Employment: The Challenges and Ways Forward into the 21st Century. White Paper*, (London: Office of the Commission of the European Communities, 1993), p.15; Commission of the European Communities, *Com(94) 333 Final Brussels, 27 July 1994. European Social Policy – A Way Forward for the Union – a White Paper*, (London: Office of the Commission of the European Communities, 1994), p.5.
24. For a characteristic presentation of this proposition, see Alan Walters, 'Economic versus Monetary Union' in Stephen Hill (ed.), *Visions of Europe: Summing up the Political Choices*, (London: Duckworth, 1993).
25. Thatcher, *Downing Street*, pp.690–1.
26. Proposed most recently in European Research Group *A Europe of Nations*, p.8.
27. *Positive European Group Statement 2 February 1995* (London: House of Commons, 1995); *Action Centre for Europe Mission Statement* (Whittle-le-Woods: Action Centre for Europe, 1995). ACE had Lord Whitelaw, who led the party's Britain in Europe campaign in the 1975 referendum, as Patron, Lord Howe as President, and both Kenneth Clarke and David Hunt on its Advisory Board. At Clarke's suggestion, its first working party and published report were on the single currency. Lord Kingsdown, formerly Thatcher's Governor of the Bank of England, chaired the working party.
28. For advocacy of 'pooling' sovereignty see Geoffery Howe, 'Sovereignty and Interdependence: Britain's Place in the World' *International Affairs* Vol.66, No.4 (1990), pp 678, 687; Ian Gilmour, *Dancing with Dogma: Britain under Thatcherism*, (London: Pocket Books, 1993), pp.323–5; Michael Heseltine, *Where there's a Will*, (London: Arrow Books, 1990), pp.273–4. For opposite views see Keith Minogue *Is Sovereignty a Big Bad Wolf?* (London: The Bruges Group, 1990), p.20. European Foundation, *The Bournemouth Speeches: Bill Cash MP, Sir James Goldsmith MEP, Rt Hon Lord Tebbit*, (London: European Foundation, 1994), pp.7–8.; and several essays in Hill, *Visions.*
29. Thatcher *Downing Street*; also Nicholas Ridley, *My Style of Government: the Thatcher Years*, (London: Fontana, 1992) p.194 *et passim*; Spicer, *Treaty*, pp.96, 100.
30. For further exploration of this point using our survey evidence, see David Baker, Imogen Fountain, Andrew Gamble and Steve Ludlam, 'Sovereignty: the San Andreas Fault of Conservative Ideology?', Political Studies Association Annual Conference, York, April 1995.
31. Baker *et al.*, 'Mapping'.

An Analysis of Britain's Party Manifestos for Europe, 1979–94

Scott D. Clarke

Introduction

Britain's major political parties have traditionally adopted a cautious approach in fighting elections to the European Parliament. The relative impotency of the European Parliament within the process of European Community decision-making has not encouraged Britain's parties to campaign to any great extent or with much vigour.[1] Rather than exacerbate or draw attention to already existing intra-party divisions on EC issues both the Conservative Party and the Labour Party have tended to campaign for European elections in a relatively low-key manner. Even the Liberal Democrats, traditionally the party most committed to the concept of a European Parliament, have failed to approach the European elections with the same energy and drive that they normally demonstrate during campaigns for the national parliament.

As a policy area the EC has continued to cause Britain's major parties considerable difficulty.[2] In particular, the Conservative and Labour parties have both experienced intense internal party conflict over the desired future direction of European integration.[3] This was particularly evident within the Labour Party during the early 1980s as the European issue became entangled in a much larger struggle for control of the party leadership. In more recent years the Conservative Party has found itself rocked by the obstructionist tactics of several Euro-sceptics within the party over the Maastricht Treaty and Britain's commitment to a single European currency.

The difficulties experienced by Britain's major parties over the European question have made elections to the European Parliament all the more challenging. Due to the widening scope of EC activity British parties can no longer afford to avoid European issues simply because of the internal difficulties that they may cause. More importantly, recent developments in the process of European integration have served to strengthen the powers of the European Parliament. It is now of considerable political importance for Britain's major parties to achieve sufficient representation within the European Parliament.

The aim of this article is to analyse and compare the European election manifestos of Britain's three major parties from 1979–94. More specifically, computer-assisted content analysis is applied to the text of the twelve manifestos involved in order to measure changes to their thematic composition and general orientation over four successive European elections. It is hoped that such an analysis will further our understanding of the changing nature of the parties' European policies as well as illustrate major alterations in the parties' approach to the European elections.

Manifestos for European Elections

Manifestos play a key role in British electoral politics. The drafting of the manifesto occupies every party for years in advance of a general election. Moreover, the themes and issues addressed within each party manifesto customarily serve as the thematic foundation for the party's electoral campaign.[4] It is also on the basis of manifestos that parties in government are held accountable for their actions.

However, many aspects of general election manifestos do not apply to party manifestos for Europe. In particular, the low political salience of EC decision-making means that those elected to the European Parliament are not likely to be held accountable by their electors for promises made during the campaign. Moreover, no government emerges from elections to the European Parliament that can be judged by its adherence to promises.[5]

Nevertheless, an analysis of European election manifestos is interesting for two reasons. First, party manifestos provide a useful measure of a party's approach to an election campaign, so an examination of European election manifestos should shed some light on the changing nature of Britain's European election campaigns.[6] Secondly, such an analysis develops our understanding of party European policy, and further provides a measure of the convergence of national and European policy areas.

The drafting of the European manifestos has proved to be a particularly important issue in the development of party European policy. During the 1979 elections to the European Parliament the Labour Party found itself engulfed in a bitter struggle between anti-Marketeers and pro-Marketeers over the control of the manifesto.[7] While pro-Marketeers were anxious for the Labour leadership to demonstrate its European commitment by signing up to a transnational manifesto prepared by the Confederation of the Socialist Parties of the European Community, anti-Marketeers were reluctant for the NEC to surrender any control over Labour's European campaign. After a bitter feud within the party the NEC won control over the writing of the manifesto although Tony Benn, on behalf of the Labour Party, also signed a Euro-socialist declaration of principles. The end result was an anti-European manifesto that denounced the Common Agricultural Policy as 'an expensive farce'; declared that Community membership had 'gravely weakened' Britain's 'right to democratic government'; and promised that the Labour Party would 'vigorously oppose any moves towards federalism'.

By contrast, the Conservative Party's manifesto in 1979 underlined the party's deep commitment to the European Community. In particular, the Conservative manifesto for Europe emphasized the party's unequivocal commitment to EC membership and a continued co-operation with member countries. Several observers have commented that in view of Labour's hostility towards Europe, membership in the EC came to be seen as part of the Conservative Party's political repertoire.[8] As such the Conservative Party's manifesto opposed the confrontation tactics pursued by the Labour Party in dealing with the EC, and argued that the Conservative Party would increase the country's influence within the EC by adopting a more constructive approach to Community affairs.

The Liberal Party's manifesto in 1979 was by far the most European of the three. The Liberals subscribed to a trans-national manifesto which emphasized their overall European commitment. Because of the lack of domestic consideration within this joint manifesto the Liberal Party also produced a four page supplement, within which .they stressed that it was the only British party that was united and fully committed to the idea of European unity.

The 1984 Labour manifesto for Europe continued the party's anti-European stance, demanding the immediate reform of CAP as well as a drastic alteration to Britain's contribributions to the EC budget. The Conservative manifesto, on the other hand, chose to exploit the warring factions within the Labour Party over the European question. It also called for an improvement in EC co-operation on foreign policy and a strengthening of Britain's world role through the Community.

The 1989 and 1994 Euro-election manifestos demonstrated a drastic alteration in party European policy. In particular, the Labour Party abandoned its anti-Europeanism in favour of a more positive approach to Europe. It called for a strengthening of EC institutions, more co-operation on social policy and the creation of a more democratic Community. In addition, Labour used both of these manifestos to draw attention to domestic economic problems and the issue of Tory mismanagement. The Conservative Party, on the other hand, adopted a much tougher position on the EC, calling for additional reforms of the EC institutional structure and warning against the effects of further integration on the British national interest. The Liberal Democrats were the only party to maintain a consistent position on European integration during this period, in both manifestos re-establishing their commitment to further integration and to the construction of a federal Europe.

Research Methodology

The remainder of this article will be a discussion of content anlaysis as applied to the text of the twelve British party manifestos for Europe between 1979–1994. Content analysis is defined by Robert Weber as a research methodology that 'utilizes a set of procedures to make valid inferences from text'.[9] For the purposes of this study content analysis will enable us to examine and evaluate the style and substance of European election manifestos from a comparative perspective.

There is a well-established tradition of content analysis of political party manifestos. In particular, the European Consortium for Political Research constituted a Manifesto Research Group as long ago as 1979 in order to evaluate the policy positions of parties in some 21 liberal-democratic countries including Great Britain, from 1945 through to 1983.[10] More recently, Richard Topf has published a content analysis of the general election manifestos of Britain's major parties between 1979 and 1992.[11] '

However, despite the obvious similarities, there are sufficient methodological differences between these two projects and the research reported in this article. One of the most fundamental and important decisions involved in content analysis concerns the definition of the basic unit of text to be classified. In the ECPR project, the core unit of analysis was the 'quasi-sentence', every manifesto being coded according to a schema of seven possible policy domains.[12] On the other hand, Topf's analysis of Britain's general election manifestos involved the coding of words or short phrases within a sentence. Once each phrase had been coded the codings were then computer-generated, with qualitative checks for ambiguities of meaning in context.

For the purposes of this study the nature and context of 'themes' existing within each of the twelve manifestos is examined. Holsti defines a theme as a unit of text 'having no more than one each of the following elements: the perceiver; the perceived, or agent of action; the action; and the target of the action.'[13] Once a unit of analysis was identified it was coded according to a specific set of classifications. These classifications were: the theme; the evaluation of the theme; the European/domestic context; and the time dimension involved. This form of coding, although labour intensive, ensures the researcher greater accuracy in determining the context of specific sentences or sections of text.[14]

Increase in Length and Scope

During the last fifteen years there has been a gradual Europeanization of British politics. As a result, there are few remaining domestic policy areas that are not somehow enmeshed with the politics of European integration. The emergence of this important European dimension into British politics has had a notable impact on the parties' approach to European affairs. In particular, the increase in the number of European issues now relevant to national politics has forced parties to expand their issue focus in both national and European elections.[15] As the European issue becomes more complex and wide ranging so it could be predicted that party manifestos will continue to grow, both in length and scope of topic areas.[16] This process is likely to be accelerated by the growing media and public interest in European issues in general.

While it would be feasible to test this hypothesis by comparing the word lengths of party European election manifestos over time it is more beneficial to concentrate on the appearance and repetition of specific themes. The number of themes appearing in a given manifesto and the frequency with which they are repeated informs the researcher not only of the general length of the manifesto but also of the range of topics discussed.

TABLE 1
TOTAL NUMBER OF THEMES

Year	Conservative	Labour	Liberal/Alliance Liberal Democrat
1979	85	73	75
1984	90	142	112
1989	220	150	106
1994	163	181	144

Table 1 lists the total number of themes or units appearing in each party manifesto for Europe since 1979. As may be seen, although the general trend is indeed towards ever-longer documents, there are specific reversals in the trend, the most notable one appearing in the Conservative Party's 1994 European manifesto, in terms of both the number of themes discussed and the overall word length. However, the reduction in the number of discussed themes between 1989 and 1994 probably had more to do with the complexity of the European issue in 1989 vis-à-vis Maastricht than with any permanent reversal of trend towards smaller European manifestos. Although the number of themes appearing in the 1989 Social and Liberal Democrat manifesto was slightly less than that appearing in 1984 the difference is hardly worth noting. For the most part, the above figures support the general hypothesis of ever-longer manifestos. Moreover, this trend reflects both the widening scope of

EC activity and the growing importance of European elections for Britain's major parties.

The growing length and widening scope of European election manifestos also points to the increasing seriousness with which major parties are approaching elections to the European Parliament. Due to the increasing powers of the European Parliament and the increase in salience of EC issues for members of the public, political parties have been forced to put forward more decisive policy alternatives on European issues.[17] Moreover, the manner in which parties carry out their campaigning for European elections is beginning to resemble that of general elections, both in terms of strategy and overall energy. Party Euro manifestos are not only increasing in length but are also beginning to adopt more attractive titles (see appendix) and have generally become more readable, reflecting the parties' expectation that a much larger section of society will devote attention to their official election statements now that elections to the European Parliament appear to carry greater political importance.

Analysis of Theme Dimensions

European manifestos were examined within the context of specific theme dimensions, adopting a straightforward analytical approach. Each unit of analysis was coded according to a schema of eighteen possible themes. A content analysis was then carried out on all words within each separate unit of analysis. Some of the categories used for this purpose related to domains of political action in which issues can arise, such as economics, agriculture, energy, security. Others were connected to European institutions, such as the European Parliament and the Commission. A third group of categories was directly related to the elections themselves, including comments on the parties contesting them and the strategies and problems involved in waging campaigns. Yet others singled out more ideological statements, including positions taken on the nature of European politics and 'visions' of what Europe is or could become.[18]

Table 2 shows the thematical composition of each party election manifesto for Europe since 1979. A number of features stand out from this analysis. First and foremost, of the eighteen theme dimensions, economic issues, agriculture and ideological 'visions of Europe' statements predominate in every manifesto since 1979. The primacy given to economic issues by all three parties is perhaps not surprising considering the significance of the EC for most areas of the domestic economy. Furthermore, economic issues usually generate the greatest amount of media and public interest.[19]

TABLE 2
THEMATIC COMPOSITION (PERCENTAGE OF TOTAL UNITS)

Themes	Conservative				Labour				Liberal/All			
	79	84	89	94	79	84	89	94	79	84	89	94
Economic	18	42	26	16	29	27	20	23	18	22	18	16
Ideological 'visions of Europe'	15	7	9	17	14	4	15	17	13	3	18	7
European Parliament	7	2	1	1	5	1	1	3	8	4	2	1
EC General	12	3	2	8	23	9	1	8	19	7	5	4
International Relations	3	8	3	4	3	8	11	3	3	8	11	3
Party Political	18	6	8	12	1	9	17	9	5	2	10	8
Education	0	0	2	2	0	2	3	0	0	1	2	6
Science and Technology	0	2	1	2	0	0	2	0	0	1	4	1
Agriculture	11	14	14	9	19	6	6	5	7	15	5	3
Energy	6	4	4	1	3	1	0	0	2	1	3	3
Transportation	0	3	4	4	0	2	1	0	0	0	1	4
Health	0	0	1	0	0	4	1	4	0	1	0	3
Environment	1	6	14	6	0	6	11	6	16	13	13	7
Social	1	0	3	1	1	11	15	7	10	9	9	25
Elections & Campaigning	4	3	0	0	0	4	1	2	1	1	1	1
Law	1	0	4	10	0	0	1	1	0	0	0	0
Security & Defence	1	3	5	8	0	6	0	2	16	13	0	5
Broadcasting	0	0	1	0	0	0	0	0	0	0	0	0
Total Units	85	90	220	163	73	142	150	181	82	112	106	144

The high salience of economic issues in each of the manifestos justifies a more detailed investigation of this thematic category. For this reason, the units coded as 'economic' were regrouped into eleven categories: unemployment, work and unions, economic management, trade, community relations, industrial sectors and regional development, state of the economy, inflation, income and taxation. For each of the parties, and in each of the elections, the greatest emphasis was placed on economic issues dealing with specific industrial sectors and regional development. The Conservative Party gave much consideration to international trade in 1979 and 1984, which further reflected Mrs. Thatcher's concern for strengthening the external trading arrangements of Europe as well as her commitment to a more 'open' Community. In contrast, the Labour Party used these two elections to highlight the problem of domestic employment. The Liberal/Alliance, on the other hand, has devoted more attention to income and taxation than either of the other two parties, particularly in 1994. An additional qualitative examination of these policy themes reveals that the focus of both the Labour Party and Liberal Democrat manifestos in 1984 and 1989 was largely a response to domestic economic difficulties. The Labour Party in particular viewed the two elections as an opportunity to draw attention to the high rate of inflation and the increasing level of unemployment under the Conservative Government.[20]

An analysis of the economic focus of the three major parties' European manifestos during this period is interesting not only for the questions raised about the growing politicization of EC economic activity but also for the light it sheds on the parties' individual response to both domestic and European economic conditions. The wide range of economic policy spheres discussed within each of the manifestos appears to reflect the overall enlargement of EC economic activity. However, a closer investigation of the manifestos reveals that the majority of references to economic issues appear within a domestic context.

Another major focus of most European election manifestos involved the party promoting its ideological 'vision of Europe'. This vision ranged from the Conservative Party's support for European co-operation during the early 1980s to the Liberal Party's consistent enthusiasm for a federal Europe. Interestingly, the number of 'ideological' statements appearing within the manifestos has increased during the last two election campaigns. The increase in 'ideological' statements can be attributed partly to the growing debate surrounding the future direction of European integration. In particular, the ratification of the Maastricht Treaty has placed additional pressure on all three major parties to disclose their preference for Britain's future relationship to the EC.

An interesting feature of this analysis is that the parties do not generally prioritize the same themes during the same election. Moreover, a shift in issue prioritization by one party from one election to the next is seldom followed by a similar shift by another party. However, certain trends are notable in the results. In particular, there has been increase in the number of references to the environment and social policy on the part of all three parties since 1979, largely due to the widening scope of EC activity into both of the policy areas during recent years.

Evaluation of Themes

All thematic references were also classified according to whether evaluative remarks of some kind – positive, negative, or mixed – were associated with them. This type of analysis is useful for indicating the extent to which Britain's major parties have adopted a positive or negative style of campaigning for elections to the European Parliament.

TABLE 3
EVALUATION OF THEMES (PERCENTAGE OF TOTAL UNITS)

Evaluation	Conservative					Labour				Liberal/All		
	79	84	89	94		79	84	89	94	79	84	89	94
Positive	34	28	41	20		4	4	11	22	16	12	27	13
Negative	24	18	12	18		38	33	41	33	11	15	13	28
Mixed/Neutral	42	54	47	62		58	64	45	45	73	73	59	59
Total Units	85	90	220	163		73	142	150	181	82	112	106	144

The results of the analysis is set out in Table 3, showing that for the most part all three major parties tend to approach the various themes from a mixed or neutral perspective. This is particularly the case for the Liberal/Alliance. In 1984, 73 per cent of the Liberal/Alliance manifesto was coded as either neutral or mixed.

In addition, these results show the Labour Party to be the most negative of the three major parties. This negativity may be attributed to the fact that Labour has, in the past, used the European elections as a means of attacking the policies of the Conservative Party. In contrast, the fact that the Conservative Party manifestos usually contain the largest percentage of positive remarks can be attributed to the fact that they have tended to use the manifestos as a means of defending their past record of government.

The predominance of mixed/neutral statements in all twelve manifestos provides an interesting contrast with the parties' general election manifestos over the same period. Political parties frequently use their general election manifestos to exploit problems in the policy positions of opposing parties as well as to attack or defend the actions of the current government. Therefore, party conflict and controversy are a major part of general election manifestos.[21] The relative neutrality of Britain's European election manifestos can largely be attributed to two important factors. First, the complexity of European issues makes it difficult for parties to put forward distinct policy alternatives, so party rhetoric surrounding European issues tends to involve broad, abstract and non-controversial policy statements.[22] Secondly, the continuing internal divisions within the Conservative and Labour parties on EC issues hinder the articulation of unambigous policy positions on Europe.[23] In order to avoid escalating internal party conflict over European integration both parties have tended to steer campaign policy statements away from areas of potential controversy.

European or Domestic Perspectives

In this section of the analysis each thematic statement has been coded according to whether it displays a European, domestic or mixed perspective. For the most part the European/domestic orientation of each unit of analysis was clearly stated. When the orientation of a particular unit was unclear, the unit was coded as having a mixed orientation. Also coded as 'mixed' were units that dealt with the specific impact of European issues on British politics, or the impact of British politics on Europe.

TABLE 4
EUROPEAN OR DOMESTIC PERSPECTIVES (PERCENTAGE OF TOTAL UNITS)

Perspective	Conservative				Labour				Liberal/All			
	79	84	89	94	79	84	89	94	79	84	89	94
Domestic	14	14	19	15	1	42	40	20	3	6	10	65
Mixed	32	16	16	13	30	19	29	15	8	5	12	9
European	56	72	65	67	67	18	30	59	89	90	77	26
Other	0	0	0	5	2	3	2	4	0	0	0	0
Total Units	85	90	220	163	73	142	150	181	82	112	106	144

The results of this analysis are set out in Table 4. In almost all of the manifestos the parties favoured a European orientation over a national one. This was particularly true for the Conservative Party which favoured a strong European orientation in all four of its manifestos for Europe. The Liberal/Alliance also displayed a strong European orientation in their manifestos although their focus shifted heavily in favour of domestic issues in 1994. The Labour Party showed the most inconsistency by moving from a strong European orientation in 1979 towards a more national focus in 1984 and 1989. In 1994 the party returned to its earlier European orientation.

The low percentage of domestic-oriented statements by all three major parties in 1979 is at least partly due to the context in which the elections were set. The 1979 Euro-elections in the UK had been fought in the wake of a national general election held only five weeks previously. Consequently, all three major parties were reluctant to distract attention away from their Westminster campaign.[24] Moreover, none of the parties were prepared to put forward a manifesto that might contradict the nature of their general election manifesto, nor did they wish to risk exploiting differences within their own internal ranks in the wake of a national election.[25] Rather than concentrating on domestic issues which were already the focus of the Westminster campaign, the 1979 Euro-election manifestos devoted more space to outlining the parties' approach to the EC. Interestingly, the strong European orientation of the 1979 Euro-election manifestos contradicts the argument of several observers that national considerations had dominated the campaign.[26] While this may be true of many aspects of the campaign it does not hold true for the manifestos themselves.

The strong domestic orientation of the Labour Party's Euro-election manifestos in 1984 and 1989 further illustrated the party's determination to exploit the record of the Conservative government on domestic issues.[27] Unlike the 1979 Euro-election which was held only a few weeks after a general election, both the 1984 and 1989 Euro-elections served as mid-term evaluations of the Conservative government. Consequently, the Labour Party and to a lesser extent the Liberal Democrats used the EP election manifestos to highlight problems with the Conservative government's management of the economy as well as their poor record on the environment, education, social services, and health care. The strong European orientation of the Conservative Party's Euro-election manifestos, on the other hand, served to reinforce the party's determination to be seen as a committed supporter of European integration but also as the party most equipped the obtain the best deal for Britain.

An interesting feature of this analysis is the heavy leaning of each of the parties towards either a national or European orientation. The parties seem to prefer a strong orientation in favour of one perspective or the other, as opposed to a balance between the two. Moreover, there are few similarities in the way in which parties choose to approach the same election. With the exception of the 1979 European election, where all three parties favoured a strong European orientation, the parties approached the elections from varying perspectives. Their reluctance to enter into direct confrontation with each other during the European elections appears to reflect their discomfort with a wide range of EC policy areas. By playing to their own strengths all three parties have been able to avoid a damaging increase in intra-party conflict during their campaigning for elections to the European Parliament.

Evaluations of European and Domestic Issues

In this stage of the analysis each evaluative statement is examined within the context of its European/domestic orientation. Each unit of analysis has been separated according to its European/domestic orientation and then further separated according to whether it involved a positive, negative, or mixed/neutral evaluation. In order to create a meaningful statistic the ratio of positive/negative evaluations for each orientation has been calculated.[28]

TABLE 5
EVALUATION OF THEMES BY EUROPEAN/DOMESTIC CONTEXT (RATIO PERCENTAGES)

Perspective	Conservative				Labour				Liberal/All			
	79	84	89	94	79	84	89	94	79	84	89	94
Domestic	-.17	.17	.51	.48	–	-.43	-.48	-.76	-.13	-.67	-.72	-.34
Mixed	.25	.07	.24	-.02	-.15	-.26	-.37	-.11	.22	.29	-.10	.15
European	.16	.09	.16	.04	-.45	-.12	-.04	.14	.18	.02	.03	.22
Other	–	–	–	–	–	–	–	–	–	–	–	–
Total Units	85	90	220	163	73	142	150	181	82	112	106	144

Table 5 shows the results of this analysis. On domestic issues, negative statements were much more frequent than positive ones in both the Labour Party and Liberal/Alliance manifestos for all European elections. A large percentage of these statements involved a specific reference to the performance of the national government. In contrast, positive statements outweighed all others for the Conservative Party in every election other than 1979.

On European issues the Labour Party has shown a significant reduction in the number of negative statements since 1979. Another striking feature of this analysis is the consistency of positive/negative evaluations for the Conservative Party between 1979 and 1994. While the predominance of positive statements within the Liberal/Alliance manifestos is not particularly surprising, one might have expected the number to be a little higher.

The shift in Labour Party policy towards Europe following the 1983 general election was followed by a significant and continuous reduction in the proportion of negative statements regarding Europe in its next three European election manifestos. In fact, the Labour Party's 1994 Manifesto for Europe displayed a more positive attitude towards the EC than the Conservative Party European election manifesto of the same year. Although this is partly a result of Labour's growing Europeanism the effects of the Conservative Party's own internal divisions cannot be understated. The influence of the Conservative Party's Euro-sceptics was a major contributor to the party's indifferent approach to European integration as revealed within its 1994 European election manifesto.

Table 5 also supports the earlier hypothesis that the large proportion of domestic policy statements is primarily due to the Opposition parties using the Euro-elections as a means of attacking the record of the Conservative Government. Perhaps not surprisingly then, within the Labour Party's manifestos the proportion of negative statements with a domestic orientation has continued to increase as the Conservative Party's period in government has lengthened.

Time Dimension

In examining the thematic references made within each manifesto it is useful to consider the time dimension in which they are made. For this reason each unit of analysis has been coded according to its specific time dimension: past, present, future, mixed and unspecified. Once again, the time dimension of each unit of analysis was clearly stated. If difficulty arose in applying a specific time dimension to a particular unit then the unit was coded as having an 'unspecified' time dimension. The time dimension of each unit of analysis was then examined with reference to the nature of the evaluation. In other words, once a unit had been categorized according to a specific time dimension it was sub-grouped according to whether it involved a positive, negative or mixed/neutral evaluation.

TABLE 6
EVALUATION OF THEMES WITH DIFFERENT TIME PERSPECTIVES (RATIO PERCENTAGES)

	Conservative				Labour				Liberal/All			
	79	84	89	94	79	84	89	94	79	84	89	94
Reference to future	.31	.04	.16	.03	.18	.26	-.05	.24	.31	.25	.22	.13
Reference to present	.07	.07	.04	.12	-.03	-.61	-.61	-.72	-.08	-.39	.37	-.58
Reference to past	-.78	.40	.61	.66	.13	-.65	-.63	.17	-.03	-.50	-.30	-.10
Mixed or unspecified time reference	.23	.15	.07	.09	-.24	-.17	-.53	.02	.12	-.01	.0	-.04
Total Units	85	90	220	163	73	142	150	181	82	112	106	144

Table 6 shows the results of this analysis. Of the three parties the Liberal/Alliance demonstrated the greatest optimism about the future. However, since 1979 there has been a gradual reduction in the number of positive references to the future made by the party.

Party evaluations of the present are particularly interesting. While the number of positive references to the present has steadily increased in the Conservative Party since 1979, the other two parties have slid in the opposite direction. An examination of the domestic/European orientation of these references shows that the majority of negative evaluations regarding the present, made by Labour and the Liberal/Alliance, involve a criticism of the domestic situation. Overall, there are only small differences in the types of evaluations made by the three parties in respect of the present state of the EC.

Evaluations of the past by the three parties also tends to be dominated by domestic matters. For this reason it is not surprising to observe a predominance of positive evaluations of the past within all four Conservative manifestos for Europe. Moreover, the percentage of positive references to the past made by the Conservative Party appears to increase as their number of years in Government grows.

Conclusion

In the study of Britain's elections to the European Parliament, the content of Britain's European election manifestos has been somewhat neglected. This investigation has aimed to bring about a better understanding of the individual parties' approach to European elections. Moreover, through an examination of the changes to the content of these manifestos several firm conclusions can be drawn about the evolution of party European policy between 1979 and 1994.

In particular, the results of the content analysis show that national considerations have continued to play a dominant role in the parties' Euro-election campaigns. This holds true particularly for the Labour Party which has generally looked upon the European elections as a mid-term test of the Conservative government's popularity. As a result, it has tended to orient its Euro manifestos towards an all-out attack on Conservative domestic policy. Moreover, the increasing European orientation of Labour's Euro-manifestos appears to have been at least partly due to the internal difficulties within the Conservative Party over the Maastricht Treaty. Labour's determination to exploit the Conservative Party's internal conflict over Europe has overshadowed any attempt by Labour to strengthen its own European commitments within the context of the Euro-elections. Nonetheless, the increase in European policy statements within the Labour Party manifestos also reflects the neutralization of its own internal divisions on EC issues. Without the continuous threat of internal divisions over European policy, Labour has been able to construct its European election manifestos around much clearer and decisive policy declarations.

Similar motivations appear to have existed behind the Conservative Party's manifestos for Europe. In both 1979 and 1984 large sections of the Conservative's Euro election manifestos were targeted at uncertainties within the Labour Party over Europe. As such, both manifestos were primarily oriented towards European issues. In 1989 and 1994 the trend continued as the Conservatives attempted to project themselves as the only party committed to preserving the national interest.

The changing style and nature of Britain's European election manifestos since 1979 reveals the evolution of the parties' European policies in this period. The widening scope of party European manifestos since 1984 is particularly impressive. If nothing else the increase in the number of observed themes within the manifestos suggests that parties have begun to respond positively to the extension of EC activity. Moreover, this analysis confirms the gradual convergence of domestic and European spheres of policy making. It has become near to impossible for British parties to formulate decisive policy on domestic issues without considering and evaluating the presence of a growing European dimension of decision-making.

APPENDIX: DATA SOURCES

Conservative Manifesto for Europe 1979
Labour Manifesto for Europe 1979
Liberal Programme for Europe 1979, and Liberal Manifesto for Europe 1979
'The Strong Voice in Europe', Conservative Manifesto for Europe 1984
Labour's Manifesto for the European Elections 1984
'Let's Get Europe Working Together', SDP/Liberal Alliance Manifesto for Europe 1984
'Leading Europe into the 1990s', Conservative Manifesto for Europe 1989
'Meeting the Challenge in Europe', Labour's manifesto for the European Elections 1989
'Manifesto for a People's Europe', The Social and Liberal Democrat Programme for the European Elections 1989
Conservative Manifesto for Europe 1994
'Make Europe Work for us', Labour's Election Manifesto for the European Elections 1994
'Unlocking Britain's Potential: Make Europe Work for us', Liberal Democrat European Election Manifesto 1994

NOTES

1. See for instance, David Butler and Paul Jowett, *Party Strategies in Britain: A Study of the 1984 European Elections* (London: Macmillan, 1985). Given the temporal focus of this article, European Community (EC) is used throughout, as opposed to the more recent European Union (EU).
2. See for instance Stephen George, *An Awkward Partner: Britain in the European Community* (Oxford: Oxford University Press, 1990); also see Nigel Ashford, 'Political Parties' in Stephen George (ed.), *Britain and the European Community: The Politics of Semi-Detachment* (Oxford: Clarendon Press, 1992), pp.119–48.
3. See for instance Ben Rosamond 'Labour and the European Community: Learning to be European? *Politics*, Vol.10, 1990, pp.25–32; See also N. Ashford, 'Political Parties'.
4. Richard Topf, 'Party Manifestos', in Anthony Heath *et al.* (eds), *Labour's Last Chance? The 1992 Election and Beyond* (Aldershot, Hants: Dartmouth, 1994), p.150–51.
5. David Butler and David Marquand, *European Elections and British Politics* (London: Longman, 1981), p.119.
6. See Michael Burgess and Adrian Lee, 'The United Kingdom', in Juliet Lodge (ed.),*The 1989 Election of the European Parliament* (London: Macmillan, 1990), pp.190–209.
7. For a useful discussion of the struggle within the Labour Party over the composition of the 1979 Euro-election manifesto see David Butler and David Marquand, *European Elections*, Ch.4.
8. See for instance Ian Gordon, 'The United Kingdom' in Karlheinz Reif, *Ten European Elections* (Aldershot: Gower, 1985), pp.167.
9. Robert Weber, *Basic Content Analysis* (Beverly Hills, Calif: Sage, 1985), p.1.
10. The most recent version of the Group's database was deposited in the ESRC Data Archive in 1992; See Ian Budge, *ECPR Party Manifestos Project* [computer file], 3rd edition (Colchester: ESRC Data Archive, 1992).
11. Richard Topf, 'Party Manifestos'.
12. For a further discussion of these policy domains see Ian Budge, *ECPR Party Manifestos*.
13. O.R. Holsti, 'Content Analysis for the Social Sciences and Humanities' (Reading, MA: Addison Wesley), p.136.
14. K. Krippendorf, *Content Analysis* (Beverly Hills, Calif: Sage, 1980).
15. Nigel Ashford, 'Political Parties'.
16. A similar prediction is made by Richard Topf in reference to British general election manifestos; See R. Topf, 'Party Manifestos', p.150.
17. Richard S. Flickinger, 'British Political Parties and Public Attitudes Towards the European Community: Leading, Following or Getting Out of the Way?', in David Broughton *et al.*

(eds), *British Elections and Parties Yearbook, 1994* (London: Frank Cass, 1995), pp.197–214.

18. Similar themes were observed in a content analysis of statements made by politicians and television broadcasters during the 1979 elections to the European Parliament; See for instance, K. Siune, 'The Campaigns on Television: What Was Said and Who Said It', in J.G. Blumler (ed), *Communicating to Voters: Television in the First European Parliamentary Elections* (London: Sage, 1983), Ch.12.

19. See Kevin Featherstone, *Socialist Parties and European Integration: A Comparative History* (Manchester: Manchester University Press, 1988).

20. Michael Burgess and Adrian Lee, 'The United Kingdom'.

21. I. Budge, D. Robertson, and D. Hearl (eds), *Ideology, Strategy and Party Change* (Cambridge: Cambridge University Press, 1987).

22. See for instance David Butler and Paul Jowett, *Party Strategies*.

23. See Richard S. Flickinger, 'British Parties and European Attitudes'.

24. See David Butler and David Marquand, pp.109–110.

25. Ibid.

26. See, for instance, Derek Hearl, 'The United Kingdom' in Juliet Lodge (ed.), *Direct Elections to the European Parliament, 1984* (London: Macmillan, 1986), p.248.

27. Michael Burgess and Adrian Lee, p.192.

28. The ratio is calculated by a formula which Hostaetter used to indicate the majority opinion in population surveys:

$$M = p+ - p-/100.$$

Where p+ = percentage of positive evaluations and

p- = percentage of negative evaluations.

This formula was adopted for the analysis because it takes into consideration the percentage of neutral evaluations within each orientation.

Thatcherism and the Scottish Question

James Mitchell and Lynn G. Bennie

Introduction

The decline of the Conservatives in Scotland has been remarkable. From its peak in 1955 when the party won 50.1 per cent of the vote the party's support has ebbed away. Elections in 1970, 1979 and 1992 saw slight improvements on previous election performances but did not interrupt the long-term decline of the party. This article deals with Thatcherism and the Scottish Question. By bringing together ideas drawn from literature on Thatcherism and the Scottish Question it is hoped to shed some light on both. The focus is on Thatcherism and anti-Thatcherism as social movements, rather than on the parties. The article begins with a discussion of the debate on Thatcherism and proceeds to consider the Scottish dimension in British politics before analysing the relationship between the two using public opinion surveys and election data. The aim is to consider whether Thatcherism in some sense helps explain attitudes towards Scotland's constitutional status.

Thatcherism

'Thatcherism,' according to Skidelsky, 'suggests both a set of beliefs and a momentum to reorder society according to those beliefs, driven by the commitment of a remarkable political personality.'[1] A number of disputes on the nature of Thatcherism follow from this: the nature of the set of beliefs is disputed; the extent to which it has been propelled by the remarkable political personality of Mrs Thatcher is also disputed. In short, defining Thatcherism presents problems. A number of definitions are considered in this article. Whether Thatcherism has impinged on the 'Scottish dimension', itself a disputed idea, may depend on what is meant by the term.

The most obvious starting point would be to focus on the 'remarkable personality' of Mrs Thatcher and consider whether Thatcherism's failure in Scotland can be explained in this way. The personal aspects of Thatcherism have been noted by Kavanagh, specifically her 'no nonsense style of leadership' and hostility to compromise.[2] Was there any particularly Scottish reaction against this? Was there some facet of Mrs Thatcher's make up, her 'Englishness' for example, which provoked hostility amongst Scots?

There are arguments over the nature of the set of beliefs which make up

Thatcherism. Whether it involves (or involved – on this there is debate) the 'free economy and strong state'[3] is less relevant, in the context of this article, than whether a public perception exists that this is what it involves. Of relevance here is not the programme but how the programme is perceived. If so, how might this relate to Scotland's constitutional status? In this respect, arguments concerned with the appeal of Thatcherism – usually blind to any specifically Scottish dimension – are important. Hall's work, suggesting that Thatcherism involved a 'hegemonic project' which challenged the foregoing consensus, is significant.[4] If Thatcherism represents a successful project, it would have to be conceded that it has had its limitations. In Scotland it would appear that there has been a marked reluctance to accept the project, even amongst those socio-economic groups who accepted it in England. One hypothesis is that an alternative hegemonic project may have developed in Scotland in reaction to Thatcherism and, if so, Scottish nationalism may have played a significant part in this alternative. Jessop and his colleagues saw Thatcherism in terms of a 'chain of equivalencies':

market = free choice = freedom and liberty = anti-statism = put an end to creeping collectivism[5]

Identifying either a weak link in the chain or some alternative chain of equivalencies in Scotland (the reaction to Thatcherism) might be a fruitful way of making sense of the Scottish dimension. John Gray, an exponent of new right ideas, has acknowledged that they do not constitute a single coherent body of ideas but are rather an 'eclectic mixture of themes and policies brought together, in Britain and elsewhere, more by the contingencies of circumstances than by logic or sustained reasoning'.[6] These contingencies have been the focus of attention of a number of commentators.[7] At the broadest level, there is some agreement that Britain is in economic decline and that Thatcherism is a response to this decline. Central to this is the notion of a 'great national crusade to make Britain "Great" once more'.[8] The British nationalism of Thatcherism causes problems because of the difficulties inherent in the notion of Britishness in Scotland. This may help explain the weakness of Thatcherism in Scotland.

One definition of Thatcherism which makes explicit reference to territorial politics is found in Bulpitt's work, where it is discussed in terms of statecraft: 'the art of winning elections and achieving some necessary degree of governing competence in office... It is concerned primarily to resolve the electoral and governing problems facing a party at any particular time.'[9] The main dimensions of statecraft are listed as party management, a winning electoral strategy, political hegemony argument, a governing competence, another winning electoral strategy.[10] In terms of governing competence, this has involved a mixture of seemingly contradictory positions: offloading

problems and strengthening power at the centre. Understanding the
governance of Scotland in Bulpitt's terms might go some way to providing
answers as to why the Conservatives have fared so badly north of the border.
The notion of a 'Two Nations' strategy[11] and Bulpitt's conception of
Conservative 'statecraft'[12] suggest a cynical electoral strategy. Jessop et al.
see this 'taking the form of unification of a privileged nation of "good
citizens" and "hard workers" against a contained and subordinate nation
which extends beyond the inner cities and their ethnic minorities to include
much of the non-skilled working class outside the South East.'[13]

Though the above emerged from a radical Marxist perspective, a similar
view has been expressed by the Canadian liberal economist J.K.Galbraith.[14]
Bulpitt refers to the Conservatives' '"Edessa complex" – the necessity to
withdraw from territory impossible to defend'.[15] Though he appears to be
referring to withdrawal in terms of public policy this had implications for an
electoral strategy, a central component of Bulpitt's understanding of
Thatcherism. The territorial implications of such an electoral strategy for
Scotland are important.

A further interpretation of Thatcherism which follows from Stuart Hall's
analysis and, perhaps unexpectedly, finds some echoes in Bulpitt's work, is
that of Jessop et al. and Peter Taylor. Jessop and his colleagues consider the
'complex and uneven impact on such societal cleavages as productive/
parasitic, rich/poor, North/South, employed/unemployed, etc.'[16] Taylor argues
that the uneven development of Britain and the simple plurality electoral
system have resulted in the Conservative government being considered a
'"southern government" formed by a new regional party.'[17] The impact on the
rest of Britain – and particularly Scotland where an alternative regionalism
capable of mobilizing around national identity exists – might, as Taylor has
suggested, lead to a 'territorial crisis'.[18]

This discussion of Thatcherism has been brief but has outlined some
possible avenues for considering the Scottish dimension. First, there is the
extent to which the personality of Margaret Thatcher may have been a factor
in provoking Scottish hostility to her party. Second, the extent to which there
is any relationship between the ideological programme of Thatcherism,
accepting the difficulties which exist in defining this programme, and the
Scottish dimension. In particular, the extent to which Thatcherism is a
manifestation of a form of British/English nationalism which has little appeal
north of the border needs to be considered. Identifying opposition to
Thatcherism in Scotland need not mean that it provoked an alternative
'hegemonic project' with constitutional reform as a central plank. It will be
necessary to consider the relationship between support for reform and
left/progressive policies. Consideration of an alternative 'chain of
equivalencies' will be necessary. The politics of the opposition might amount

to little more than oppositional politics, attacking the government without offering an alternative. The extent to which a coherent alternative hegemonic project has emerged will be considered.

The Scottish Dimension

There has been no 'missionary nation-building ideology' in the UK.[19] The Conservative Party traditionally accepted and indeed encouraged Scottish political distinctiveness. The foundation and development of Scottish central administration, a willingness to 'play the Scottish card' against Labour when in office, and a determination to maintain a distinct Scottish profile north of the border were all part of the Conservative (Unionist) Party's past.[20] Conservatives understood better than others that the UK was not a unitary state but a union state.[21] Matters dealt with by the Scottish Office might be seen as coming under the rubric of 'low politics' in Bulpitt's dual polity model – as areas in which the centre was content to devolve responsibility.[22] This description might have been applicable in an earlier period, but the advent of British economic decline meant that it became blurred. The Thatcherite response was to demand controls on public expenditure. Matters of high politics were to be protected while matters of low politics – especially where the localities were left to make the cuts – would face financial constraints removing much of their previous autonomy.

In opposition, Conservative politicians attacked Labour for neglecting and being insensitive to Scottish aspirations. Playing the 'Scottish card' is a well established part of opposition politics north of the border, but even in government Conservatives have traditionally been willing to make concessions to Scottish distinctiveness. Perhaps most important in the past were the material opportunities which the union offered – jobs in the Empire and later through the welfare state and state intervention. The post war settlement and Keynesian welfare state, central to many discussions of Thatcherism, were important in making Britain attractive to Scots. These very *British* institutions were referred to by Conservatives (and Labour) before the late 1970s when they argued against home rule, which was presented as a threat not only to the integrity of the British state but also to the welfare state and to economic wellbeing.

The 1979 election marked a change, though as in other areas it was gradual. The official line in the devolution referendum and subsequent general election was that the Conservatives still favoured a measure of devolution. Opposition, it was claimed, was to the Labour government's proposals and not the principle of devolution (which at that stage was taken to mean a Scottish legislature, though Conservatives later argued that they supported 'devolution to individuals'). Nonetheless, the rhetoric of

Thatcherism was rarely heard from the team of ministers under George Younger at the Scottish Office. Younger's approach in the early years was similar to that later adopted by Peter Walker in Wales. The Thatcherite aspects of public policy in the 1979–83 Parliament touched on the responsibilities of the Scottish Office less so than in later parliaments, making it easier for the Scottish Office to be semi-detached. Thatcherites maintained that Younger protected lame ducks and that the Scottish Office was the 'wettest department in Whitehall'.[23]

In the early 1980s there were efforts to acknowledge the Scottish dimension, through the establishment of the Scottish Affairs Select Committee and by allowing the Scottish Grand committee to meet in Edinburgh. In time this was replaced by a less sensitive approach. Throughout the 1980s there were a number of occasions when the Conservatives could have played the Scottish card yet failed to do so. A succession of administrative changes increasing the remit of the Scottish Office were brought about, but without the great fanfare which had accompanied similar measures in the past.[24] But the Scottish Office could not be entirely isolated. Relations with local authorities were poor and, throughout the Thatcher period, Conservative councillors were reduced in number. The symbolically important steel industry was run down, despite the considerable body of Scottish opinion which argued for government action in its defence.[25] Against this background, the changes in parliamentary procedure, outlined above, were hardly likely to be noticed.

In time, the Thatcherite agenda advanced into those areas of competence which in Scotland were the responsibility of the Scottish Office. The process was gradual but culminated in the poll tax, a measure passed in the dying days of the 1983–87 Parliament. A gulf of opinion opened up between the opposition and Thatcherite Conservatives with little doubt as to which side the Scottish public took. The accusation that Scotland was being used as a testing ground for unpopular measures was made by the opposition. Nigel Lawson complained that large areas of Scottish life were 'sheltered from market forces and exhibit a culture of dependence rather than that of enterprise'.[26] Mrs Thatcher informed Scots that they were privileged to be subsidized by the 'marvellously tolerant English'.[27] If Thatcherism came to have a Scottish dimension it was the development of an integrationist perspective which radically reassessed Scotland's position in the union.

After the 1987 election backbench English Tories intervened increasingly in Scottish debates. The change was dramatic. These Tory MPs had no conception of the UK as a union state and favoured integration of Scotland into England. Their rhetoric could only have harmed the Conservative cause north of the border. Added to this was the rise of Michael Forsyth, MP for Stirling from 1983. His education policies at the Scottish Office in the late

1980s provoked controversy and resulted in the invention of a new word, when the main teaching union, the Educational Institute of Scotland, accused him of the 'Englishing' of Scottish education.[28]

Nevertheless, the continued existence of elements of a union state meant that Scottish representation at Westminster could not be entirely ignored. Scotland could not be 'written off', partly because there were areas where Thatcherism would be appealing and partly because 'governing competence' would be compromised if the party's support fell too low. With only ten MPs after 1987, the Conservatives were hard pressed to find ministers to head the Scottish Office and sit on parliamentary committees. The Scottish Affairs Select Committee, presented as part of the Conservatives' willingness to take the Scottish dimension seriously, had to be abandoned. Any fewer Scottish Tory MPs might conceivably have turned a political problem into a constitutional crisis.

TABLE 1
PREFERRED GOVERNMENT FOR SCOTLAND: AVERAGE LEVELS OF SUPPORT BY YEAR (%)

Year	Independence	Scottish Assembly	No Change
1981	24	48	28
1983	23	50	21
1987	26	46	20
1992	39	36	22

Note: DK/NA not included so percentages may not add up to 100.
Source: ICM Research Ltd., conducted for the *Scotsman* and STV.

There has always been a Scottish dimension to politics in Britain, but in recent times the Scottish dimension has been equated with support for a Scottish Parliament. It was possible for Conservatives to play the Scottish card in the past without having to support a Scottish legislature. But this no longer seems possible, due mainly to the fact that support for a Scottish Parliament has grown (see Table 1).

Thatcherism and the Scottish Public

Having discussed the different meanings of Thatcherism and the changing nature of the Scottish dimension, we need to consider the links between the two, by an examination of the different meanings of Thatcherism in relation to public opinion, and also by assessing the relationship between Thatcherism and support for constitutional change – most notably whether an anti-Thatcherite, pro-Scottish Parliament consensus exists.

Thatcherism as Personality

Following the 1987 election, a leaked report by the Conservative Party's two vice presidents maintained that the party was perceived to be 'English and anti-Scottish' and that this was personified by Mrs Thatcher.[29] This conformed with popular wisdom, and with journalistic reports, suggesting that Mrs Thatcher herself was the problem. Her unpopularity in Scotland, most notably during the later years of her premiership, was considerable. It is useful to compare Mrs Thatcher's standing with that of John Major. Polls conducted in 1989 and 1991 discovered a potentially significant Thatcher effect. The belief existed that she had little understanding of, and less sympathy for, Scottish interests. This is most strikingly illustrated by comparing a poll taken in September 1989, on how Scots thought Mrs Thatcher viewed Scotland, with another poll in June 1991 which asked the same questions about John Major. As Table 2 makes clear, Mrs Thatcher was not well liked in Scotland. The figures indicate a perception that Mrs Thatcher did not regard Scottish interests as important, resulting in Scots being treated as 'second class citizens'. Major, on the other hand, elicits a much lower degree of resentment. Indeed, a minority of respondents in 1991 (41 per cent) felt that Scots were treated as second class citizens by Major. This contrasts with the substantial 77 per cent who had this impression under Mrs Thatcher in 1989.

TABLE 2
WHAT THE PRIME MINISTER THINKS OF US (%)

	Agree strongly	Agree slightly	Neither agree nor disagree	Disagree slightly	Disagree strongly
PM has the best interests of Scotland at heart	4 (5)	6 (21)	5 (12)	15 (24)	69 (32)
PM regards Scotland as unimportant in his/her future political plans	50 (21)	18 (19)	5 (8)	13 (30)	11 (16)
PM deserves respect for what he/she has achieved	16 (17)	29 (38)	10 (13)	11 (11)	32 (16)
PM treats the Scots as second-class citizens	61 (23)	16 (18)	4 (11)	9 (24)	8 (19)
I would be more inclined to vote Tory if PM showed more interest in Scottish affairs	16 (15)	24 (24)	10 (10)	10 (11)	35 (34)
The Tories will do better in Scotland now Major is party leader	(11)	(26)	(10)	(16)	(30)

Note: Both surveys were commissioned by the *Glasgow Herald*, the first in August 1989, the second (in brackets) in June 1991. Question wording did not vary except that in 1989 they related to Margaret Thatcher and in 1991 to John Major. The 1989 survey had a sample of 962 adults interviewed in 38 constituencies throughout Scotland over the period 24–29 August 1989. The 1991 survey sampled 1,015 adults in 39 constituencies in 23–28 May, 1991. Don't Know/Non-Applicable not included so percentages may not add up to 100.

Source: Glasgow Herald 20 September 1989; 19 June 1991.

Election data on Scottish attitudes to party leaders in 1987 and 1992 (see Table 3) reveal that Thatcher was regarded as a strong but 'extreme' and rather uncaring leader who tended to look after one class only. By contrast Major was regarded as less class oriented, rather more moderate and substantially more caring (with the Labour leader in 1992, Neil Kinnock, regarded as the most caring of all).

TABLE 3
ATTITUDES OF SCOTTISH RESPONDENTS TO LEADERS, 1987 AND 1992 (%)

	Thatcher 1987	Major 1992	Kinnock 1992
Extreme	75	20	40
Moderate	18	72	53
Neither/both	4	3	3
DK/NA	3	4	4
Looks after one class	72	54	41
Looks after all classes	25	41	52
Neither/both	1	1	3
DK/NA	2	3	4
Capable of strong leadership	96	63	42
Not capable	3	32	53
Neither/both	0	1	1
DK/NA	1	4	4
Caring	40	68	77
Uncaring	54	25	17
Neither/both	4	4	3
DK/NA	2	2	3

Note: Don't Know/Non-Applicable not included so percentages may not add up to 100.
Source: Scottish Election Study

This evidence goes some way to suggest that the personality of Thatcher did indeed have a negative effect on Scottish perceptions of the Conservative Party. However, the fact remains that the change of leadership did not enhance support for the Conservatives. As the poll findings indicated in 1991 – and as the 1992 election result showed – a new leader, who was generally viewed in a more positive light, did not mean that the party did any better. Despite the relative popularity of Major, the Tories still had a dismal performance in Scotland in 1992. Either Mrs Thatcher's influence was still being felt or else her personal impact was less than imagined. If Thatcherism is defined primarily in terms of the personality of Mrs Thatcher then the Conservatives might have been expected to perform better in 1992 with a much more popular leader. The evidence from Scotland suggests that Thatcherism amounts to more than personality traits.

Thatcherism as British Nationalism

What of the claim that support for change in Scotland is in some way a response to Thatcher's British nationalism, to her 'great national crusade to make Britain "great" once more'? It might be expected that Thatcher's national crusade was incompatible with long established feelings of 'Scottishness' north of the border. In 1992, 51 per cent of Scottish Election Study respondents thought of themselves as Scottish compared with 35 per cent who considered themselves British. Does this incompatibility help explain the weakness of Thatcherism in Scotland?

TABLE 4
NATIONAL IDENTITY AND THE VOTE IN SCOTLAND, 1992 (%)

	Scottish not British	Scottish more than British	Equal Scottish and British	British more than Scottish	British not Scottish
Conservative	10	14	34	50	58
Labour	30	36	30	22	12
Liberal Democrat	4	11	10	9	15
SNP	38	22	11	6	4
Total (N)	184	384	314	32	26

Note: There was no comparable question in 1979. Don't Know/Non-Applicable not included so percentages may not add up to 100.

Source: Scottish Election Study

As Table 4 reveals, it is certainly the case that in 1992 Conservative supporters regarded themselves as British more than Scottish. Conversely, voters who considered themselves more Scottish than British were much more likely to vote for one of the parties in favour of constitutional change. What is more relevant is that Conservative support, while shrinking in overall size between 1979 and 1992, has become distinctly more 'British', while supporters of the opposition parties have become more 'Scottish'. This Scottish/British split along party lines has intensified since 1979, with two consequences for the Conservative vote: it is more British and less Scottish than it was in 1979, but there are also fewer Conservative votes, perhaps as a consequence.

Thatcherism as a 'two nation' electoral strategy

Opinion polls and the SES results of 1979 and 1992 lend weight to the argument that Thatcherism is a two-nation electoral strategy. In 1979, 52 per cent of Scots felt they could trust the Conservatives 'on Scottish Affairs'.[30] A poll in August 1990 found that only 13 per cent of respondents in Scotland felt that the Conservatives ensured that 'Scottish interests are properly served in the UK government'.[31] This same poll found that 79 per cent of respondents saw the Conservative Party as 'mainly an English party with little relevance to Scotland'.

Overall, evidence of an 'Edessa complex' electoral strategy is bound to be partly circumstantial but it is possible to identify the existence of a perception amongst Scots that the Conservatives were 'anti-Scottish', that Thatcher mainly represented the interests of the English. There is some support for the claim that an alternative regionalism has developed, mobilized around national identity. There is evidence that Scots believe that the Conservatives treat Scotland contemptuously and that the Conservative electoral strategy has been based on winning votes in England at the expense of Scotland. In 1992, 72 per cent of Scots considered Scotland to be less well off compared to Britain as a whole. This does not mean, of course, that the Conservatives had an 'Edessa' strategy; rather that the Scots perceived that a 'two nation' political strategy existed. This is significant from an electoral politics standpoint.

Thatcherism as Free Market Ideology

As we have seen already, attempts to identify the ideological nature of Thatcher's programme are fraught with difficulties. While embracing many free-market new-right ideas, Thatcherism also reflected aspects of traditional conservatism. The result of this is that the principles behind Thatcher's ideological programme are difficult to summarize. Data from the 1992 British and Scottish Election Studies allow us to assess any differences in Scottish public opinion. The results point to a difference of emphasis in Scottish attitudes towards welfare and state intervention. Comparing Scottish and English responses on a range of issues relating to state intervention reveals the Scots as consistently more 'statist': they are more likely to favour nationalized industries; they are more critical of big business in Britain; they are more likely to believe that the government has a responsibility to provide jobs and a good standard of living; and they are much more likely to believe in the need for an equalization of incomes. Table 5 provides examples of attitudes in Scotland and England, indicating a greater desire on the part of the Scots for a redistribution of wealth, a cooler response to the development of private welfare provision and a stronger commitment to government spending. It would appear that, ideologically, the Thatcherite programme lacked appeal in Scotland. The perception that Scottish public attitudes were progressive as compared with 'Tory England' seems quite accurate.

TABLE 5
SCOTTISH AND ENGLISH ATTITUDES, 1992 (%)

	Scottish Definitely/probably	English Definitely/probably
Income and wealth should be redistributed	60	45
Govt should get rid of private education	27	16
Govt should encourage private medicine	24	31
	Definitely	Definitely
Govt should spend more fighting poverty	62	53
Govt should put more money into NHS	71	63
	Strongly agree	Strongly agree
Govt should spend more to create jobs	36	25

Note: Don't Know/Non-Applicable not included so percentages may not add up to 100.
Sources: Scottish and British Election Studies

An Anti-Thatcherite Scottish Alternative ?

Of central importance here is not only whether Scots have been reluctant to accept the project of ideas offered to them by Thatcherism, but also whether there is evidence of an alternative 'chain of equivalencies' in Scotland. Specifically, does any alternative Scottish hegemony include support for constitutional reform? If an alternative movement has emerged, the chain of equivalencies expected might be:

anti-Conservative = Scottishness = support for state intervention = support for constitutional change

The results of the 1992 SES indicate that support for constitutional reform is in some way related to progressive attitudes. In 1992, respondents who were in favour of change to Scotland's constitutional status were consistently left of centre on issues like government spending and public ownership of industry. Significantly, this group was considerably more to the left on these issues than those respondents against any form of constitutional reform. Regression analysis of support for reform suggests that negative attitudes towards privatization and the desire to see a redistribution of wealth are the most important of the left–right variables in relation to attitudes towards constitutional change (Table 6).

TABLE 6

REGRESSION ANALYSIS OF SUPPORT FOR CONSTITUTIONAL CHANGE IN SCOTLAND AND LEFT–RIGHT ATTITUDES

Independent Variables	Support for Change
Privatization gone too far	0.15 **
Redistribute income and wealth	0.10 **
Spend more on education	0.08 *
Get rid of private education	0.10 **
Spend less on poverty	- 0.08 *
Encourage private medicine	- 0.05
Spend more on NHS	0.05
R^2	0.13
N: 869	

* Significant at the 0.05 level
** Significant at the 0.01 level

Note: Don't Know/Non-Applicable not included so percentages may not add up to 100.
Source: Scottish Election Study

How important are Scottish progressive attitudes overall when it comes to explaining support for constitutional change? The nature of the support for change can be considered in terms of its socio-economic, ideological or party political complexion. In 1992 its features suggest that it is related to issues on the 'conventional' left–right axis, with supporters of change tending to hold leftist views. Support for change is stronger among working class respondents than among the middle class, though the differences are not great. Party identification, attitudes towards the Conservative Party, age, attitudes towards privatization and national identity all help to explain support for constitutional change.

The results (see Table 7) suggest that 'not identifying with the Conservatives' is the most outstanding feature of those who favour constitutional change, even more so than identifying with the SNP. The next most notable feature of support for change is another negative relationship – 'not feeling more British than Scottish'. Anti-privatization feelings also feature amongst those supporting a Scottish Parliament, which reinforces our previous findings. The analysis suggests that age is also relevant. We can tentatively conclude, therefore, that support for constitutional change involves negative attitudes towards Thatcherism, in the sense of its free market ideology and British nationalism.

TABLE 7
REGRESSION ANALYSIS OF SUPPORT FOR CONSTITUTIONAL CHANGE IN SCOTLAND

Independent Variables	Support for Change
Age	-0.08 **
Low income	0.02
Feel more British than Scottish	-0.10 **
Privatization gone too far	0.08 *
Conservatives uncaring	0.07
Against Conservative Party	0.05
Identify with Conservatives	-0.21 **
Identify with SNP	0.16 **
Identify with Labour	0.07
R^2	0.25
N: 893	

* Significant at the 0.05 level
** Significant at the 0.01 level

Note: Don't Know/Non-Applicable not included so percentages may not add up to 100.
Source: Scottish Election Study

Conclusion

In her memoirs, Mrs Thatcher acknowledged that she had difficulties in Scotland and that the Scots proved unreceptive to Thatcherism.[32] However, it is important to distinguish between the variety of Thatcherisms on offer. What was it that made Thatcherism unpopular? The evidence presented here suggests that we must be careful in equating Thatcherism with Mrs Thatcher herself. She was deeply unpopular but so too was the party, even after it elected a new leader. Thatcherism may well have been seen as a form of British nationalism and as such was unpopular in Scotland. The importance of the Scottish dimension and the perception that the Conservatives had a two-nation strategy is sustained by our data. There is some support for the view that there has been an emergence of an alternative 'chain of equivalencies' backing a national social movement in response to Thatcherism. In short, there is a relationship between anti-Conservative attitudes, support for the opposition parties, Scottishness, support for state intervention and support for constitutional change.

NOTES

1. Robert Skidelsky, *Thatcherism* (London: Chatto & Windus, 1988) p.2.
2. This is one of three usages of the term 'Thatcherism' identified by Dennis Kavanagh *Thatcherism and British Politics* (Oxford: Oxford University Press, 1987) p.9.
3. Andrew Gamble, *The Free Economy and the Strong State,* second edition (Houndmills: Macmillan, 1994).
4. Stuart Hall and Martin Jacques (eds.) *The Politics of Thatcherism* (London: Lawrence and Wishart, 1987).
5. Bob Jessop, Kevin Bonnett, Simon Bromley and Tom Ling, *Thatcherism: A Tale of Two Nations* (Cambridge: Polity Press, 1988) p.73.
6. John Gray, *Beyond the New Right: Markets, Government and the Common Environment* (London: Routledge, 1993) p.v.
7. See discussion in Jessop *et al., Thatcherism,* Ch.2.
8. Stuart Hall, 'The Great Moving Right Show', Hall and Jacques (eds.) *Politics of Thatcherism,* p.30.
9. Jim Bulpitt, 'The Discipline of the New Democracy: Mrs Thatcher's Domestic Statecraft', *Political Studies,* Vol.34 (1986), p.21.
10. Ibid., pp.21–22.
11. Jessop, *et al., Thatcherism,* p.78.
12. Bulpitt, 'The Discipline'.
13. Jessop, *et al., Thatcherism,* p.87.
14. J.K. Galbraith, *The Culture of Contentment* (London: Penguin, 1993). Though the book focuses on the USA, Galbraith argues that there is evidence of the same phenomenon in Britain, see pp.151–152.
15. Bulpitt, 'The Discipline', p.33. In a footnote he explains the Edessa complex: 'The County of Edessa was one of the states set up by the Crusaders early in the 12th century. In contemporary language it was a "front-line" statelet, impossible to defend, and was soon recaptured by the Muslims.'
16. Jessop, *et al., Thatcherism,* p.87.
17. Peter Taylor, 'Changing Political Relations' in Paul Coke (ed.) *Policy and Change in Thatcher's Britain* (Oxford: Pergamon, 1992) pp.51–52.
18. Ibid., p.52.
19. Michael Keating *State and Regional Nationalism: Territorial Politics and the European State* (Hemel Hempstead: Harvester Wheatsheaf, 1988) p.71.
20. James Mitchell, *Conservatives and the Union* (Edinburgh: Edinburgh University Press, 1990).
21. This distinction is drawn from Stein Rokkan and Derek Urwin, 'Introduction: Centre and Peripheries in Western Europe', in idem (eds) *The Politics of Territorial Identity* (London: Sage, 1982) p.11. A unitary state is defined as one 'built up around one unambiguous political centre which enjoys economic dominance and pursues a more or less undeviating policy of administrative standardization. All areas of the state are treated alike, and all institutions are directly under the control of the centre.' A union state, on the other hand, is 'not the result of straightforward dynastic conquest. Incorporation of at least parts of its territory has been achieved through personal dynastic union, for example by treaty, marriage or inheritance. Integration is less than perfect. While administrative standardization prevails over most of the territory, the consequences of personal union entail the survival in some areas of pre-union rights and institutional infrastructures which preserve some degree of regional autonomy and serve as agencies of indigenous elite recruitment.' See discussion in James Mitchell 'Conservatism in Twentieth Century Scotland: Society, Ideology and the Union', in Michael Lynch (ed.) *Scotland, 1850–1979: Society, Politics and the Union* (London: Historical Association, 1993).
22. Jim Bulpitt, *Territory and Power in the United Kingdom* (Manchester: Manchester University Press, 1983).
23. Godfrey Barker, 'Lame ducks in a grouse moor sanctuary', *Daily Telegraph* 21 March 1984.

24. Brian Hogwood, 'Whatever Happened to Regional Government? Developments in Regional Administration in Britain since 1979', *Strathclyde Papers on Government and Politics* No. 97, 1994.
25. Chris Moore and Simon Booth, *Managing Competition: Meso-corporatism, Pluralism, and the Negotiated Order in Scotland* (Oxford: Oxford University Press, 1989) Ch.5.
26. *Glasgow Herald*, 24 November 1987.
27. *Daily Express*, 25 April 1990.
28. *Scotsman* and *Glasgow Herald* 10 October 1988.
29. *Scotsman* and *Glasgow Herald* 10 September 1987.
30. Scottish Election Study 1979. Sample of 729.
31. *The Scotsman* 27 August 1990. Sample of 1,000 people interviewed in 50 randomly selected constituencies throughout Scotland on 20–21 August by Market Reseach Scotland.
32. Margaret Thatcher, *The Downing Street Years* (London: Harper Collins, 1993) pp.618–27.

From Mass Propaganda to Political Marketing: The Transformation of Labour Party Election Campaigning

Dominic Wring

The rise and growing importance of political marketing is self evident in many of the major western democracies.[1] The innovative Conservative party campaign effort of 1979 is sometimes referred to as a major watershed in the development of the phenomenon in Britain.[2] Results of that election proved a vital component in the respective success of both the agency and client organization. Victory heralded the beginning of three Thatcher led majority governments as well as the start of a period of commercial success for the party's consultants, Saatchi and Saatchi, culminating in their emergence as the largest advertising agency in the world.[3] The relationship between the Saatchi team and their most famous clients initiated considerable media interest in the process of professionalized political communications, with the implication that the partnership had been crucial to the Conservatives' good fortune. The execution of the 1983 and 1987 general elections consolidated the idea that marketing consultants were becoming an indispensable part of the modern electoral process. In particular television documentaries such as Michael Cockerell's *The Marketing of Margaret* helped to provoke interest in the new style of campaigning among a previously disinterested Labour leadership.[4]

Partly due to the proliferation of media interest in the subject, political marketing is sometimes equated with sophisticated advertising or 'slick' campaigning. A good deal of election coverage has become increasingly preoccupied with the perceived domination of style over substance and image over issue. However, while it is true that some marketing approaches to campaigning use 'slick' methods, it is by no means axiomatic that all of them should or do pursue the glossy formula. Marketing is more than just presentational devices and advertising – it also relates to product management. Furthermore the process represents not only a set of techniques but also an approach to managing organizational relationships with their publics.[5] In 1985 the American Marketing Association issued a redefinition of its subject, adding the crucial word 'ideas' to the list of product concerns which further legitimized the application of marketing to electoral politics: 'Marketing is the process of planning and executing the conception, pricing, promotion and distribution of ideas, goods and services to create exchanges that satisfy individual and organizational objectives.'[6]

Arguably the process has begun to play a more significant and central part in contemporary British politics than is suggested by such terms as 'spin doctoring', 'image making' or 'power dressing'. Undoubtedly these techniques form an important (and more obvious) part of some campaigns but they are far from being the sole functions or representations of a political marketing exercise. Increasingly marketing is becoming a central part of strategy as political leaderships attempt to determine, refine and prioritize policy and goals. It is this process of the incorporation of marketing technique and philosophy into party organizational thinking to which this article now turns. The study will make reference to the historical development of the Labour party as a campaigning unit.

If the term 'market' is taken literally, Labour began to market itself to a mass electorate in 1918, the year that saw both the introduction of universal suffrage and the first major restructuring of the party apparatus. From this point it is possible to compare the evolution of the Labour party campaign machine with the marketing development of a firm operating in a business environment.

The Stages of Political Marketing Evolution

In seeking to clarify the stages of political marketing development in Britain it is useful to refer to Avraham Shama's account of changes in American presidential election organization.[7] Shama likens the conventional model of commercial marketing development in a firm to the stages in the evolution of a campaigning political party. Consequently three distinctive phases of electioneering can be identified, each directly comparable with the product, sales and market stages of orientation in business marketing. The analogy builds on a theme originally popularized by the democratic theorist Joseph Schumpeter: 'Party and machine politicians are simply the response to the fact that the electoral mass is incapable of action other than a stampede, and they constitute an attempt to regulate political competition exactly similar to the corresponding practices of a trade association.'[8]

Shama characterizes the period 1940–60 in American presidential politics as the 'candidate orientation' stage in that campaign organization resembles a business engaged in a product led marketing strategy. Under this mode of operation politicians began to employ advisors, sometimes professional advertisers, whose chief task was to magnify the candidates' media presence in the belief that the 'number of exposures and length of exposures were taken as the key for victory in the campaign'. The 'product'-focused approach to campaigning was preoccupied with maximizing name recognition through heavy promotional activity rather than addressing and seeking to assess voters and 'their political needs and wants'.

The era of 'sales management' orientation established itself in the 1960s. During this period campaigners started to develop more rigorous plans which in turn led them to adopt scientific methods of opinion research. Polling was used to solicit information from voters, particularly in respect of how they accessed, used and responded to political communications. Organizers also began to consider techniques for segmenting and targeting voters according to demographic variables. This 'selling concept' approach to electioneering was aimed at presenting a more sophisticated message to a better defined audience though, like the preceding 'candidate orientation' stage of marketing development, its ultimate aims lay in maximizing the politician's exposure to the voters.

Shama develops his analysis by arguing that, as with innovative and successful firms in the commercial sector, politicians can be seen to acquire a 'market orientation' as they embrace a third and more advanced form of campaigning: 'The new marketing concept is interested in the basic political needs and wants of the voters with the intention of offering them candidates who are capable of satisfying these needs and wants or changing existing candidates to meet these needs and wants.'[9] Shama observes that, in seeking to adopt the marketing concept, political organizations use opinion research in order to develop long term plans and strategic goals rather than just presentational ideas for the last few weeks of an election campaign. Furthermore sophisticated demographic and psychographic market research starts to be fed into the design of the product, be it in relation to the image of a candidate, party or policy platform on which they stand. Marketing techniques such as positioning, segmentation and product development also begin to be more fully integrated into electoral strategy. Shama contrasts this phase of political marketing development with its predecessors in that targets other than just the electorate become the focus of activity. Consequently efforts become partly preoccupied with influencing opinion in the party itself, among interest groups and, crucially, the mass media. The relatively novel term 'political marketing' is arguably more credibly used with the realization of this stage in campaign orientation.

By using Shama's framework, it is possible to discern a similar trend in the development of political marketing in other countries, notably Britain. In particular the evolution of the Labour Party organization can be analysed with respect to the changing nature of its electoral approach.

The Era of Mass Propaganda

The first stage of Labour's organizational development, comparable to a product led (or candidate orientation) marketing approach, can be traced from the introduction of universal suffrage in 1918 to the advent of mass television nearly forty years later. Analysis of Labour campaigning in this period makes it possible to identify the antecedents of modern political marketing. Electioneering activity was commonly referred to as an exercise in 'propaganda', a word which did not have the pejorative connotations it has since acquired. The term is of particular use in describing the one-directional flow of communication from political elites to the electorate, prior to the growth of widespread public opinion research. Qualter defines propaganda as: 'The deliberate attempt by the few to influence the attitudes and behaviour of the many by the manipulation of symbolic communication.'[10]

Prior to assessing the conduct of electioneering in the propaganda era it is worth examining two of the most important environmental factors conditioning the development of Labour campaigning in this period: the nature of headquarters reorganization and the party's relationship with the mass media.

Party Organization and Election Campaigning

The Great War had a profound effect on the way British politicians, including the Labour leadership, viewed the potential of propaganda as a tool of persuasion. Similarly, the passage of the 1918 Representation of the Peoples' Act, guaranteeing universal male suffrage and extending the franchise to some women, also helped increase party organizers' interest in the techniques of mass political communication. This changed electoral environment coincided with the first major overhaul and extension of Labour Party headquarters' activity.[11] Labour formed a Press and Publicity Department in October 1917, just prior to a wholesale review of organizational structure. Former religious journalist, Herbert Tracey, headed the new department prior to the appointment of W.W. Henderson in 1921. A reinvigorated party organization quickly won praise for its efforts during the 1918 election.[13] The 1923 and 1929 general election campaigns provided the party with more tangible rewards in the form of its first minority administrations. Soon after the formation of the second government, the Foreign (and party) Secretary Arthur Henderson attributed part of Labour's success to 'an unequal standard of organizational and electioneering efficiency'.[14] Similarly, Dean McHenry, an American scholar writing on the development of Labour party in the 1930s, observed that the organization 'perhaps surpasses in effectiveness the most highly perfected American political machines sustained by spoils'.[15]

Labour and the Mass Media

The study of party political communication has been understandably dominated by discussions of the impact of the mass media. Even prior to the beginning of the twentieth century there were significant changes in the partisan nature of political coverage. Recognizing a trend towards more selective and biased reporting in the privately owned print media, Matthews observed that: 'politics began to be more packaged for consumption by the readership of the newspaper'.[16] The Labour Party, in particular, became a major target for press hostility in the form of compromising stories, the most infamous of which became known as the 'Zinoviev letter', where a forged document, published on the front page of the *Daily Mail* days before the general election of 1924, was widely perceived to have discredited the then minority Labour government with the taint of being pro Moscow.[17] Neither did the rise of a heavily regulated state radio broadcasting service, in the shape of John Reith's British Broadcasting Corporation, instil much confidence in a Labour Party whose view of the mass media was coloured by the antics of a hitherto dominant print media.[18] By the 1930s initial apathy towards the BBC began to develop into hostility, with Labour organizers openly questioning the allegedly unjust allocation of party broadcasts in the 1931 general election[19] and the coverage of Russian affairs in 1933.[20] If the media provided few opportunities for Labour to promote its message to the British public, the party realized it would have to develop other methods of political communication. Consequently strategists began to assess ways of directly informing the public about the democratic socialist case. The embryo of political marketing development lies in this debate and some of the experimentation with campaign methodology that took place during the period.

The Development of Party Propaganda Technique

Traditional methods of voter canvassing – meetings, doorstepping and leafleting – provided the basis of Labour Party campaigning prior to the advent of the 'television election' in the latter half of the 1950s. However, while practical propaganda plans were dominated by these long established techniques coupled with the narrow calculations of leading politicians, strategists started to appreciate the possibilities presented by the 'new media'. Consequently consideration began to be given to advertising, film making, image projection and design as well as a rudimentary approach to segmenting and targeting sections of the electorate. Symbolically in 1924 the party commissioned a competition to design its first logo with the winning entry materializing in the form of the shovel, torch and quill design which still appears above the gates of the current headquarters in Walworth Road.[21] A year later party leader Ramsey Macdonald (in perhaps a prophetic move) attempted to change the traditional party song, launching a contest in the *Daily Herald* to find a replacement for The Red Flag. Despite receiving some 300 entries Labour decided to keep its anthem.[22] In addition leading figures such as Philip Snowden articulated the need for Labour propagandists to make image laden themes a part of their campaign work:

> It is so very easy to bore an audience with facts and figures and statistics. The person who uses facts in speaking or writing should remember that the way to impress is to give a mental picture of 'relativity'. That is an awful word, but what I mean to say is this: To say that we have 1,423,819 persons unemployed gives no striking and impressive mental picture. But if you say that the number of unemployed could be formed into a procession, four abreast, which would reach from London to Liverpool, you leave a permanent impression on your hearers' minds.[23]

It was a leading Fabian and political scientist, Graham Wallas (pioneer of the phrase 'party image'), who noted that 'advertisement and party politics are becoming more and more closely assimilated in method'.[24] Practical evidence of this came in the 1929 election with the formal introduction of political advertising into the British electoral process, in the shape of the employment of the S.H. Benson agency by the Conservatives.[25] Labour strategists also began to consider the implications of using advertising other than in terms of traditional poster propaganda. Several party thinkers began to explore what one of them called this 'subtle and immeasurable thing' in recognition of the wider societal and political importance of the new phenomenon: 'few people realize the tremendous force which advertisement has become in modern society, nor the terrific amounts of brains, energy and money that is put into it'.[26]

The national party apparatus, however, was not responsible for the most innovative and important Labour advertising campaign of the inter-war period. 1934 had seen the return of a Labour administration led by Herbert Morrison at County Hall, London. Subsequently Morrison sought to overhaul the image of the authority, setting up a new publicity department and employing advertising and public relations techniques in the process.[27] In the following London County Council elections of 1937 the leader extended the use of professional communications to the capital's Labour party business in what was, his biographers argue, 'the most professional campaign ever fought'.[28] In securing an impressive re-election victory, Morrison was helped by a group of sympathetic publicity consultants which included Robert Fraser, George Wansborough and Clem Leslie coupled with funds from the T&GWU and NUGMW unions.[29] The campaign team produced high quality material promoting the leader and their chosen core campaign themes of education and housing: the message was summed up in one arresting poster image featuring Morrison accompanied by children in front of newly built LCC flats. Early marketing commentators, in the form of Advertising Monthly, applauded the campaign, declaring that it had '[set the] standard and made the running for the advertising world itself'.[30]

While propaganda was still predominantly thought of in print terms, politicians began to recognize the potential of film as a vehicle for political persuasion. Soon after the First World War the Labour Party appointed a group to consider the possible uses of cinematic documentary. Reporting in 1920 Sidney Webb, Chair of the Labour Propaganda Committee, declared:

> During the War the Cinematograph became a powerful instrument of propaganda in the hands of the Government. The experience gained in this attractive and striking method of publicity is now being used by capitalist interests in various ways to undermine and check the progress of Labour throughout the country...[31]

As with advertising, key initiatives came from the non executive level of party organization. Several groups of supporters such as the Socialist Film Council and ILP Masses and Stage Film Guild sought to promote the medium in the earlier part of the 1930s.[32] Despite these efforts, Labour never effectively developed a programme to counter the Conservatives' fleet of cinema vans which became a popular feature of inter-war propaganda.[33] After the 1935 election defeat the subsequent three annual party conferences played host to important film events. In turn these led to the involvement of documentary makers such as Paul Rotha in discussions about Labour's propaganda methods. J.S. Middleton, Arthur Henderson's successor as party secretary, became convinced of the importance of film as a political medium after attending one of the conference events. The culmination of this activity came with the inauguration of the Workers' Film Association (WFA) in 1938.[34] The WFA was formed after a period of collaboration between the Labour Party, trades unions and experienced film makers in the co operative movement. Though the group had initially intended to help the Labour Party in its election campaigning, the burden of its anti fascist propaganda activity (and ultimately the war) put an end to these plans.[35]

Prior to the proliferation of opinion polling as a method of campaign feedback after the Second World War, Hugh Berrington characterized politicians' relationship to their electorate as a 'Dialogue of the Deaf'.[36] Despite this shortage of data on voters, Labour campaigners actively sought and found ways to better define and target their propaganda at sections of the public. In these activities some of them engaged in a rudimentary type of 'market research' which drew on canvass returns and previous election results. The most important contribution to organizational thinking on the subject came in 1922 with the publication of 'Stratified Electioneering' by Sidney Webb, leading Labour intellectual and creative inspiration behind the recently adopted party constitution. In his influential article Webb sought to develop an elementary approach to targeting selected audiences with relevant messages:

> we should, as far as possible, 'stratify' our electioneering: appealing to each section of the electorate in the language which that section understands; emphasizing just the points in which that section is interested; subordinating the questions that each section finds dull or unpleasant; addressing to each section the literature most appropriate to it; and generally seeking to substitute, for the 'greyness' of mass propaganda, the warmer and more individual colours of each man's speciality.[37]

This conceptualization, a basic form of political 'market segmentation', made a notable impression on party strategists and earned the rare honour of a reprint nearly a decade after its initial appearance in the agents' journal *Labour Organiser*. Several people took up the analysis, including the agent Frank Edwards who showed how it was possible to organize constituency campaigns on the basis of targeting sub groups of weak Conservatives, Liberals, religious observers and workers by occupation.[38] Similarly Harold Croft, a highly influential member of the National Union of Labour Organizers, included the stratified electioneering approach in his widely distributed campaign handbook, *The Conduct of Elections*, while party secretary Arthur Henderson devoted one pre election address of Lancashire agents to expounding Webb's concept.[39] The historical significance of stratified electioneering lies in its importance as a precursor to the development of more sophisticated means of political opinion research and segmentation after 1945.

The Development of the Media Campaign

The advent of television broadcasting in Britain in the 1950s coincided with a proliferation of advertising communications. Both had an immediate impact on society, not least in the sphere of electoral politics. In his model Shama identifies the emergence of a 'sales management' approach to electioneering comparable to the development of what British commentators have termed the 'media campaign'. Consequently the main Westminster parties began to invest in private opinion research and advertising consultancy in order to refine and better target their message. Writing on European party organizational change at this time, Kirchheimer viewed the emerging trend in electioneering as: 'fulfilling in politics a role analogous to that of a major brand in the marketing of a universally needed and highly standardized article of mass consumption.'[40]

The new style of media campaigning helped transform the nature of electoral organization. Identifying what he termed a 'contagion from the right', Epstein cited the importance of the development of 'counter organizational tendencies' as agents of party change. Subsequently European parties began to eschew the importance of mass membership campaigning as they moved to adopt modern methods of communication through the employment of advertising and public relations advisers. In concluding his analysis Epstein foresaw the emergence of American style 'middle class cadre type organizations'.[41] Such a course of development can be detected in British politics during and after the 1950s and 1960s.

The 1959 General Election

The decade following the 1955 election has been identified as a key watershed in the development of presentational politics in Britain. This period also marked the entrenchment of conventional marketing in the sphere of civil and economic life, perhaps best encapsulated in terms such as 'consumerism' and 'the affluent society'. The 1959 British general election' and events leading up to it provided early evidence of the beginning of a major strategic shift in the nature of electioneering.[42] Conservative Central Office, working in conjunction with leading London advertising agents Colman Prentis and Varley, launched what was generally perceived to be an effective campaign based around the slogan 'Life's Better Under the Conservatives, Don't Let Labour Ruin It'.[43] For its part the Labour Party did not formally embrace such techniques but did commence experimentation with innovative television Party Election Broadcasts (PEBs). The project was supervised by a Broadcasting Advisory Committee which included three MPs with backgrounds in the media – namely Tony Benn, Woodrow Wyatt and Christopher Mayhew (presenter of the first ever small screen Labour PEB during the 1951 general election). Commenting on the 1987 Labour campaign Benn recalled the importance of his earlier party work, describing himself as: 'the Peter Mandelson–Bryan Gould of the 1959 election. I fought a brilliant campaign and lost'.[44]

Both before and after the 1959 general election the nature and desirability of political advertising became the focus of some debate. Commentators such as Richard Crossman denounced the promotion of Prime Minister Macmillan as a debasement of political debate akin to the selling of detergents.[45] His fellow Labour MP Alice Bacon, chair of the party National Executive Committee's publicity sub committee, attacked the Conservatives' relationship to the CPV agency in a trenchant parliamentary speech: 'The Conservative Party has placed itself in the hands of an advertising agency which produced the so called image of the Tory Party by advertising methods. I believe this to be doing something alien to our British democracy.'[46]

Other sections of the party were less inclined to voice partisan criticisms of the Conservatives' professional communications; for them the issue was one of ideological contradiction between what was seen as the capitalist process, with its consumerist tools, and the Labour movement's historic commitment to a socialist vision of society. Writing in 1960, Dennis Potter helped voice the moral indignation on the left for what was perceived to be the encroachment of slick advertising and salesmanship into the political process: 'The Prime Minister, Harold Macmillan, is sold on the hoardings of the Mayfair agents of Colman, Prentis and Varley... the techniques of persuasion, the ideology of the acquisitive society, have taken on new and more dangerous dimensions.'[47]

Labour Embrace the 'Selling Concept'

In the immediate aftermath of the 1959 general election defeat, debates over advertising and publicity strategy were unsurprisingly dwarfed by rows between revisionist and traditionalist sections of the Labour Party concerning defence policy and Clause Four.[48] Nevertheless one aspect of modern marketing technique – opinion research – did make some impression during the heated debates over the future and image of the party. In particular the publication of *Must Labour Lose?*, a venture originally commissioned by the key Gaitskellite journal *Socialist Commentary*, helped highlight the relevance of political opinion research in giving credence to the revisionist case.[49] One of the report's authors, Mark Abrams, offered polling evidence which suggested that Labour should reconsider certain standpoints. Specifically the research indicated the party would benefit from shedding its commitments to allegedly unpopular policies such as nationalization. *Must Labour Lose?* and its methods were not without its critics particularly among traditional socialists who, sharing Aneurin Bevan's view that polling was responsible for 'taking the poetry out of politics', condemned market research and what they saw as the objectification of the voter as a 'political consumer'.[50] Others disagreed more with Abrams' results and sought to defend the policy of state ownership by citing Gallup data which cast doubt on the argument that this aspect of Labour's programme had helped foster the public's negative perceptions of the party.[51] Opinion polling had begun to permeate and inform internal political debates, a factor which served to legitimize the techniques and usage of market research within the organization.

Just three years after Bacon's statement in the House of Commons Labour embraced advertising and opinion research methods as part of its presentational push under Harold Wilson. The leader, a more consensual figure than his predecessor Hugh Gaitskell, was one of the key factors behind the consolidation of the new approach to party strategy.[52] Consequently he was able to encourage the assembly of a formidable team of professional publicity consultants including advisors such as David Kingsley. Significantly, Wilson incorporated former advisors to Gaitskell such as pollster Mark Abrams and the new party Director of Publicity, John Harris, into positions of influence in a revitalized campaign machine. The Conservatives' success at the 1959 election and the Kennedy 'New Frontier' presidential campaign both helped underline the need for an assessment of professional political communications methods inside the party.[53] Support for an overhaul of party presentation came in the form of articles in several influential publications including *Socialist Commentary*, the Fabian Society pamphlet series and *The Political Quarterly*.[54] The ultimate vindication of the new strategy came with the election of a Labour government in 1964 after an upbeat and innovative campaign that helped promote Harold Wilson and his 'white heat of technology' theme.

Despite his campaign successes in 1964 and 1966, the Labour leader became the focus of criticism after the general election defeat of 1970. Some accused Wilson of running an aloof campaign without care for the rest of the party organization.[55] The Labour effort was in marked contrast to the carefully organized efforts of their Conservative opponents who broke new ground through the innovative use of sophisticated polling and advertising methods.[56] The subsequent elections in 1974 saw little in terms of presentational innovation though they did mark a cementation of the relationship between Labour and the pollsters MORI who had begun to experiment with psychographic research techniques on behalf of their political client.[57] The campaigns were to be Wilson's last in control and so marked the end of the leadership's long-standing close association with professional election advisors such as Peter Lovell Davies and Dennis Lyons.

The Consolidation of Political Marketing

The third stage of campaign development in Shama's model involves the realization of a market orientation in electioneering practices. In implementing this new approach, it is possible to identify moves towards what Panebianco calls the 'electoral–professional' ideal type of party organization. Thus, in this mode, parties become focused on appealing to the 'opinion electorate' rather than their own ideological or membership predilections.[58] During the 1980s the Labour Party radically reorganized itself.[59] A key component of this transformation was a two-step integration of modern marketing into its campaign structures. Initially, in the build up to, and during, the 1987 campaign, sophisticated advertising and opinion research methods were reintroduced to the organization. Secondly, despite suffering a further defeat, the election served to enhance the leadership to the extent that they were able to introduce a market led approach into party strategy during the Policy Review.

The Adoption of Sophisticated Techniques

In contrast to the smooth running Conservative election campaigns of 1979 and 1983, both Labour efforts proved difficult to manage, lacked strategic clarity and were dogged by organizational inertia. Ironically the 1983 election, which resulted in Labour's heaviest defeat since 1931, was the first to see the party formally retain an advertising agency, Johnny Wright and Partners. Later, making his inaugural party conference speech as leader, Neil Kinnock invoked the memory of the result in declaring 'Just remember how you felt then, and think to yourselves: "June the ninth, 1983 – never ever again will we experience that."' The campaign became a by word for all of Labour's strategic and political failings of the previous years and henceforth acted as a major motivating force behind the reconstruction of the party machine under its new leadership.

Within a year of the 1983 debacle, Labour sympathizers from the world of marketing formed an informal 'breakfast group' to discuss the party's communications problem.[60] By early 1985 internal pressure groups such as the Labour Co-ordinating Committee were calling for the integration of marketing techniques into party strategic thinking, a view endorsed in a successful motion to the annual conference later that year.[61] Reflecting on his experiences in the 1983 campaign, Nick Grant, the retiring Director of Publicity, recognized a major re-think was underway: 'Labour has, at last, come to terms with the need for a clear concise marketing approach – not in order "to sell politics like soap powder", but in order to understand the need to develop political marketing as part of the science of communication in the multi media society in the Britain of the 1980s and 1990s.'[62]

This desire for a new approach to campaigning was highlighted in a memo on party communications prepared by advertising consultant Philip Gould for Grant's successor, Peter Mandelson. The paper offered an in depth critique of various presentational and organizational failings and proved instrumental in setting up the Shadow Communications Agency (SCA) in 1986, consisting of a number of advertising and marketing specialists all of whom offered their services to Labour on a voluntary basis.[63] Working closely with Mandelson and his new Campaigns and Communications Directorate at Labour headquarters, the SCA co ordinated a series of events such as the 'Freedom and Fairness' publicity offensive in an attempt to give the party an image overhaul, complete with a new red rose logo, in preparation for the forthcoming general election.[64]

The 1987 election has been identified as a major watershed in the adoption of marketing by Labour.[65] Certainly, in terms of technique, the campaign saw the party develop sophisticated machinery geared to the twin tasks of news management and firming up electoral support. In the words of two key strategists their achievement had been to devise 'one of the most effective pieces of disciplined communication of modern British politics'.[66] In addition the coherent use of marketing tools to promote the party during the campaign surprised the Conservatives, foiled the Alliance parties and helped stabilize Neil Kinnock's hold on the leadership. Despite having led the party to its third major defeat in a row, Kinnock was the recipient of some of the praise for Labour's professional campaign. Given that polling and communication activity was perceived to have been one of the few positive aspects of party endeavours at the time, it is perhaps not surprising that it became a key element in the leadership's modernization strategy during the following parliamentary term. In organizational terms this process of professionalization afforded the Labour leader (not to mention his successors) 'an institutionalized battery of resources upon which he can draw to enhance his grip over the process of developing party policy and strategy'.[67]

Characteristic of the politician credited with describing the 1983 manifesto as 'the longest suicide note in history', Gerald Kaufman pointedly concluded that the 1987 campaign had been 'a facade'.[68] In his view the party had not changed enough since 1983, and presentational reforms needed to be supported by a major review of political commitments. This assertion is supported by Swindells and Jardine's contention that, in contrast to the Conservatives, Labour did not 'market' itself but sought to build a campaign around the 'particular narratives of deprivation and poverty and the moral worth of British socialism'.[69] Commenting after the campaign, Peter Mandelson concluded that Labour needed to extend the use of technique and develop a marketing outlook, especially in respect of its 'product' – the leadership, image and party manifesto: 'Next time, however, we will need to get further in marketing the party on the basis of our programme for government than our professionalism and passion have taken us so far in opposition.'[70]

The Policy Review Process

Following on from his first election defeat as leader, and after consultation with close colleagues such as NEC member Tom Sawyer, Neil Kinnock launched Labour's Policy Review. The whole exercise, closely monitored by the leadership team, dominated internal party political thinking up until the 1992 election. While the Review formally committed Labour to accepting the workings of the market in the sphere of economic life it also marked a turning point in the party's embrace of another 'market' – in the political domain. Using the criteria set out by Shama, Labour shifted from a sophisticated selling approach to adopt a market orientation devoted to satisfying, in the words of one informed account of the period, 'the needs and concerns of groups of voters'.[71] The monitoring of public opinion throughout the Review process was to prove crucial in this respect.

Prior to the convening of Policy Review, principally through the formation of individual subject groups, the entire Labour leadership in the shape of a joint meeting between members of the Shadow Cabinet and the ruling National Executive Committee were left in little doubt as to what specially commissioned opinion research was saying about their party. The research was, in its implicit advocacy of the need for changes in political strategy, reminiscent of the *Must Labour Lose?* report, itself a product of a third electoral defeat. The SCA (and associates) briefing, entitled *Britain and Labour in the 1990s*, influenced the parameters of the subsequent party and review groups discussions of policy in such a way that 'political demands would be inseparable from the communications imperative'.[72] This extensive report of public opinion identified a declining base of popular support and the perennial concern of poor party image as Labour's key problems.[73] Opinion research was commissioned and made available to the policy discussion groups throughout the ensuing review process. Party policy was changed in several areas of perceived electoral weakness, notably in relation to defence, the economy and industrial relations.[74] Eric Shaw concludes that, as a result of the Policy Review process, Labour developed into a 'responsive' as opposed to an 'educative' party after embracing what he terms an 'electoral imperative' on the basis that: 'No significant development of policy was considered without the most careful attention to likely public responses.'[75]

The final stages of the Policy Review involved the promotion of a new, revised party programme. Campaign co ordinator Jack Cunningham heralded the renewal of Labour for the 1990s in a series of 'pre manifesto' relaunches beginning with the 'Meet the Challenge, Make the Change' campaign of 1989.[76]

After 1992

The 1992 election registered a serious blow to the 'new model' Labour Party and marked the end of Neil Kinnock's leadership. Yet the organizational changes and thinking that he pioneered have outlasted his period in office. The 'electoral imperative', an apt description of the market orientation embedded in the party's strategy for the 1992 campaign, proved to be one of the factors that played a role in conditioning the cautious debate following the election of John Smith as Labour leader.

Despite the generally bad publicity the polling industry received after failing to predict the 1992 election result, the credibility of market research techniques was apparently not totally damaged inside the Labour Party. Interestingly the party inquiry (in conjunction with the SCA) into the fourth defeat used qualitative opinion research undertaken during and after the campaign to try and discover the reasons behind the unexpected fourth Tory victory. Some of the findings, in the form of focus group feedback, were leaked to the press and helped to set an agenda about the reasons behind the party's setback.[77] Despite the limitations inherent in this type of research, the results were reported by sections of the media as an authoritative source particularly in the absence of other short term scientific explanations for the setback. Press coverage of the work helped vindicate the leadership's modernization strategy, blaming past disunity and associations with minority causes for Labour's defeat.[78] In addition the research was reported to contain evidence which implied that links to the trades union movement had proved detrimental to the party's electoral fortunes. The claims contrast with the more modest conclusions of the British Election Study which indicate that Labour suffered as a result of failing to clarify its message.[79] Nevertheless the focus group post mortem on the party's unexpected 1992 defeat helped shape the political agenda following the election of John Smith as Kinnock's successor.

Besides shaping debate within the party, modern political marketing has also helped redefine the power structures in favour of the leader: the holder of the office not only plays an organizational role but also becomes a central part of the product offering himself.[80] Consequently even a relatively consensual leader figure such as John Smith was able to initiate, lead and win major debates in his party with some ease. Smith was at the forefront of a 'One Member One Vote' campaign which, while being primarily about changing the rules governing parliamentary candidate selections and leadership elections, was widely interpreted as the party seeking to weaken its links to its financial sponsors, the affiliated trades unions.[81] Similarly a Social Justice Commission was set up to evaluate party policy and possibly allow the instigation of changes to long held commitments on the welfare state and universal benefits.

Perhaps the clearest evidence of the fundamental shift that has taken place within the Labour Party came with the election of Tony Blair as leader. The 1994 ballot for the leadership, involving nearly a million party members and trades unionists, gave a clear majority vote in each section to the candidate of the so called 'modernizers'. In winning the contest, Blair had been identified in the print media as the prospective leader most likely to win the votes of disaffected Tory and weak Liberal Democrat supporters.

Shama noted that, in adopting a market led approach to campaigning, communications become targeted at groups other than the general public, such as the party (in particular those who vote in leadership elections), interest groups (affiliates such as the trades unions) and the agenda setting mass media. Labour's adoption of such an orientation has helped alter the nature of the party (as well as the overall political environment it operates in) over the course of the last decade. In this way the non party media, especially the national press, have been able to play an increasingly influential role in internal matters including the recent leadership contests. Thus, in 1994, the newspapers read by the bulk of Labour Party members were able to help by running features in sympathy with the central message of Blair's case, founded as it was on the belief that he could best realize the party's aspiration to win governmental office.[82]

The market led renewal strategy pioneered by Kinnock and developed by his successors has not been without its critics in the party. Dissent focuses on two closely related arguments over the political and organizational consequences of Labour adopting a modern marketing campaign approach. Some dissenters, notably Ben Pimlott, have argued that it is unwise to devise political strategy with reference to market research findings on the grounds that such a method is likely to stifle the development of ideas and policies designed to challenge rather than mirror electoral opinion.[83] Other Labour supporters such as Teresa Pearce, a delegate to the 1992 party conference, have questioned the perceived lack of accountability within the party in terms of its policy formulation and presentation:

> We have allowed ourselves to be marketed by paid image makers, but in whose image are we are being made? It is not an image I recognize. It is not an image I want to recognize. We should beware of the paid image maker. These are people, mainly middle class graduates, who have learned their socialism from market research and opinion polls.[84]

Conclusion

The basic premise of this paper has been to compare the development of the Labour Party as a campaigning organization with that of a commercial firm engaged in marketing. Since its first major overhaul of organizational structures in 1918, Labour has been in the business of using marketing techniques in its bid to win electoral support. Marketing did not become a feature of British political life in either the 1959, 1979 or 1992 elections; rather, as Shama observes, it was the basic orientation of the campaigns which changed in light of developments in the market or wider environment. Philip Kotler, one of the leading authorities on marketing, contends: 'Campaigning has always had a marketing character. The "new methodology" is not the introduction of marketing methods into politics, but an increased sophistication and acceleration of their use.'[85]

Clearly though there was a decisive shift in the nature of Labour party organization in the periods 1962–64 and more recently after the 1987 defeat. Arguably the adoption of a modern political marketing strategy in the run up to the 1992 general election was a watershed in the building of a more centralized, disciplined organization. The change, intended to make Labour electable, has been a contributory factor to the emergence of a strong leadership and more passive party.

NOTES

1. Shaun Bowler and David M. Farrell (eds), *Electoral Strategies and Political Marketing* (Hampshire: Macmillan, 1992).
2. Martin Harrop, 'Political Marketing', *Parliamentary Affairs*, Vol.43, No.3 (1990).
3. Philip Kleinman, *The Saatchi and Saatchi Story* (London: Weidenfeld and Nicolson, 1987). By the end of the 1980s the Saatchi brothers' fortunes, like those of their political client, were on the wane.
4. See Michael Cockerell, 'The Marketing of Margaret', *The Listener*, 16 June 1983. The documentary had an impact on the thinking of senior Labour figures such as Robin Cook, the newly appointed party Campaigns Co-ordinator.
5. Geoff Lancaster and Lester Massingham, *Essentials of Marketing* (Berkshire: McGraw-Hill, 1993, second edition), p.5. Analysis of presentation techniques sometimes forms the basis of commentary on political marketing, see Rodney Tyler, *Campaign: The Selling of the Prime Minister* (London: Grafton, 1987).
6. Quoted in Seymour Fine (ed.) *Marketing the Public Sector* (New Jersey: Transaction, 1992) p.1.
7. Avraham Shama, 'The Marketing of Political Candidates', *Journal of the Academy of Marketing Sciences*, Vol.4, No.4 (1976), pp.764–77.
8. Joseph Schumpeter, *Capitalism, Socialism and Democracy* (London: Unwin, 1943), p.283.
9. Shama, 'The Marketing of Political Candidates', p.771. It should be noted that while the consumer is the focus of the marketing approach, the AMA definition of the concept (see note 6) also takes due account of the existence of organizational (party) objectives. In this way political marketing strategies are not necessarily predicated on the simplistic idea of slavishly following public opinion: recent Conservative campaigns are a good case in point. See Margaret Scammell, 'The Phenomenom of Political Marketing: The Thatcher Contribution', *Contemporary Record*, Vol.8, No.1, pp.23–43.
10. Terence Qualter, *Opinion Control in the Western Democracies* (London: Macmillan, 1985), p.124.
11. Robert McKenzie, *British Political Parties* (London: William Heinemann, 1955), p.563.
12. Ralph Casey, 'British Politics: Some Lessons in Campaign Propaganda', *Public Opinion Quarterly*, Spring (1944).
13. Ross McKibbin, *The Evolution of the Labour Party 1910–24* (Oxford: Oxford University Press, 1974), p.124.
14. *Labour Organiser*, No.100, October 1929.
15. Dean McHenry, *The Labour Party in Transition 1931–38* (London: George Routlege & Sons, 1938), p.303.
16. H.C.G. Matthew, 'Rhetoric and Politics in Great Britain, 1860–1950', in P.J. Waller (ed.) *Politics and Social Change in Modern Britain* (Sussex: Harvester Press, 1987).
17. A. Jones, 'The Zinoviev Letter', *Talking Politics*, Vol.5, No.1, Autumn (1992).
18. *Labour Organiser*, No.79, January 1928.
19. *Labour Organiser*, No.126, December 1931.
20. *Labour Organiser*, No.143, May 1933.
21. *Labour Organiser*, No.42, May 1924.
22. John Gorman, *Images of Labour* (London: Scorpion, 1985), p.28.
23. *Labour Organiser*, No.19, April 1922.
24. Graham Wallas, *Human Nature in Politics* (London: Constable, 1948 edition; first published 1908), p.87.
25. Michael Pinto-Duschinsky, *British Political Finance, 1830–1980* (Washington: American Enterprise Institute, 1981), p.98.

122 BRITISH ELECTIONS AND PARTIES YEARBOOK 1995

26. *Labour Organiser*, No.178, April 1936.
27. Bernard Donoghue and George Jones, *Herbert Morrison: Portrait of a Politician* (London: Weidenfeld and Nicolson, 1973), p.207.
28. Ibid., pp.209–10.
29. Fifty years after Herbert Morrison revolutionized his local authority and party publicity machines, similar pioneering campaign methods were being introduced by Ken Livingstone, his Labour successor at County Hall, in an attempt to save the Greater London Council. Likewise, the use of a committee of advertising experts in the 1937 London elections was replicated in Labour's high profile 1987 national campaign. Interestingly the latter effort was managed by Morrison's grandson, Peter Mandelson, a party official often credited with introducing professional methods into the Labour Party.
30. *Labour Organiser*, No.193, July 1937.
31. Quoted in Bert Hogenkamp, *Deadly Parallels: Film and the Left in Britain, 1929–1939* (London: Lawrence & Wishart, 1986), p.18.
32. Stephen Jones, *The British Labour Movement and Film, 1918–1939* (London: Routledge and Kegan Paul, 1987), pp.141–2.
33. T.J. Hollins, 'The Conservative Party and Film Propaganda Between the Wars', *English Historical Review* (1981), pp.359–69.
34. Alan Burton, *The People's Cinema: Film and the Co-operative Movement* (London: British Film Institute, 1994), pp.44–45.
35. Jones, *The British Labour Movement*, pp.153–4.
36. Hugh Berrington, 'Dialogue of the Deaf? The Elite and the Electorate in Mid-Century Britain', in Dennis Kavanagh (ed.) *Electoral Politics* (London: Macmillan, 1992).
37. *Labour Organiser*, No.22, July 1922.
38. *Labour Organiser*, No.54, June 1925.
39. *Labour Organiser*, No.89, November 1928.
40. Otto Kirchheimer, 'The Transformation of the Western European Party Systems', in J. La Palombra and M. Weiner (eds.) *Political Parties and Political Development* (New Jersey: Princeton University Press, 1966).
41. Leon Epstein, *Political Parties in Western Democracies* (London: Pall Mall, 1967), p.257.
42. Richard Rose, *Influencing Voters: A Study of Campaign Rationality* (London: Faber and Faber, 1967). It is significant that this book, the most penetrating analysis of the new media mode of campaigning in Britain, appeared soon after the emergence of the phenomenon in the post-war era.
43. David Butler and Richard Rose, *The British General Election of 1959* (London: Macmillan, 1960).
44. *The Guardian*, 11 July 1992.
45. Butler and Rose, *The British General Election of 1959*, p.27.
46. Rose, *Influencing Voters*, p.14.
47. Dennis Potter, *The Glittering Coffin* (London: Victor Gollancz, 1960), p.15.
48. For background on the major actors in this period see: Mark Jenkins, *Bevanism: Labour's High Tide* (Nottingham: Spokesman, 1979); and Stephen Haseler, *The Gaitskellites* (London: Macmillan, 1969).
49. Mark Abrams and Richard Rose with Rita Hinden, *Must Labour Lose?* (London: Penguin, 1960).
50. Raphael Samuel, 'Dr Abrams and the End of Politics', *New Left Review*, No.5, September (1960).
51. Geoffrey Gibson, 'Voting Habits are Examined', *Labour Organiser*, No.486, December (1962). See also the edition from December 1960.
52. Stephen Fielding, 'The Evolution of "Wilsonism": "White heat" and White Collars', in R. Coopey, S. Fielding and N.Tiratsoo (eds.), *The Wilson Governments, 1964–70* (London: Pinter, 1993).
53. On the Kennedy election campaign see Theodore White, *The Making of the President 1960* (London: Jonathan Cape, 1962).
54. See for instance Christopher Rowland, 'Labour Publicity', *Political Quarterly*, Vol.31, July (1960).

55. Labour MP Leo Abse called for an inquiry into Wilson's behaviour during the campaign. See Dick Leonard, 'The Labour Campaign', in H.R. Penniman (ed.) *Britain at the Polls 1974* (Washington: American Enterprise Institute, 1975).

56. Barry Day, 'The Politics of Communication or the Communication of Politics', in Robert Worcester and Martin Harrop (eds.), *Political Communication: The General Election of 1979* (London: Allen & Unwin, 1982).

57. Robert Worcester, *British Public Opinion* (Oxford: Blackwell, 1991), p.48.

58. Angelo Panebianco, *Political Parties: Organization and Power* (Cambridge: Cambridge University Press, 1988), pp.263–4. The point about the difference between modern political marketing and earlier forms of electioneering is perhaps reinforced by Rose's study of campaign rationality (see note 42) which concluded that the 'media' approach (the focus of his research) was restricted by parties' reticence to use opinion research as a feedback mechanism.

59. See Paul Webb, 'Election Campaigning, Organisational Transformation and the Professionalisation of the Labour Party', *European Journal of Political Research*, Vol.21, pp.267–288 (1992); also Adrian Sackman, 'Managers and Professionals in Neil Kinnock's Labour Party 1983–87: A Case Study of Campaign Management', paper presented at the European Consortium of Political Research joint sessions, Leiden, April (1993); and John Wilton, 'Labour in the 1980s: the Effect of Professionalisation on Party Campaigning', paper presented at the Political Studies Association Conference, Leicester, April (1993).

60. *The Guardian*, 2 October 1989.

61. *The Guardian*, 30 January 1985; *Labour Party Annual Conference Report* (London: Labour Party, 1985).

62. Nick Grant, 'A Comment on Labour's Campaign', in Ivor Crewe and Martin Harrop (eds.) *Political Communication and the General Election of 1983* (Cambridge: Cambridge University Press, 1986).

63. David Butler and Dennis Kavanagh, *The British General Election of 1987* (London: Macmillan, 1988).

64. Andrew Grice, 'Political Advertising: How Labour Staged a Marketing Revolution', *Campaign*, 30 May 1986.

65. Harrop, 'Political Marketing'.

66. Patricia Hewitt and Peter Mandelson, 'The Labour Campaign', in Ivor Crewe and Martin Harrop (eds.), *Political Communication in the 1987 General Election Campaign* (Cambridge: Cambridge University Press, 1989).

67. Paul Webb, 'Party Organizational Change in Britain: The Iron Law of Centralization?' in Richard Katz and Peter Mair (eds.), *How Parties Organize* (London: Sage, 1994).

68. Remark made in an interview shown on London Weekend Television's series *Kinnock: The Inside Story*, broadcast on the ITV network, August 1993.

69. Julia Swindells and Lisa Jardine, *What's Left: Women in Culture and the Labour Movement* (London: Routledge, 1990), p.viii.

70. Peter Mandelson, 'Marketing Labour', *Contemporary Record*, Winter (1988). Press reports highlighting discussions over the need for the party to make serious changes to its policies began to appear soon after the 1987 defeat, for instance 'Labour Told to Adapt Policy or Face Defeat', *The Times*, 27 July 1987.

71. Colin Hughes and Patrick Wintour, *Labour Rebuilt: the New Model Party* (London: Fourth Estate, 1990), p.46.

72. Ibid., p.54. See also discussion of the importance of the research, pp.60–63. The documentary series *Kinnock: The Inside Story* (see note 68) placed particular emphasis on the impact of this research on the Policy Review process. Furthermore, the polling provided a clear and coherent source of information when contrasted with other Review inputs such as the quickly abandoned *Labour Listens* exercise.

73. David Butler and Dennis Kavanagh, *The British General Election of 1992* (London: Macmillan, 1992), p.60.

74. Hughes and Wintour, *Labour Rebuilt*. Polling was fed to important review group discussions on defence (p.109), the economy (pp.137–8) and party image (p.153).

75. Eric Shaw, 'Towards Renewal? The British Labour Party's Policy Review', *West European*

Politics, Vol.16, No.1, January (1993); the phrases 'educative' and 'responsive' come from the same author's 'The Triumph of Professionalism? Labour's Communications Strategy and the 1992 Election Campaign', paper presented to the European Consortium of Political Research, Leiden, April (1993).

76. Jack Cunningham, 'Get the Message', *New Socialist*, October/November (1990).
77. Reports of the polling appeared in several titles including *The Guardian*, 12 June 1992, *The Financial Times*, 17 June and *The Sunday Times*, 21 June.
78. Commentary in *The Guardian*, 12 June 1992, indicated that floating voters saw the party as 'too old fashioned, too tied to the past, too linked to minorities and old images of the trades unions'. The debate over the uses of focus group research methods is discussed in J.L. Drayton *et al.*, 'The Focus Group: A Controversial Research Technique', *Graduate Management Review*, Winter (1989); also D.L. Morgan (ed.), *Successful Focus Groups* (London: Sage, 1993).
79. Anthony Heath *et al*, *Labour's Last Chance?* (London: Dartmouth, 1994).
80. Michael Foley, *The Rise of the British Presidency* (Manchester: Manchester University Press, 1993).
81. Andy McSmith, *John Smith* (London: Mandarin, 1994).
82. Patrick Seyd and Paul Whiteley, *Labour's Grassroots* (Oxford: Clarendon, 1992), p.37. Over 60% of party members were reported as either readers of *The Guardian* or *Daily Mirror/Record* titles. Both these papers, together with sections of the non-Labour supporting press, ran several features in sympathy with Blair and the message of his campaign, see Tariq Ali, 'The British Clinton?', *New Statesman and Society*, 20 May 1994.
83. Ben Pimlott, 'The Future of the Left', in Robert Skidelsky (ed.) *Thatcherism* (London: Chatto and Windus, 1988).
84. Labour Party, *Annual Conference Report* (London: Labour Party, 1992), p.68. For a detailed discussion on the opposition to the modernization strategy, see Richard Heffernan and Mike Marqusee, *Defeat from the Jaws of Victory: Inside Kinnock's Labour Party* (London: Verso, 1992).
85. Philip Kotler, 'Voter Marketing: Attracting Votes', in *Marketing for Non-profit Organizations* (New Jersey: Prentice-Hall, 1982).

Political Communications in British Election Campaigns: Reconsidering Media Effects

Pippa Norris

The central argument of this article is that we need to reconsider how we assess the influence of political communications in British election campaigns. We have established a substantial literature focusing on the *production* of election communications, including the role of journalists, party managers and campaign professionals, and the broader institutional framework governing political coverage in Britain.[1] Moreover, there are a number of studies of the *contents* of newspaper and television coverage in terms of partisan balance, and the battle over the campaign agenda.[2] Nevertheless we know far less about the subtle, complex and diverse *effects* on the electorate of campaign coverage and interpersonal communications.

Existing research in Britain, reflecting the concerns of thirty years ago, usually adopts an unduly narrow conception of media 'effects', conceived as the influence of the media on the vote. The dominant model remains the simple one of 'stimulus-response', without taking account of intervening conditions such as the source, contents, and user.[3] In the United States most recent mainstream studies of voting behaviour and public opinion have absorbed political communications as an integral part of their analysis.[4] There are some classic studies of Britain in the 1960s,[5] which deserve to be re-examined during the changed context of modern television-saturated campaigns. Yet with some notable exceptions,[6] it is striking how far most recent mainstream research on British voting behaviour has excluded the influence of political communications.[7] Like Sherlock Holmes' dog which did not bark, work on media effects has been remarkable mainly by its absence. This neglect needs to be overcome through theoretical and methodological innovations.

To argue this case the first section of this article sets out the theoretical framework and sketches the major literature on the impact of the media on British voting behaviour. The next section explores evidence from the 1992 British Election Study. Media influence is conceptualized as a sequential process from message through successive steps (information, agenda setting, framing, persuasion) to an attitudinal or behavioural response. The conclusion suggests we need to develop a more imaginative multi-method research design to unravel problems of reciprocal causality in political communications.

Theoretical Context

This article works from the perspective of the 'constructionist' approach, which regards election campaigns as a dynamic interaction between three agencies: parties, the electorate and the media.[8] Each part of the trilogy plays a distinct role in setting the political agenda. Parties seek to attract, reinforce and mobilize supporters through prioritizing issues. Voters actively employ established schema to sift information and weigh choices within a campaign. And the media provide the essential linkage mediating between parties and voters.

In exceptional circumstances politicians can bypass the media, meeting individuals face-to-face at campaign rallies or canvassing. Party activists continue to invest in local campaigns.[9] But these activities, which only ever reached a few anyway, have declined in Britain.[10] Interpersonal communications such as family political discussions may prove important, but much of this information ultimately derives from the media.[11] Parties, the media and the electorate bring their agenda to the election, and the campaign resolves which priorities predominate. In effective democratic campaigns, party and voter agendas move closer together, with the media serving as marriage broker.

This linkage function has to be seen as a process of mutual interaction. Media messages are predominately 'top-down' during an election, telling voters about parties, for example by reporting press conferences, policy debates, or campaign rallies. But the direction is also 'bottom-up', informing party leaders about public concerns through coverage of opinion polls, phone-in programmes, and vox pop interviews. Seen in this light, the quality of the campaign debate is important, not just for determining the winning party, but also as an integral part of representative democracy.

Media coverage therefore matters in the most obvious sense by influencing voting choice, and thus the outcome for the winning party in government. This has been the primary preoccupation with previous studies in Britain. But arguably even more important, by influencing citizens' knowledge about the policy options available, their sense of civic engagement, and their participation in the electoral process, media coverage matters for the quality of British democracy. Elections thereby function as a form of civic education for leaders and led. Democratic campaigns are the principle opportunity for politicians and voters to speak to, and learn about, each other. Poor coverage, whether excessively negative, superficial, or biased, may damage trust in the political system, and erode the ability of political leaders to connect with public concerns.

Review of the Literature

What does the previous literature tell us about these issues? As McLeod,

Kosicki and Pan suggest,[12] there is great diversity in the research questions, theoretical styles and methods of evidence within the 'media effects' literature.[13] Much of the research has been developed in the United States, then extrapolated elsewhere. At the broadest level commentators commonly distinguish between three broad schools of thought. Pre-war theories of propaganda, impressed by the rapid growth and potential reach of mass communications, stressed that the public could easily be swayed by media techniques.[14] In reaction to this, post-war American studies, analysing the first systematic survey evidence, stressed theories of minimal consequences, which down-played media influence.[15]

Research since the 1970s can be placed between these extremes. Recent studies in the United States have discovered limited but specific consequences, particularly agenda-setting effects.[16] The newer literature suggests that the media influences public opinion through four main avenues: enabling people to keep up with what is happening in the world (learning), defining the major political issues of the day (agenda-setting), influencing who gets blamed or rewarded for events in the news (framing responsibility), and finally shaping people's political choices (persuasion).[17] These four categories represent a sequence of effects in a dynamic process: from growing awareness of a problem (such as global warming, conflict in Bosnia, or rising interest rates), to rising concern about these issues, to assigning responsibility for them (whether the British government could have done more to prevent these problems). Finally, this process may persuade voters, if people feel the government has failed to tackle a critical issue.

LEARNING> AGENDA SETTING> FRAMING RESPONSIBILITY> PERSUASION

Of these factors, most attention in the British literature has been devoted to the media's (particularly newspapers') partisan powers of persuasion, without taking into account the intermediate steps which may, or may not, lead to changes or reinforcement in voting behaviour.

The neglect of media effects in Britain has probably been driven by a variety of factors. One reason is the continued strength of the 'Michigan' model, with its focus on long-term partisan identification, despite the battering this theory experienced in the 1980s. Moreover, there is widespread scepticism about whether social science can isolate the influence of the media if the effects are complex, pervasive and long-term.[18] Further, in Britain the field of electoral behaviour is dominated by survey methods, despite their limitations when dealing with short-term change.[19] Newton noted the well-established difficulties of isolating media messages from surrounding events during the campaign, and the complex problem of disentangling the reciprocal relationship between media use and political attitudes.[20] This problem will continue in the absence of more tightly controlled experiments, focus groups or personal interviews which can isolate the short-term effects of specific messages. This neglect has left a vacuum at the heart of our understanding of the linkages between parties and voters. Commentators widely acknowledge the dominance of television in modern British campaigns, but at the same time we admit that we know little about its role. British writers commonly extrapolate from the US research on media effects to Britain,[21] although without testing this may be highly misleading given the institutional context of British elections, with major differences in the length of campaigns, strength of party loyalties, role of candidates, role of money, regulations of television advertising, and diversity of media markets.

The available research in Britain in recent years allows some tentative conclusions about media influences on the vote. Based on the 1983 and 1987 BES, Newton found a significant link between newspaper readership and voting choice, after controlling for political attitudes.[22] Using aggregate data, Webber noted a relationship between readership of the popular tabloids (the *Mirror* and the *Sun*), and constituency party swing.[23] Dunleavy and Husbands argued that the relationship between the vote and readership was too strong to be attributable mainly to self-selection.[24] Based on the 1987–92 BES panel, Curtice and Semetko concluded that over the longer term newspapers had a modest influence upon their readers' voting choice, as well as their economic evaluations.[25] Sanders, Marsh and Ward, as well as Gavin, suggest that media coverage shapes perceptions of the economy, thereby producing an indirect effect on the vote.[26] Studies have most commonly focused on the partisan impact of newspapers, where we might expect to find the strongest relationship, although it is difficult to disentangle the direction of causal effects: people may vote for a party influenced by the political content of newspapers, but they may also buy a newspaper sympathetic to their party choice, or both.

Miller produced the most thorough recent study of a wide range of media effects.[27] Based on a panel survey and content analysis in the 1987 British general election Miller concluded that television coverage had little influence on agenda-setting or perceptions of party credibility. Yet the press, but not television, had a significant impact on voting choice and on party and leadership images.[28] The literature therefore suggests newspapers have a modest but significant influence upon voting choice in Britain, although the effect of television is less well established. The influence of the British media on learning, agenda-setting, persuasion, and political participation therefore deserves to be re-examined in the context of the last campaign.

Re-examining Media Effects in the 1992 Campaign

To analyse these issues we can use the 1992 British General Election Study (BES). The BES *cross-sectional survey* interviewed 3,534 respondents after the 1992 election, asking a wide range of items designed to tap patterns of media use. The television scale in this analysis sums ten separate items, such as how often people watched television news, listened to radio news, and watched party political broadcasts (see Table 1). These items proved reasonably reliable as a scale (Cronbach's Alpha =.66). The survey also asked people about their readership of daily morning newspapers (type of paper, frequency of use, attention to political coverage, and perceptions of partisan bias). Again simple measures were developed by combining frequency of use plus attention to newspapers. The analysis of effects in the cross-sectional survey is limited without time-series data. For this we can turn to the five-wave *panel survey*.[29] During the campaign people were asked about their media use and attention, which produced simple newspaper and television scales.

Learning Effects on Political Information

What do voters learn from campaign communication? The answer depends very much upon what is defined as 'knowledge': whether the research tests for the acquisition of specific factual 'information' (for example, the name of the leader of the opposition) or a more general understanding of British politics (such as the position of parties on the major issues). Harrop suggested that the impact of attention to television news and the press is strongest on levels of cognitive knowledge.[30] If so, we would expect that the most regular and attentive viewers of television news would be among the most informed citizens, concerning specific political events, the identity of party leaders, and general awareness of the political system.

One test of political knowledge is the ten point 'political quiz' in the 1992 BES. This included a series of general statements which people had to judge true or false, ranging from fairly simple items ('The leader of the Labour party is Neil Kinnock') through more general constitutional statements ('British prime ministers are appointed by the Queen'). We might expect the social background and prior interest of respondents to influence both their political knowledge and their use of the media. The model therefore included measures of social class, education, age, and gender. Interest was measured by how much respondents cared which party won the general election. After controlling for these factors, what impact did television usage have on general levels of political knowledge?

TABLE 1
POLITICAL INFORMATION EFFECTS

	ALL	R4 Today	BBC2 News-night	BBC1 9 News	BBC1 6 News	ITN News at 10	ITN 5:40	Ch4 News	Quality paper	Tabloid paper
Class	.20	.20	.22	.21	.22	.21	.22	.22	.23	.21
Education	.26	.25	.27	.28	.27	.28	.28	.27	.31	.24
Gender	.27	.27	.27	.27	.27	.27	.27	.27	.23	.26
Age	.20	.19	.21	.22	.22	.22	.24	.21	.05	.23
Interest	.13	.14	.14	.14	.15	.15	.14	.14	.08	.15
Media Use	.10	.14	.08	.09	.03	.02	.02	.07	.01	.02
Adjusted R^2	.32	.34	.33	.33	.32	.32	.32	.33	.29	.27

Note: The figures represent standardized beta coefficients in a two-stage ordinary least squared regression model with scores on the Politics Quiz as the dependent variable. All coefficients are significant at the 0.1 level unless otherwise indicated.
Variables are defined as follows:
Class: respondent's Goldthorpe Heath classification.
Education: respondent's highest educational qualification.
Interest: whether respondent cared which party won the election (0/1).
Media use: how often respondent watched/listened to the specified programme per week.
Source: 1992 BES Cross-sectional

The results of the regression analysis in Table 1 show that the strongest influences on political knowledge are education, gender, class, age and interest, as might be expected. Nevertheless the model also shows that after controlling for these factors, those most attentive to television news also scored highly on the political knowledge scale. The overall model proved reasonably satisfactory (Adjusted R^2 =.32).

Three main issues of interpretation arise from the results. First, this pattern showed considerable variation once we looked in more detail at the source of television news programme. Levels of information proved most strongly associated with the 'high-brow' programmes such as listening to *Today* on Radio 4, and watching *Newsnight* on BBC2, the BBC1 *9:00 News*, and Channel 4's *7:00 News*. But the evidence is mixed: it remains unclear why there was not a similar pattern among those who tuned into the *ITN News at Ten* which is pitched at around the same level, or the slightly softer early evening BBC1 and ITN news.

The second question concerns how we interpret the direction of causality where there was a significant association between knowledge and viewership. Regular viewers of the news might be expected to learn more about the political system. Yet, equally plausibly, those who were more knowledgeable about British politics might be expected to watch the news on a regular basis.

Without a more precise gauge of what was learned from specific transmissions, or time-series data measuring changes in political knowledge *or* media use during the campaign, it is difficult to interpret this evidence.

Lastly, it might be expected that there would be a stronger relationship between the print media and levels of political information, because reading newspapers is normally seen as a more demanding activity than watching television. The quality press includes a far wider range of stories, and covers these in more depth, than broadcast news. Nevertheless previous research into the relative information value of print and television news has produced mixed results. After controlling for social background and interest, this study found no significant association between newspaper readership (quality or tabloid) and scores on the political knowledge scale, which seems counter-intuitive. Overall therefore the limited evidence in the BES provides unclear conclusions about the impact of media use on the acquisition of information. These findings remain difficult to interpret for methodological reasons. As will be argued in the conclusion, rather than survey measures of knowledge and media use, with the 'effects' of media coverage measured well after the event, we need more detailed studies of what is learned and understood from specific media messages concerning particular events, using focus groups and experiments to supplement panel survey data.

Agenda-Setting Effects

The idea that the media plays a critical role in agenda-setting has a long history. In Cohen's words: 'The press is significantly more than a purveyor of information and opinion. It may not be successful in telling its readers what to think, but it is stunningly successful in telling them what to think about.'[31] The most convincing evidence of agenda-setting comes from experiments by Iyengar and others who have found that a slight shift in the priorities of news coverage can produce a significant change in viewers' beliefs about the importance of these issues.[32] Yet survey evidence in Britain tends to provide little support for this view. In the 1987 general election Miller found that television's agenda was very different from the public agenda, with a far greater focus on security issues. Nevertheless the television coverage of defence had only a very modest impact on public worry about this issue. Moreover, public concern about health and education preceded television's switch towards these issues. Miller concluded that the public and television agendas remained poles apart throughout the 1987 campaign.[33]

To re-examine agenda-setting effects in the last campaign we can measure changes in issue priority in the 1987–92 panel survey. Content analysis of television news found that the most prominent issue on all channels was the economy, with considerable attention devoted to taxation.[34] A similar pattern was clear in front-page lead stories about the election.[35] In addition the explosion of publicity around 'the war of Jennifer's ear' gave a large boost to coverage of health and social services. In 1987 defence played a major role in the campaign.[36] In 1992, in marked contrast, following the fall of the Berlin wall, changes in Central and Eastern Europe, and new relations with Russia, the issue of defence almost dropped out of sight on television coverage. Therefore what was the overall impact of the media's agenda on public priorities?

TABLE 2
AGENDA SETTING EFFECTS

Change 1987–92	Taxation		Health/ Soc Serv		Defence	
	Lo TV	Hi TV	Lo TV	Hi TV	Lo TV	Hi TV
Less salient	1.1	0.6	5.4	5.6	19.0	21.3
No change	92.1	91.9	71.7	72.4	79.7	77.5
More salient	6.8	7.5	22.9	22.0	1.3	1.2
	100.0	100.0	100.0	100.0	100.0	100.0

Notes: Question: 'At time of general election, importance of ... as an issue facing Britain?' Change in 'most important' issue.

Source: 1987–92 BES Panel Survey N=1604

Without detailed time-series data to see whether changes in news coverage followed – or preceded – public concern, it is difficult to resolve this question. Nevertheless we can analyse whether public concern about these issues changed from 1987–92, and whether the shift was strongest among the most attentive television viewers. People were asked about the most important issues facing Britain in each election survey. Public concern about defence clearly declined substantially between elections, while at the same time increased priority was given to health and social services, and taxation. Changes in the media and public agendas were therefore associated. But, as shown in Table 2, there is no evidence that the media set the public agenda. The changes in priority given to the issues of defence, health, and taxation were found equally among those most and least attentive to television news during the campaign. The agendas of the media, the parties and the public shifted between elections, but it is not clear from this evidence who led, (if anybody), and who followed.

Persuasion and Voting Choice

Most previous work on media effects in Britain has focused on the vote, particularly the impact of Tory tabloid newspapers on the Conservative lead in successive elections.[37] There has been far less analysis of the influence of television on the vote. To see whether more regular viewers of television news were persuaded to switch parties we can analyse a voter transition matrix of vote change in the 1987–92 elections, based on the panel survey.

TABLE 3
VOTER PERSUASION EFFECTS, 1987–92

1992 Election

	Con	Lab	LDem	Other	Didn't vote	
LOW TV						
Con 1987 vote	78.3	4.7	8.8	2.6	5.6	100.0
Lab 1987 vote	4.1	75.8	7.2	4.2	8.7	100.0
LDem 1987 vote	13.6	16.8	60.9	3.0	5.7	100.0
HIGH TV						
Con 1987 vote	82.1	5.0	6.9	1.7	4.3	100.0
Lab 1987 vote	3.5	82.4	6.7	2.8	4.6	100.0
LDem 1987 vote	16.4	31.5	45.9	2.7	3.5	100.0

Source: 1987–92 BES Panel Survey N=1604

The results suggest an intriguing pattern (see Table 3). The most regular viewers of television news were slightly more likely to remain Labour and Conservative supporters than those who watched less television. In contrast, among Liberal Democrat voters in 1987, those who watched more television news were more likely to desert their party than those who watched less. The principle, although not exclusive, beneficiaries were the Labour party. We can speculate about possible explanations for this pattern, but these initial results suggest television reinforced support most strongly for the major parties.

Participation, Political Efficacy and Satisfaction

Lastly, what is the effect of the media on public participation, efficacy and satisfaction with the political process? One of the primary functions of the media's coverage of the campaign is to increase information about the choices on offer, stimulating interest in public involvement in the process. Yet in the United States, Patterson has strongly argued that the increasingly negative slant of television coverage has produced a growing cynicism and disillusionment with American government and public life.[38] What is the evidence in Britain?

TABLE 4
POLITICAL SATISFACTION EFFECTS

	TV Usage		Newspaper Usage	
Change 1987–92	Low	High	Low	High
Less satisfaction	17.4	17.0	19.0	15.1
No change	61.4	62.5	59.7	64.8
More satisfaction	21.2	20.5	21.3	20.1
	100.0	100.0	100.0	100.0

Note: Question: 'All in all, how well or badly do you think the system of democracy in Britain works these days?'

Source: 1987–92 BES Panel Survey N=1604

We can measure changes in overall satisfaction with the British political system by the question asked in the 1987–92 BES Panel survey: 'All in all, how well or badly do you think the system of democracy in Britain works these days?' As shown in Table 4, many people changed their mind about this issue between 1987 and 1992. But the change was not unidirectional: about equal proportions were more or less satisfied with British democracy. Moreover, this pattern was not significantly associated with regular use of television or newspapers. If anything, stronger media use was modestly related to slightly greater satisfaction with the system.

TABLE 5
POLITICAL PARTICIPATION, EFFICACY AND TELEVISION USAGE

	Vote Turnout	Political Efficacy
	Beta	Beta
Class	.02	.18**
Age	.08*	.21**
Gender	.04	.13**
Education	.04	.26**
Television use	.14**	.19**
Adjusted R2	.03	.24

Note: The figures represent standardized beta coefficients in an ordinary least squared regression model. (See Table 1 for coding.) Turnout is defined as reported turnout (0/1). Political efficacy is a scale from items Q220a to Q220e. **=coefficient significant at 0.01 level; *= significant at 0.05 level.

Source: 1992 BES Cross-sectional Survey N=3534

A similar pattern is found if we turn to television use and electoral participation. As shown in Table 5, the regression model includes variables for class, age, gender and education, which may all be expected to influence both turnout and media use. After controlling for these factors, television viewership proved to be significantly related to (reported) voter turnout, and indeed to be a better predictor than any of the social background variables. Television use was also significantly related to political efficacy – the sense that citizens could influence government and the political process. Nevertheless, as with earlier evidence, questions remain about how we interpret this relationship. Watching politicians debate the major issues during the campaign may stimulate viewers to feel better informed, more aware of the choices on offer, and therefore better equipped to exercise choice at the ballot box. Nevertheless, those most interested in voting, and who want to influence the process, may be more likely to watch campaign news. From this evidence, the old issues of reciprocal causality remain unresolved.

Conclusion

To summarize the positive findings of this analysis, we can conclude that there seems to be a significant link between watching television news and levels of political knowledge, participation and efficacy in Britain. Nevertheless the evidence concerning learning is not always consistent (for example across programmes), and the study found no support for the agenda-setting effects which are often stressed in US studies. The analysis also suggests that television may have had a modest impact on the vote, since the most attentive viewers were slightly more likely to switch away from the Liberal Democrats between elections. Yet overall we should treat these results with caution because there remain serious problems in disentangling causality through survey measures which cannot relate detailed media messages to specific media effects. Any progress in this area needs to radically rethink the most appropriate research design to gauge media effects.

   One serious limitation of previous work is the way media production, contents and effects are usually fragmented into separate studies, rather than treated as an integrated and comprehensive process of political communications. When treating these aspects separately it is too easy to study the contents of political communications, for example the political bias of the tabloid press, and assume that this has some impact on the audience. It is also easy to look at changes in the production of political communications, for example the growth of professional campaign consultants within parties, and assume this has a significant influence on the contents. Looking at any single element in isolation can provide only a partial and inadequate picture.

   The conclusion of this article is that we need to consider alternative

136 BRITISH ELECTIONS AND PARTIES YEARBOOK 1995

approaches to disentangling the effects of the media. Focus groups have been widely adopted in market research, as a way of supplementing public opinion poll data.[39] The advantages are more precise control over the 'stimulus' (for example, discussion of a particular party political broadcast or a documentary programme) and more subtle and detailed qualitative information about how people interpret and understand media messages. Their systematic use within British campaigns would be a valuable addition to existing research, particularly to suggest innovative items which could be tested more widely through conventional survey data.

Experimental and quasi-experimental research designs provide stronger tests of communication effects. By manipulating one variable, then observing its effects, studies can isolate causal factors. Iyengar and Kinder, for example, by altering the amount of television news coverage devoted to particular issues, demonstrated an agenda-setting effect.[40] The weakness of experiments concern the limited representativeness of small samples, and the artificiality of participation, which makes it difficult to generalize from the results to 'natural' settings. Nevertheless a combination of multi-method approaches – including experimental designs and focus groups to analyse short-term learning and interpersonal communication, panel surveys of public opinion and attitudinal change, content analysis of television and the press, and participant observation of news rooms and party strategy headquarters – seems the most promising avenue for new communications research.

NOTES

1. Ivor Crewe and Martin Harrop (eds), *Political Communications: The General Election Campaign of 1983* (Cambridge: Cambridge University Press, 1986); Ivor Crewe and Martin Harrop (eds), *Political Communications: The General Election Campaign of 1987* (Cambridge: Cambridge University Press, 1989); Ivor Crewe and Brian Gosschalk (eds), *Political Communications: The General Election Campaign of 1992* (Cambridge: Cambridge University Press, 1995); David Butler and Dennis Kavanagh, *The British General Election of 1992* (London: Macmillan, 1992).
2. Holli Semetko, Jay G. Blumer, Michael Gurevitch and David H. Weaver, *The Formation of Campaign Agendas: A Comparative Analysis of Party and Media Roles in Recent American and British Elections* (Hillsdale, NJ: Lawrence Erlbaum Associates, 1991); Holli Semetko, Margaret Scammell and Tom Nossiter, 'The Media's Coverage of the Campaign' in Anthony Heath, Roger Jowell and John Curtice with Bridget Taylor, *Labour's Last Chance: The 1992 Election and Beyond* (Hants: Dartmouth, 1994); William L. Miller, *Media and Voters: The Audience, Content and Influence of Press and Television at the 1987 General Election* (Oxford: Clarendon Press, 1991).
3. Denis McQuail, *Mass Communication Theory* (London: Sage, 1992) pp.260–1.
4. See, for example, William C. Mayer, *The Changing American Mind* (Ann Arbor: University of Michigan Press, 1992); Samuel L. Popkin, *The Reasoning Voter* (Chicago: University of Chicago Press, 1994); John R. Zaller, *The Nature and Origins of Mass Opinion* (Cambridge: Cambridge University Press, 1993); Benjamin Page and Robert Shapiro, *The Rational Public* (Chicago: University of Chicago Press, 1992).
5. Jay Blumler and Dennis McQuail, *Television in Politics* (London: Faber and Faber, 1968); J.

Trenaman and Dennis McQuail, *Television and the Public Image* (London: Methuen, 1961).

6. Patrick Dunleavy and Christopher Husbands, *British Democracy at the Crossroads* (London: Allen and Unwin, 1985); Heath *et al.., Labour's Last Chance?;* Hilde Himmelweit, Patrick Humphreys and Marianne Jaeger, *How Voters Decide* (Milton Keynes: Open University Press, 1985); Miller, *Media and Voters;* William Miller *et al., How Voters Change: The 1987 British Election Campaign in Perspective* (Oxford: Clarendon Press, 1990).

7. David Denver and Gordon Hands (eds), *Issues and Controversies in British Voting Behaviour* (Herts: Harvester Wheatsheaf, 1992); Mark Franklin, *The Decline of Class Voting in Britain* (Oxford: Clarendon Press, 1985); Anthony Heath, Roger Jowell and John Curtice, *How Britain Votes* (Oxford: Pergamon Press, 1985); Anthony Heath *et al., Understanding Political Change* (Oxford: Pergamon Press, 1991); David Robertson, *Class and the British Electorate* (Oxford: Basil Blackwell, 1984); Richard Rose and Ian McAllister, *The Loyalties of Voters* (London: Sage, 1990); Bo Särlvik and Ivor Crewe, *Decade of Dealignment* (Cambridge: Cambridge University Press, 1983).

8. Ann Crigler, Marion Just and Timothy Cook, 'Constructing Campaign Discourse: News Coverage and Citizen Perspectives in the 1992 Presidential Election', ICA conference, Washington DC, May 1993; Marion Just *et al., Crosstalk: the Media, Politicians and Voters in the 1992 Campaign* (Chicago: University of Chicago Press, forthcoming); Russell Neuman, Marion Just and Ann Crigler, *Common Knowledge* (Chicago: University of Chicago Press, 1992). See also Shaun Bowler and David M. Farrell (eds), *Electoral Strategies and Political Marketing* (Basingstoke: Macmillan, 1992); Peter Esaisson, '120 Years of Swedish Election Campaigns', *Scandinavian Political Studies* 14, 1991, pp.261–78.

9. David Denver and Gordon Hands, 'Measuring the Intensity and Effectiveness of Constituency Campaigning in the 1992 General Election' in David Denver *et al.* (eds), *British Elections and Parties Yearbook, 1993* (Herts: Harvester Wheatsheaf, 1993).

10. David Butler, *British General Elections since 1945* (Oxford: Basil Blackwell, 1989), p.112.

11. Silvo Lenart, *Shaping Political Attitudes* (Thousand Oaks, CA: Sage, 1994).

12. Jack M. McLeod, Gerald M.Kosicki and Zhangdang Pan, 'On Understanding and Misunderstanding Media Effects', in James Curran and Michael Gurevitch (eds) *Mass Media and Society* (London: Edward Arnold, 1991).

13. McQuail, *Mass Communication Theory*, pp.251–95.

14. Harold Lasswell, 'Propaganda', *Encyclopedia of the Social Sciences* (New York: Macmillan, 1934); Walter Lippmann, *Public Opinion* (New York: Harcourt, Brace, Jovanovich, 1922).

15. Bernard Berelson, Paul Lazarsfeld and William McPhee, *Voting, A Study of Opinion Formation in a Presidential Campaign* (Chicago, Chicago University Press: 1954); Joseph Klapper, *The Effects of Mass Communications* (New York: Free Press, 1960); P.Lazarsfeld, B. Berelson and H.Gaudet, *The People's Choice* (New York: Columbia University Press, 1948).

16. M. E. McCoombs and D.Shaw, 'The Agenda Setting Function of the Mass Media', *Public Opinion Quarterly* , Vol.36, 1972, pp.176–87.

17. Stephen Ansolabehere, Roy Behr and Shanto Iyengar, *The Media Game* (New York: Macmillan, 1993); Shanto Iyengar and Donald Kinder, *News that Matters* (Chicago, University of Chicago Press, 1987); Shanto Iyengar, *Is Anyone Responsible? How Television Frames Political Issues* (Chicago: University of Chicago Press, 1991).

18. David Denver, *Elections and Voting Behaviour in Britain* (London: Philip Allen, London, 1989), p.105.

19. Carl Hovland, 'Reconciling Conflicting Results from Survey and Experimental Studies of Attitude Change', *American Psychologist*, Vol.14, 1959, pp.198–217; Larry M. Bartels, 'Messages Received: The Political Impact of Media Exposure', *American Political Science Review* Vol. 87, No.2, 1993, pp.267–85.

20. Ken Newton, 'Political Communications', in Ian Budge and David McKay (eds) *The Developing British Political System: The 1990s* (London: Longman, 1993).

21. Martin Harrop, 'Voters', in Jean Seaton and Ben Pimlott (eds), *The Media in British Politics* (Aldershott: Avebury, 1987); Ralph Negrine, *Politics and the Mass Media in Britain* (London: Routledge, 1989).

22. Ken Newton, 'Do People Read Everything They Believe in the Papers? Newspapers and

Voters in the 1983 and 1987 Elections', in Ivor Crewe *et al.* (eds), *British Elections and Parties Yearbook, 1991* (Herts.: Harvester Wheatsheaf, 1991).

23. John Curtice and Michael Steed, 'Appendix A', in David Butler and Dennis Kavanagh, *The British General Election of 1992* (Basingstoke: Macmillan, 1992); Richard Webber, 'The 1992 General Election: Constituency Results and Local Patterns of National Newspaper Readership', in David Denver *et al.* (eds), *British Elections and Parties Yearbook 1993* (Herts.: Harvester Wheatsheaf, 1993).

24. Dunleavy and Husbands, *British Democracy at the Crossroads*, p.114.

25. John Curtice and Holli Semetko, 'The Impact of the Media', in Heath *et al.* (eds), *Labour's Last Chance?*

26. Neil T. Gavin, 'Television News and the Economy: The Pre-Campaign Coverage', *Parliamentary Affairs*, Vol.45, No.4, 1992, pp.596–611; David Sanders, David Marsh and Hugh Ward, 'The Electoral Impact of Press Coverage of the Economy, 1979–87', *British Journal of Political Science*, Vol.23 (1993), pp.175–210.

27. Miller, *Media and Voters*; Miller *et al., How Voters Change.*

28. Miller, *Media and Voters*, p.198; Miller *et al., How Voters Change*, p.232.

29. For technical details, see Heath *et al., Must Labour Lose?.* Respondents to the 1987 British Election study were re-interviewed as follows: by telephone during the 1992 election campaign (N.1323); by telephone a few days after the campaign (N.1,324); face-to-face following the election (N.1,608); a self-completion supplement (N.1564). The ten-item media scale was constructed from the following items:

    • Q207a-g. How often do you watch/listen to the following television/radio programmes: BBC1 9:00 News, BBC1 6:00 News, ITN News at Ten, ITN 5.40pm News, BBC2 Newsnight, Channel 4 7:00 News, Radio 4 Today programme.

    • Q208. Leading up to a general election, a lot of time on television news is spent on politics and the election campaign. How much attention do you generally pay to these items?

    • Q210a How often have you seen additional television programmes about the election campaign? Party Election Broadcasts; Interviews with John Major, Neil Kinnock or Paddy Ashdown.

    The 1987–92 panel survey includes a more restricted range of items on media usage than the cross-sectional survey.

30. Martin Harrop, 'Voters'.

31. Bernard C. Cohen, *The Press and Foreign Policy* (Princeton, NJ: Princeton University Press, 1963), p.13.

32. Iyengar and Kinder, *News that Matters*; Iyengar, *Is Anyone Responsible?.*

33. Miller, *Media and Voters.*

34. Martin Harrison, 'Politics on the Air', in Butler and Kavanagh, *The British General Election of 1992*; Holli Semetko, Margaret Scammell and Tom Nossiter, 'The Media's coverage of the campaign', in Heath *et al., Labour's Last Chance?*

35. Martin Harrop and Margaret Scammel, 'A Tabloid War', in Butler and Kavanagh, *The British General Election of 1992*, p.201; Semetko *et al.,* 'The Media's Coverage of the Campaign', p.28.

36. Martin Harrison, 'Broadcasting', in David Butler and Dennis Kavanagh, *The British General Election of 1987* (London: Macmillan, 1988).

37. See, for example, Curtice and Semetko, 'The Impact of the Media'.

38. Thomas E. Patterson, *Out of Order* (New York: Knopf, 1993).

39. Richard A. Krueger, *Focus Groups: A Practical Guide for Applied Research* (Newbury Park, CA.: Sage, 1988); Michael W. Traugott, 'The Use of Focus Groups to Supplement Campaign Coverage', American Political Science Association, annual meeting, Chicago, 1992.

40. Iyengar and Kinder, *News that Matters*; Iyengar, *Is Anyone Responsible?*

What Future for the Opinion Polls?
The Lessons of the MRS Inquiry

John Curtice

The 1992 general election was a disaster for the opinion poll industry. Four British polls published on the morning of polling day on average put Labour ahead of the Conservatives, albeit only by one percentage point. In the event the Conservatives were a comfortable seven and a half points ahead. The error was even worse than the last time the polls were seen to have got it 'wrong' in 1970; then the final polls on average put Labour four points ahead whereas the result showed a two and a half point Conservative lead. Moreover, at least on that occasion one company, ORC, was within a point and a half of the result. In 1992 the company which came closest, Gallup, was still seven points adrift in its estimate of the Conservatives' lead (see Table 1).

TABLE 1
THE FINAL POLLS IN 1992

	Fieldwork Dates	Sample	Con %	Lab %	LDem %	Oth %	C lead %
NOP	7–8/4	1,746	39	42	17	2	-3
ICM	8/4	2,186	38	38	20	4	0
MORI	7–8/4	1,731	38	39	20	3	-1
Gallup	7–8/4	2,478	38.5	38	20	3.5	+0.5
Average			38	39	19	3	-1
Election (GB)			42.8	35.2	18.3	3.7	+7.6

Source: The Opinion Polls and the 1992 General Election: A Report to the Market Research Society (London: Market Research Society, 1994).

Not surprisingly this record attracted plenty of criticism and questions from the press. Within the market research industry it aroused horror. Political polling is a relatively small part of that industry, but it is by far the most visible. The pollsters' own polls revealed that public confidence in their work was severely dented by the election result.[1] The wider industry was concerned that it had also damaged confidence in the results of commercial market research more generally. The Market Research Society, the professional association for all market researchers, had already been active in the 1987 election in trying to uphold standards in the conduct of opinion polls. It acted swiftly to try and find out what had gone wrong in 1992. Within hours of the outcome it had established a working party which it was hoped would be able to make a statement within a week![2] In the event it published an interim report after two months[3] and its final report took some two years to prepare.[4] But now that their lengthy deliberations have borne fruit, what can we say about what went wrong, and what are the implications for the future of opinion polls?

Late Swing?

One possible reason why the polls could have got it wrong is that there was a sudden late swing to the Conservatives. After all, the polls had detected the possibility that a late swing was occurring in their final polls and perhaps this had continued more rapidly in the final hours before polling took place. Many an anecdote was told of voters who entered the polling booth intending to vote Labour but who, when faced with the prospect that they might be voting for tax increases, found their hands were moved to place their cross against the Conservatives. Others, including Neil Kinnock himself, felt that the last minute attacks on the Labour leader in the Tory tabloid press had dissuaded people from voting Labour. And many Liberal Democrats, disappointed at their failure to secure the balance of power argued that some of their supporters had been frightened into the Conservative camp by the prospect of a Labour government and/or the chaos of a hung parliament.[5]

The working party was not concerned to establish why there might have been a late swing but simply whether or not it had occurred and if so, how large it was.[6] This task however was crucial. For if there had been a substantial late swing, then it could be argued that the polls were in fact correct at the time that they were taken and their methods could be given a clean bill of health. No poll can ever claim to do more than measure opinion at the time it is taken, and all companies already conduct their surveys as late as they possibly can before polling day. Late swing may be inconvenient for those who expect the polls to forecast the outcome of the election, but if it exists there is little that can be done to take it into account.

But how can one ascertain the existence of a late swing? Ideally one would reinterview those who had been interviewed by the polling companies in their final polls to see how they had actually voted. We could then examine whether or not they actually voted the same way as they said they would before polling day, and if so who benefited. Unfortunately this exercise was only undertaken for one of the four final polls. ICM succeeded in recontacting just over half of the people they had interviewed in their final poll. This revealed that voters' last minute decisions did benefit the Conservatives–not however simply as a result of voters switching parties, which is the only kind of switching that can unambiguously be described as a 'late swing'–but rather because those who had failed to indicate how they would vote before polling day also ended up being more likely to vote Conservative. Some of these had said they wouldn't vote, and others had said they did not know how they would vote. Whether either represents late swing, rather than simply a greater reluctance on the part of Conservative voters to declare their voting intention, is a moot point. However, according to ICM's figures, the difference between what people said they would do and what they actually did could only account for two of the Conservatives' seven and a half points lead – that is a late swing of one per cent to the Conservatives. It explains no more than one-quarter of the error in the polls (see Table 2).

TABLE 2
THE LESSONS OF ICM'S RECALL

	Con %	Lab %	Con lead %
Original poll result	38	38	0
Result after allowing for:			
Differential turnout	39	39	0
Switching between parties	40	39	+1
Late deciders	40	38	+2

Differential turnout: The net impact of those who decided not to vote when they had said they would when interviewed before polling day and of those who decided to vote when they had said they would not.

Switching between parties: The net impact of those who said when interviewed beforehand that they would vote for one party but who reported after polling day that they had actually voted for a different party.

Late deciders: The net impact of the votes of those who had said beforehand that they did not know how they would vote or that they would not vote.

Source: *The Opinion Polls and the 1992 General Election, A Report to the Market Research Society* (London: Market Research Society, 1994).

ICM's evidence is, however, hardly definitive. Because they only succeeded in recontacting just over half of their original respondents we cannot be sure that those who were recontacted were typical of the rest of the sample.

Perhaps they were less – or more – inclined to switch at the last minute than those who were not recontacted. Although none of the other surveys went back to the people they interviewed in their final polls, we do have a range of other evidence from which we can attempt to corroborate ICM's estimate of the size of the last-minute swing. Two panel studies which had interviewed respondents regularly during the course of the election campaign also reinterviewed their respondents after polling day. One was undertaken by MORI, the other by NOP. In both cases their last pre-polling day interview was conducted as much as a week before polling day, so many of the changes of mind they detect could have occurred before polling day – and as we have already noted, there was some sign of a movement towards the Conservatives during the few days before the final polls were taken. Both panels indeed show a rather larger swing to the Conservatives than ICM – 2.5 per cent in the case of MORI and as much as four per cent in the NOP panel.

But both these exercises also have their methodological limitations. MORI's recall was undertaken by telephone and only recontacted 60 per cent of their original sample, while NOP recontacted less than a third. Additional evidence points towards a more conservative estimate of the late swing. Although Gallup did not reinterview the respondents in their final poll, they did conduct a fresh cross-section survey on the two days after polling day. This showed only a half point increase in the reported Conservative vote compared with their final poll. Meanwhile, the British Election Study, a non-commercial survey undertaken using a different sampling strategy from most opinion polls, also interviewed a panel of respondents before and after polling day. The pre-polling day interviews were spread out over the campaign (and were confined to voters who had also been eligible to vote in 1987), so the panel certainly does not simply measure late swing. But in any event it shows no net increase in the Conservative vote and just a two point drop in Labour's vote –well below what we would expect to see if there had been a substantial late swing.[7]

In short there is no single reliable estimate of how much late swing there was. All of the sources of evidence have their limitations and in this, as in other aspects of its work, the working party could do no more than collate and reanalyse the data that had been collected by others. But the limitations of each source are different and collectively they point in a clear direction. They all suggest that there was some late swing from Labour to the Conservatives, but equally that it was nothing like enough to account for the difference between the final polls and the eventual outcome. Indeed, the clearest evidence that late swing could not be the whole explanation comes from a handful of cross-section polls undertaken immediately after polling day. These polls asked their respondents, recruited using sampling methods similar to those used in the final campaign polls, how they had voted in the general election. So if late swing were the whole explanation and the methodology of the polls not at fault, we should find that on average the reported vote of the respondents in these polls faithfully replicates the election result. (Indeed, if there should be any error then we might expect it to be in the direction of overestimating the Conservative vote, as previous elections suggest that people tend to over-report voting for the winning party.[8]) But in fact on average these polls only produced a Conservative lead of three points and none of them overestimated the Conservative lead. Clearly, something was wrong with the polls during the election campaign (see Table 3).

TABLE 3
REPORTED VOTE IN POST-ELECTION CROSS-SECTION SAMPLES

Fieldwork	Dates	Con %	Lab %	LDem %	Oth %	C lead %
Gallup	10–11/4	39	38	19	4	+1
ICM/Rowntree	10–11/4	40	38	19	4	+2
MORI	25–28/4	39	37	18	6	+2
ICM	8–9/5	44	37	15	4	+7
Average		40.5	37.5	18	4.5	+3
Election (GB)		42.8	35.2	18.3	3.7	+7.6

Source: The Opinion Polls and the 1992 General Election: A Report to the Market Research Society (London: Market Research Society, 1994).

What went wrong?

Just as commentators provided a variety of explanations as to why there was a late swing to the Conservatives, so equally there was no shortage of accounts as to why the polls had got it wrong. It was suggested that people were ashamed to admit they were going to vote Conservative for fear of being thought selfish, and so lied to the pollsters about their true intentions.[9] It was argued that the polls had interviewed Labour supporters who had taken themselves off the electoral roll because of the poll tax. It was pointed out that British citizens who had been resident abroad for up to 20 years were now entitled to vote (and were much more likely to be Conservative than Labour sympathizers) and none of these could have been interviewed by the pollsters.

However, none of these are important explanations of what happened. To start with lying: proving whether or not people deliberately lied about how they intended to vote is of course very difficult. But we do have one, albeit imperfect, indicator of the level of dishonesty in people's answers to interviewers. The 1992 British Election Study compared respondents' own reports of whether they had actually voted or not with the marked-up electoral registers. These are the registers which are used at each polling station to record which people have been issued with a ballot paper; they are available for inspection at the Lord Chancellor's Office for twelve months after each general election.

This exercise does indeed reveal that more people 'lied' in 1992 than previously about whether or not they had voted. As many as ten per cent of those who said they had not voted in fact had done so; in 1987 the equivalent figure was only just over five per cent. By answering as they did, these respondents ensured they were not asked to say how they had voted. But these reluctant voters are far from being closet Conservatives. For although they were not asked how they had voted, they were asked to say how much they supported or opposed each of the parties. And they gave their highest marks to Labour rather than the Conservatives. So on this evidence if any group had a particular propensity to lie in order to hide their true preferences, it seems to have been Labour rather than Conservative voters.

The impact of the poll tax on electoral registration has been the subject of some controversy.[10] Certainly, the number of people on the electoral register stopped growing in the late 1980s around the time the tax was introduced, even though the Registrar General's estimate of the adult population continued to increase. However, no one has produced any reliable evidence that those who did remove themselves from the register in this period were mostly Labour voters; indeed such evidence as there is suggests they were not.[11] But even if they were disproportionately Labour, a little mental arithmetic is sufficient to see that the impact of the poll tax on the accuracy of the polls could only have been small. The difference between the number of people on the register and the adult population grew by 850,000 between 1987 and 1992. Assume that all of this additional deregistration was caused by the poll tax – that 65 per cent of these would have voted if they had been on the register, and that 75 per cent of those voting would have voted Labour. On these assumptions we find that the Conservative lead over Labour would have been just one per cent lower. So even if the polls did regularly include in their samples people who were ineligible to vote because they were not on the register (and many of them did in fact ask whether their respondents were on the register or not), this could have accounted for no more than a small part of their error.

Assessing the precise impact of the poll tax may be difficult, but ascertaining the irrelevance of overseas voters is not. The extension of the franchise to expatriate Britons has been greeted with far less enthusiasm than some had anticipated. There were just 31,942 overseas voters on the register in 1992. Even if they had all voted Conservative, they would have been worth just 0.1 per cent of the vote.

However, although these popular explanations for the inaccuracy of the polls prove to be misguided, there lies a grain of truth behind them. The claim that the polls were led astray by the poll tax or overseas voters are in essence claims that the polls failed to interview a representative sample of the electorate. And while these specific explanations may be wrong, there is evidence that the samples interviewed by the polls were in fact biased in a direction that favoured Labour. Equally, while Tory voters may not have lied, they do seem to have been more reluctant to declare their preference than Labour voters. These are the two crucial findings which have emerged from the MRS inquiry.

Sample Bias

In recent elections virtually all opinion polls have been undertaken using quota sampling. Under this method interviewers are told to interview (in a given location) a specific number of persons of a given type, such as so many men and so many women, or so many under 25 and so many over 65. But interviewers are free to interview whomsoever they like within those constraints. This is in stark contrast to random or probability sampling in which interviewers are instructed to interview a specific person (or a person at a specific address) who has been chosen (using a random selection method) in the office.

The great virtue of quota sampling is that it enables surveys to be undertaken quickly. So long as the interviewer finds the correct number of males, the correct number of females and so on, the method assumes it does not matter who those males or females are. The quota can be filled by interviewing those whom the interviewers can find on a given day or couple of days. Random surveys, in contrast, typically require weeks if not months if they are to achieve the high response rate that ensures that they are adequately representative. And given the shortness and intensity of British campaigns that is far too long a period to satisfy the news values of the pollsters' media clients.

But, if they are to work quota samples, have to fulfil two requirements. First, the proportion of persons of a given type that the interviewers are asked to interview must indeed be the same as the proportion of such persons in the population as a whole. Secondly, the variables used to set quotas must sufficiently circumscribe the freedom available to interviewers about whom to interview so that representative samples are ensured. Given too much freedom, interviewers are liable to choose to interview the kinds of people that they like to interview, people who may well be socially and politically atypical.[12] The MRS inquiry found evidence that the polls failed to satisfy both requirements in 1992.

In order to determine the proportions of persons of each type that should be interviewed, all of the polls conducted during the election campaign relied in whole or in part upon the results of the National Readership Survey. (Some press reports that the polls relied upon the out-of-date 1981 Census were wholly erroneous.) This survey is undertaken on a continuous basis using random rather than quota sampling, and thus appears to provide a convenient up-to-date source of information on the social profile of the country. However, the principal aim of the survey is to provide a measure of newspaper and magazine readership, information which is vital to the determination of advertising strategies and rates, and not to provide an accurate social profile of the nation. Its response rates are typically lower than commonly found on major government surveys which do attempt to measure social profile, such as the General Household Survey.

And comparison of the results of the 1991 National Readership Survey (NRS) with those of the 1991 Census (see Table 4) indicates that the survey may not indeed be the most accurate source of information on the social profile of the country. Most crucially, the NRS sample appears to be short of professional and managerial occupations, while it contains too many skilled manual workers. All of the companies used information from the NRS on social class as part of their quota controls. As a result all of them probably interviewed too few middle-class voters, who are of course more likely to vote Conservative than Labour (see Table 4).

TABLE 4
THE CLASS PROFILE OF THE NRS AND THE 1991 CENSUS

Registrar General's Social Class		NRS 1991 %	Census 1991 %
I	Professional etc. .	3.1	4.7
II	Managerial and technical	21.6	27.3
IIINM	Skilled non-manual	22.4	22.8
IIIM	Skilled manual	24.5	21.3
IV	Partly skilled	16.4	15.9
V	Unskilled	6.5	6.0
	Unclassified	4.7	2.0

Based on economically active persons. Those not classified were respondents for whom social class could not be ascertained or who were members of the armed forces.

Source: The Opinion Polls and the 1992 General Election– A Report to the Market Research Society (London: Market Research Society, 1994).

Equally, the NRS appears to contain too many people living in council houses – 21.5 per cent rather than the 19.5 per cent recorded by the 1991 Census. Although none of the companies used housing tenure in order to set their quotas, two of them – MORI and NOP – did subsequently weight their results so that the proportion of council tenants matched what they thought was an accurate profile of the population. Alas, they weighted not to 21.5 per cent, let alone 19.5 per cent, but to 24 per cent. The reason is simple. In setting their target they used the most recently available figure from the NRS for the proportion of *households* which are council houses rather than the proportion of *persons* (aged 18+) living in council houses. But it is the latter which matters in acquiring an accurate social profile of the nation. The proportion of households living in council houses is larger than the proportion of persons doing so because the average number of adults living in each council house is below the average size of all households.

The unrepresentativeness which seems to have been produced in the polls by the use of incorrect quotas can be seen in a couple of demographic measures. First, the polls interviewed too many council tenants (even before any weighting was applied). No less than 22 campaign polls collected details of their respondents' housing tenure. Of these only three interviewed fewer council tenants than the 19.5 per cent which appeared in the census. No less than ten interviewed 22 per cent or more. Second, none of the polls showed more than 27 per cent of their respondents living in households with two or more cars; the census found there were as many as 30 per cent.

These biases in housing tenure and in car ownership may not however simply be a consequence of setting quotas which contained too few middle-class people. They could also indicate that the quota controls used by the polls were insufficient to circumscribe interviewer choice about whom to interview. More direct evidence that the latter was also the case can be found by looking at the variation between the polls in the proportions of respondents who were found in various socio-economic groups. These proportions did not change during the short period of a three-week election campaign, so the proportions recorded in the polls should vary by no more than might be explained by sampling error. In practice there was more variation than sampling error alone would lead us to expect. The proportion of council tenants found by the polls varied from 17.5 per cent to 27 per cent. Similarly, the proportion of trade unionists varied from 15 per cent to 21 per cent.

In short, even if they were accurate, it is by no means clear that the quota controls used by the polling companies were adequate to ensure that their samples were representative, either socially or politically. This is perhaps hardly surprising when we look at those characteristics on which quotas were actually set. These were age, sex, social class and – in some polls only – employment status. Two of these, age and sex, are only very weakly associated with voting behaviour. They are in fact amongst the least important social characteristics which an opinion poll has to get right to be sure of acquiring an accurate measure of the balance of voting intentions. Far too much of the burden of ensuring that the sample is politically representative in fact falls upon social class. And to make matters worse the particular class schema used by the opinion polls, the social grade schema, is highly unreliable and is heavily dependent on the coding and probing skills of the interviewer.[13]

Differential Refusal

Approaching a representative sample is one thing. Securing a successful interview with that sample can be quite another. Some respondents will refuse to say how they are going to vote,while others will say they don't know what they are going to do. Together these two groups can constitute a significant proportion of all those interviewed. Across all of their election campaign polls the lowest proportion of refusals and 'don't knows' recorded by any company was six per cent (NOP), while the highest was 16 per cent (Harris). Traditionally in reporting their results the polls have effectively assumed that those who do not say how they intend to vote will in fact divide their support in the same way as those who do declare their voting intention. This they do by reporting the percentage support recorded for each party amongst those who do declare a vote intention. The evidence of the 1992 election suggests that this practice is no longer viable.

A number of different sources of evidence all suggest that those who refused or said that they did not know how they would vote were in the event more likely to vote Conservative than the general population. For example, in ICM's recall of those whom it had interviewed in its final poll, as many as 58 per cent of those who had refused to say before polling day how they would vote but were prepared to say after polling day how they had actually voted declared they had voted Conservative. In the British Election Study panel the equivalent figure was 59 per cent. And while the imbalance amongst the 'don't knows' appears not to have been quite so strong as this, again a number of different sources suggest they were more likely to vote Conservative than Labour.[14]

But this could only be the tip of the iceberg. If Conservative voters were less willing to declare their voting intention in an interview in which they were otherwise willing to participate, perhaps they were also less willing to participate in opinion polls at all. Refusal rates are not collected in quota surveys as a matter of course and are impossible to calculate where such surveys are conducted in the street (on spotting a clipboard, the unwilling victim may well cross the street to avoid being approached in the first place). But three recent quota surveys reported refusal rates as high as 35 per cent to 38 per cent.[15] Potentially at least the impact of 'differential refusal to participate' could be explosive.

Of course, if quota sampling works effectively, refusals to participate should not make any difference. Somebody who refuses to participate will be replaced by someone from a similar background and thus presumably with similar views. But if the criteria used for quota selection are only weakly related to voting, then we must be less confident that like is replaced with like. Here too the importance of good quota controls is evident. Unfortunately, the voting behaviour of those who refuse to participate in surveys is, like that of those who supposedly lie about their voting behaviour, very difficult to research. Two characteristics which interviewers can record about refusers are their gender and estimated age. Three recent experiments into refusers confirm the conventional wisdom that older women are more likely to refuse to participate and that older women are marginally more likely to vote Conservative.[16] But because age and gender are only weakly associated with vote, this approach can never measure differential refusal adequately.[17]

Differential refusal can in fact be thought of as part of a more general potential problem for quota polls undertaken in a relatively short period of time. For quota polls are not only confined to those who are willing to be interviewed at short notice, but also to those who can be contacted over a short-period of time in the first place. Jowell et al[18] attempt to measure the impact of this 'availability bias' by looking at the voting behaviour of those who were interviewed on first contact for the British Election Study (which used probability rather than quota sampling) and comparing their voting behaviour with those who were only contacted subsequently. Of course those who were interviewed at first contact were not socially representative. To allow for this, they weighted this group so that their social profile matched that of the opinion polls on the characteristics used to set quota controls, thereby mimicking the quota control procedure.

At first sight their findings suggest that Labour voters are more readily available to be interviewed and that existing quota controls are unable to counteract availability bias adequately. They find that the Conservative lead over Labour is six points lower amongst the election study first contacts than amongst the whole sample. But unfortunately their evidence is not as robust as it seems. First, in order to weight their first contacts, they used the quota controls set by NOP which were atypical of those adopted by other pollsters and which resulted in that company interviewing even fewer middle-class respondents than the other polls. This accounts for one of their six points. Second, the election study itself overestimated the Conservative lead over Labour by three points. Compared with the actual election result the (correctly) weighted first contacts only overestimate the Conservative lead by two points, suggestive but hardly definitive. But third, even that overestimate is not necessarily evidence of availability bias. It could just as easily reflect the inaccuracy of the quotas used.

Thus, we are left with one clear conclusion and much remaining uncertainty. Those who participated in polls but were reluctant to say how they would vote were more likely to vote Conservative. From this it seems likely, but far from certain that those who refused (or were unavailable) to participate at all were also more likely to be Conservative. It is even less clear whether or not existing quota controls were able to counteract any resulting bias that did exist.

The way forward?

As we have seen, finding out what went wrong in 1992 is itself a difficult enough task. But ascertaining how to do things better in the future is even more so. Given the infrequency of nationwide elections in Britain, pollsters have little opportunity to experiment with alternative research designs. However a number of remedies, both radical and more modest, have been proposed. Some indeed have already been adopted by one or other of the polling companies.

Perhaps the most straightforward problem for the pollsters is coping with those who fail to state a voting intention. One solution is to try and reduce the number who do so. It has been suggested that this could be done by implementing a 'secret ballot'. Instead of respondents being asked verbally by an interviewer how they would vote, they are asked to complete a ballot paper and place it in an envelope, thereby increasing the anonymity of the procedure. ICM decided to adopt the secret ballot in its monthly polls soon after the 1992 election and initially at least it consistently recorded a lower vote share for the Conservatives than other polls. More recently this has not been the case and experiments undertaken by other companies have failed to show that use of the secret ballot technique makes an appreciable difference.

Another solution is to find a better way of estimating how those who fail to declare how they would vote will actually do so. The practice adopted in 1992 effectively assumed that this group divided their support between the parties in exactly the same way as those who did indicate their voting intention. However, evidence from both ICM's recall of the respondents to its final poll and the British Election Study panel survey indicates that around 60 per cent of these respondents in fact voted the same way as they said they did in the 1987 general election. Thus it would seem sensible to collect information on respondent's past vote and to use this to infer how these respondents would vote. A procedure along these lines has now been adopted by all of the polling companies, though all except ICM give the resulting 'adjusted' figures less prominence than the 'unadjusted' figures.

Rather more difficult is ensuring that the quota controls and weights used are accurate. True, some of the mistakes made in 1992 – such as weighting by the proportion of households which are council tenants rather than the proportion of persons in such properties – are easily remediable. But the industry is faced with a difficult decision over whether it should continue to rely on the NRS as its source of information on the social profile of the nation and, if not, what the alternatives might be. One possibility would be to switch to a government source such as the General Household Survey. But government surveys do not use the social grade scheme for classifying occupations which is currently used by the polls, and so any change would require that to be abandoned as well. The MRS inquiry report suggests this may be feasible and indeed desirable, but it would require a substantial investment by the industry in new procedures. An alternative route would be for the industry to initiate its own high quality random survey designed explicitly to measure the social profile of the nation – but this would require the expenditure of considerable resources.

But the difficulties which could beset the industry without some such action have been further underlined since the 1992 election. Kellner has demonstrated that there were substantial differences in the social profile of the three quota polls being regularly conducted in the second quarter of 1994.[19] In particular, ICM's poll contained 70 per cent owner-occupiers while Gallup's contained just 64 per cent. Similarly, while 47 per cent of ICM's respondents were in the A, B or C1 social grades, only 42 per cent of Gallup's were. These differences of social profile were matched by differences in 'unadjusted' voting intention; thus ICM reported a Labour lead over the Conservatives of 27 points while Gallup recorded no less than a 36-point lead. The need for further investment in securing accurate quotas could not be clearer.

But even if the quotas are accurate, this still leaves the potential problem of the adequacy of quota controls as a means of ensuring that availability bias or interviewer discretion do not hinder the selection of a representative sample. Lynn has recently estimated that age, gender, social class and working status can account for as little as one per cent of the variance in Labour support.[20] In truth it matters relatively little whether polls achieve a representative balance of the genders or the age groups, as compared with for example owner occupiers and council tenants, *Sun* readers and *Mirror* readers, or car owners and non-owners. Yet the polls continue to rely on age and gender as quota controls, partly because they are easy for interviewers to operationalize (especially in the street) and partly because they believe that their clients, using common sense rather than social science sense, would find it difficult to accept a poll that contained far too many men or far too many young people. The MRS inquiry however recommends that the pollsters identify new variables for use in quota controls.

Equally, it is striking just how little information is collected by the polls on one important aspect of availability bias: refusal rates. These are not always easy to collect, especially in polls that use in-street interviewing, but that hardly justifies giving up on the attempt to do so. The collection of refusal rates should be part of the quality control of any survey organization in order to evaluate the success of both individual interviewers and individual surveys. And it will be essential if the industry is to succeed in improving response rates as urged by the MRS inquiry.

But perhaps even if all these changes are adopted, quota controls will still never be adequate. That leaves us with two possibilities: One is to use weighting strategies to correct for the potential unrepresentativeness of quota samples. (The other is to abandon quota sampling altogether.) Is there any way that weighting could possibly overcome the problems of the polls? One piece of information which, if it could be measured accurately, would seem to hold great promise is past vote. For how someone voted last time is the best single predictor of they how are likely to vote next time, and thus a poll which is weighted to ensure that reported past vote is in line with the results of the last election would seem unlikely to be in serious error. Weighting by past voting is indeed common practice in a number of countries.[21] But in Britain at least it has become conventional wisdom that past voting cannot be measured sufficiently accurately to be used as a weighting variable. It is argued that voters have a tendency to align their past behaviour with their current preference – and those who voted Liberal/Alliance in the past are particularly prone to do so.[22] Indeed the British Election Study panel shows that this was still true in 1992. As a result polls tend to find a deficit of declared former Liberals in their samples – but if they then weight their samples to correct for this apparent deficit they run the danger of overestimating the current level of Liberal Democrat support. This is precisely what happened to the first telephone polls undertaken in an election campaign in Britain when they used past voting as a weighting variable in an attempt to overcome the biases of telephone samples.[23]

Despite this potential pitfall, weighting by past vote is receiving serious attention once more. Polls conducted between 1992 and 1994 did not find a deficit of past Liberal Democrat voters, but they did (as during the 1992 campaign) find a deficit of past Conservative voters, fuelling concern that the pro-Labour bias apparent in 1992 continued to plague the polls. This pattern encouraged ICM in particular to institute past vote weighting as a means of overcoming the apparent bias and this method is now used in its regular polls for *The Guardian*. The poll the company conducted the day after voting at the 1994 European Parliament elections, and three days before the ballot papers were counted, was as inaccurate as the final polls in the 1992 election before weighting. After weighting by past vote, however, it overestimated the Labour lead by just two points. But weighting also made its overestimation of the Liberal Democrat vote even worse, so there must continue to be uncertainty as to how far past vote can be used successfully.

So perhaps we are left with our final alternative and should scrap the quota methodology altogether. The problem is that any alternative method will have to be capable of being implemented successfully within the time and cost constraints typically imposed upon the pollsters by their media clients. One alternative which can meet those constraints and is indeed already commonly used in polls undertaken in individual constituencies is random location sampling. Control over whom interviewers interview is achieved by requiring them to conduct the survey within a relatively small area of 150 addresses or so. These areas are chosen at random, but only after they have been sorted according to detailed census data on their social and economic profile. Thus the areas in which interviewing takes place should be a microcosm of the nation and, given the smallness of the areas within which interviewers are required to work, only very limited quota controls should be needed to ensure that interviewers contact a representative sample. But whether random location sampling can be any more successful than quota sampling is unclear. The method was used by RSL in five unpublished polls it undertook during the 1992 campaign. Their record was rather better than that of the quota polls – on average they put the Conservatives two points ahead of Labour – but their final poll (a one point Conservative lead) was no more accurate than the published quota polls. Further, constituency polls undertaken during the election campaign using random location sampling proved no more accurate than any of the other polls.

In contrast there seems little doubt that good random sampling could overcome the problems faced by the polls in 1992. This is quite apparent from the results of both the 1992 British Election Study and the 1992 wave of the British Household Panel Study.[24] The latter only underestimated the Conservatives' lead by one point while the former actually overestimated it. But the fieldwork for these studies was not only relatively expensive but was undertaken over a period of months. Where random surveys have been used in the past in commercial polls with short fieldwork periods – and correspondingly low response rates – they have proven no more accurate than quota polls.[25] However, alternative means of utilizing random sampling within the constraints imposed by a short election campaign can be envisaged. One possibility is that random sampling could be used as part of a panel design. A random sample of respondents would be interviewed over an extensive fieldwork period before the election was called. This sample could then be recontacted one or more times during the election campaign. The response rate would be likely to be low, but any resulting biases could be measured and corrected for by comparing the characteristics of those who were successfully recontacted with those of the original sample.[26] But the fieldwork would still be relatively expensive and would require that the date of the next election be guessed reasonably accurately in advance.

A second possibility, which perhaps might have been given greater attention in the MRS Report, is the deployment of telephone surveys using random digit dialling, now a standard technique in the United States. Because interviewer time does not have to be expended on moving from house to house, it would be possible to make a number of callbacks to unanswered numbers even within a relatively short fieldwork period. True, some voters are still inaccessible by telephone and these voters are much more likely to vote Labour than are the general population, but they now constitute no more than one in ten of the electorate while our knowledge of how we might weight telephone samples to overcome the anti-Labour bias is much improved.[27]

So what can we establish about the future of the opinion polls in the light of the MRS report? One thing is clear. Opinion polls will never be quite the same again. The inquiry has uncovered a number of deficiencies in the way in which the polls were conducted. And a number of changes have already been implemented to try and overcome these. The real uncertainty is how far those changes will have to go. The inquiry suggests a number of remedies but it does not give any assurances that these will be effective or sufficient to put the polls back on track. Indeed, as well as calling for improvements in the current practice of quota sampling, it also suggests that work is required to establish whether alternative methods such as random sampling might be more successful.

But that of course begs the question of what do we mean by 'successful'? Existing methods have been developed to satisfy media clients primarily interested in getting as good a headline as possible as cheaply as possible. And, encouraged by the intensity of British election campaigns, a good headline is defined as the 'latest' information on who is going to win. Yet both speed and cheapness are enemies of good quality survey research. They may also be false gods. Given that there were only small changes in party strengths over the course of the 1992 campaign,[28] one rather more expensive poll conducted gradually but accurately over the whole of the three week campaign would have provided an invaluable scoop for whoever had undertaken it. Further, most media reporting of the polls consists of the secondary reporting of the simple headline figures. But one result of the 1992 debacle has been greater methodological diversity in how polls are conducted.[29] A divergence has particularly opened up between ICM and the remainder. The MRS report suggests that such diversity may well be necessary to advance methodological knowledge, but it can lead to confusion and misreporting in the media by, for example, comparing the 'adjusted' figures of one poll with the 'unadjusted' figures of another.

The media are ultimately interested in knowing not how many votes each party will win but how many seats. Yet, under our existing electoral system, even the most accurate forecast of the national vote share cannot be guaranteed to produce a precise prediction of the outcome in terms of seats. Where such predictions are produced they are commonly based on the assumption that the swing since the last election will be the same in every constituency. Yet if the polls had been wholly accurate in 1992 then this method of forecasting seats would still have resulted in a substantial error, anticipating a Conservative majority of 71 rather than 21.[30] The typical opinion poll is far too small to produce reliable estimates of the change in party support in the degree of geographic detail needed to ensure an accurate prediction of the distribution of seats. In short, the 1992 election has not only raised important questions about the conduct of the polls but also their use by the media. Not only do the polls need to examine their methods, but the media also need to question their expectations of what polls can achieve.

ACKNOWLEDGEMENTS

Some sections of this article originally appeared in the journal *Scottish Affairs* and are re-printed with permission.

NOTES

1. *Gallup Political and Economic Index*, No.383, July 1992.
2. The original members of the working party were John Barter (formerly of NOP), Prof. Martin Collins (City University Business School), John Curtice (University of Strathclyde), John O'Brien (British Market Research Bureau) and Sue Stoessl (Director General, Market Research Society), none of whom were at the time responsible for the conduct of opinion polls but all of whom were closely acquainted with the industry. After the publication of the interim report two pollsters, Nick Sparrow (ICM) and Robert Worcester (MORI), joined the working party. Later John Barter resigned as the working party's chairman and his place was taken by David Butler (Nuffield College, Oxford). Similarly, following her resignation as Director General of the Market Research Society, Sue Stoessl was replaced by her successor in that post, Michael Warren.
3. *Interim Report of the MRS Inquiry into the 1992 General Election Polls* (London: Market Research Society, 1992).
4. *The Opinion Polls and the 1992 General Election: A Report to the Market Research Society* (London: Market Research Society, 1994).
5. J. Bullmore, 'How Clipboards Came Unstuck', *Evening Standard*, 10 April 1992; A. King, 'Tory "Super-Party" Born of Last Minute Switching', *Daily Telegraph*, 13 April 1992; D. Lipsey, 'Polls Give Clues to Motives Behind the Late Voting Shift', *The Times*, 11 April 1992; B. MacArthur, 'Perhaps It Was *The Sun* "Wot Won It" for John Major', *Sunday Times*, 12 April 1992; R. Worcester, 'Don't Blame the Opinion Pollsters', *The Times*, 13 April 1992.
6. But for an analysis which takes a sceptical view of many of the reasons offered see A. Heath, R. Jowell, J. Curtice and P. Clifford, 'False Trails and Faulty Explanations: How Late Swing Did Not Cost Labour the 1992 Election', in D. Denver, P. Norris, D. Broughton and C. Rallings (eds), *British Elections and Parties Yearbook 1993* (Hemel Hempstead: Harvester Wheatsheaf, 1993).
7. Ibid.; and R. Jowell, B. Hedges, P. Lynn, G. Farrant and A. Heath, 'The 1992 British Election: the Failure of the Polls', *Public Opinion Quarterly*, Vol.57 (1993), pp.238–63.
8. I. Crewe, 'Surveys of British Elections: Problems of Design, Response and Bias', *Essex Papers in Government and Politics*, No.6 (Colchester: University of Essex, 1983).

156   BRITISH ELECTIONS AND PARTIES YEARBOOK 1995

9. R. Harris, 'We are a Nation of Liars', *Sunday Times,* 12 April 1992.
10. See especially J. Smith and I. McLean, 'The Poll Tax and the Register', in A. Heath, R. Jowell and J. Curtice with B. Taylor (eds), *Labour's Last Chance? The 1992 Election and Beyond* (Aldershot: Dartmouth, 1994).
11. I. Crewe, 'A Nation of Liars? Opinion Polls and the 1992 Election', *Parliamentary Affairs,* Vol.45 (1992), pp.475–95; *Results of Recall Interviews Conducted after the 1992 Election* (London: ICM Research, 1992).
12. See also C. Marsh and E. Scarbrough, 'Testing Nine Hypotheses about Quota Sampling', *Journal of the Market Research Society,* Vol.32 (1991), pp.485–506.
13. S. O'Brien and R. Ford, 'Can We At Last Say Goodbye to Social Class?', *Journal of the Market Research Society,* Vol.30, No.3 (1988), pp.289–332.
14. N. Moon, 'Why Did the Polls Get it Wrong in 1992? "I Don't Know" – and "I Won't Tell You"', *NOP Research Paper* (London: National Opinion Polls, 1993).
15. *Opinion Polls and 1992 Election,* p.60.
16. Ibid, p.61.
17. See also J. Curtice and C. Payne, 'Forecasting the 1992 Election: The BBC Experience', in I. Crewe and B. Gosschalk (eds), *Political Communications: The British General Election of 1992* (Cambridge: Cambridge University Press, 1995).
18. Jowell *et al.* (see Note 7)
19. P. Kellner, 'Measuring the Electorate' (Paper presented at a conference on Opinion Polls, Nuffield College, Oxford, 10 February 1995).
20. P. Lynn, 'Evidence of the Inaccuracy of Quota Samples', *Survey Methods Centre Newsletter,* Vol.15, No.1 (1995), pp.20–23. This estimate was made after taking into account the variation between polling districts.
21. H. Taylor, 'Horses for Courses: How Survey Firms in Different Countries Measure Public Opinion with Very Different Methods' (Paper presented at a Harris Research Centre conference on Predicting General Election Results – An International Perspective, London, 26 May 1995).
22. H. Himmelweit, M. Jaegar and T. Stockdale, 'Memory for Past Vote; the Implications of a Bias in Recall', *British Journal of Political Science,* Vol.8 (1978), pp.365–84.
23. J. Clements, 'The Telephone Poll Bogeyman: A Case-Study in Election Paranoia', in I. Crewe and M. Harrop (eds), *Political Communications: The British General Election of 1983* (Cambridge: Cambridge University Press).
24. A. Brynin, 'The Stability of Voting Intentions', in N. Buck, J. Gershuny, D. Rose and J. Scott (eds), *Changing Households: The British Household Panel Survey 1990–92* (Colchester: ESRC Research Centre on Micro-Social Change, 1994).
25. R. Worcester, 'Political Polling: 95% Expertise and 5% Luck' (Paper presented at an Ordinary Discussion Meeting of the Royal Statistical Society, 14 June 1995).
26. Jowell *et al.,* (see Note 7).
27. Clements (see Note 23); W. Miller, 'The British Voter and the Telephone at the 1983 Election', *Journal of the Market Research Society,* Vol.29, No.1 (1987), pp.67–82.
28. P. Clifford and A. Heath, 'The Election Campaign', in A. Heath, R. Jowell and J. Curtice with B. Taylor (eds), *Labour's Last Chance? The 1992 Election and Beyond* (Aldershot: Dartmouth, 1994).
29. This is despite the fact that Gallup has now fallen in line with the rest of the industry by putting vote intention at the beginning of its questionnaire.
30. J. Curtice and M. Steed, 'Appendix 2: The Results Analysed', in D. Butler and D. Kavanagh, *The British General Election of 1992* (London: Macmillan, 1992), pp.347–8.

Class and Party Revisited: A New Model for Estimating Changes in Levels of Class Voting

Geoffrey Evans, Anthony Heath and Clive Payne

Introduction

The changing relationship between class and party in Britain has continued to be a topic of considerable interest and controversy. This interest reflects the role of class in extensive sociological and political debates about the emergence of post-industrial society and the kinds of electoral strategies likely to be adopted by political parties.[1] If class is losing its ability to condition electoral strategies, it heralds the possibility of new lines of division arising – reflecting other sources of distributional conflict[2] and perhaps divisions other than those over economic resources – which can in turn be expected to alter the structure of political competition.[3] It also raises questions about the stability of the party system – supposedly 'frozen' in more or less its present form since the early part of the century[4] – in the face of volatile, unstructured expressions of political preferences that have little basis in the type of cleavage structures identified by authors such as Lipset and Rokkan.[5]

In contrast to the wide-ranging implications which make the question of class of such general social scientific interest, much of the controversy surrounding the debate on class voting derives from far narrower disputes over technical issues, particularly over the statistical techniques used to measure the relationship between class and party. In this paper we aim to advance this debate by presenting a model for estimating changes in the class/party relation which avoids the pitfalls of the various measures used by protagonists on both sides of the argument. We also take the opportunity to update our previous work with results from the 1992 British General Election Study. If class dealignment is indeed occurring, then it should become more readily visible as the time series is extended and we become better able to distinguish the long-term underlying trends from the more transient fluctuations due to variations in, say, party popularity. First, however, we shall review the connection between technique and substantive conclusions which has ensured that the dealignment controversy is still active.

Class Dealignment or Continuity?
The Methodological Bases of Substantive Disputes

Class dealignment theories take different forms. Some imply that social classes are becoming more similar in their political interests and ideologies. The growth in affluence, education, and social and geographical mobility in the postwar era has supposedly brought with it a decline in the social cohesion and ideological distinctiveness of classes. Class position no longer has the importance which it once had as a basis of individual or collective political action. In some versions of this thesis, classes are thought to be less significant politically because other cross-cutting social bases of interests – especially those concerning state and private sector employment and housing tenure – have become more important,[6] whereas in others it is because all social cleavages are losing their political distinctiveness.[7] There are also renderings of the dealignment argument which focus on the growing salience of 'new politics' issues as a result of the rise of postmaterial values associated with increasing affluence.[8] The point here is that even if there were substantial class divisions over traditional left–right issues, they would not be sufficient to prevent the erosion of class differentials in political partisanship: politics has become less focused on distributional inequalities and more concerned with quality of life and liberal concerns with rights and social harmony.

Thus one set of arguments proposes that left–right issues no longer strongly divide *classes*, whereas the other emphasizes the idea that left–right issues no longer so strongly divide *parties*. That both these theories continue to flourish is evident in the many recent publications in this vein.[9] Clark and Lipset, for example, in their article 'Are Social Classes Dying?' respond in the affirmative to their eponymous question, and argue that 'Class analysis has grown increasingly inadequate in recent decades as traditional hierarchies have declined and new social differences have emerged'.[10] They conclude that politics is now 'less organized by class and more by other loyalties'.[11]

The main pieces of evidence for class dealignment have been the decline in the proportion of the electorate voting for the 'natural' party of their class[12] and the decline in the Alford index of class voting.[13] The proportion of the electorate voting for the 'natural' party of their class has usually been taken as the sum of middle-class Conservatives and working-class Labour voters expressed as a proportion of all voters.[14] This measure of 'absolute class voting' did indeed decline from 64 per cent in 1964 to a low of 52 per cent in 1983.

The second measure, the Alford index, is the difference in the proportions of the middle class and of the working class who vote Labour. It is equivalent to the slope in a linear regression equation where the probability of voting Labour is regressed on a dichotomous measure of class, and indeed some authors have also used linear regression to measure the relationship between class and vote.[15] Again, the Alford index has shown a decline from 44 in 1964 to a low point of 27 in 1987.

These conclusions about class dealignment have been challenged on a number of grounds, relating both to the measurement of class and party, and to the techniques for assessing their relation. First, the class dealignment thesis typically rests on a rather crude dichotomization of the class structure into the middle class and working class (broadly equivalent to non-manual and manual workers respectively). However, there is no reason to see classes as of only these two types. Indeed, the failure to recognize that class need not be a dichotomy is a source of considerable confusion for critics of work in 'How Britain Votes' and since. Thus the Goldthorpe schema,[16] which has formed the basis for much of the electoral research which has emerged from Nuffield College over the last decade, is based in part upon employment status but also upon carefully specified distinctions between employee classes.[17] Routine non-manual workers and Foremen & Technicians, for example, are distinctive classes, not groups which according to some critics 'cannot be placed confidently within a class model'.[18] There are, moreover, important differences within the middle and working classes in their propensity to vote Labour; within the middle class, for example, employers tend to be rather more prone to support the Conservatives than are salaried employees.

The use of a simple dichotomy also means that one cannot distinguish class dealignment from class realignment or from compositional changes within a class. Thus if the proportion of salaried employees were to increase but their relative propensity to support the Conservatives remained unchanged, the dichotomous model would nonetheless show class dealignment. Similarly, if the proportion of salaried employees remained unchanged but they became relatively less inclined to support the Conservatives, this too would show up as class dealignment. It is clearly preferable, therefore, to use a more detailed class schema.[19]

Secondly, the Alford index and the measure of absolute class voting ignore any class basis which there may be to Liberal voting. Both measures are ones which were first proposed at a time when the Conservative and Labour Parties dominated British politics and when the Liberal Party (and its successors) could reasonably be ignored. It is less clear that these measures are now appropriate in what is effectively a multiparty system. To the degree that Liberal support derives disproportionately from different classes, it is indeed a 'class party'.

Thirdly, and perhaps most importantly, the Alford index and the measure of absolute class voting fail to distinguish changes in the association between class and vote from changes in the overall sizes of the class and in the overall popularity of the parties.[20] For example, if voters were to defect from Labour to the centre parties (as they did in 1983), the measure of absolute class voting would necessarily decline. It might however be quite wrong to interpret this as evidence of a decline in the distinctiveness of class interests and ideologies; instead it might simply indicate a decline in the overall popularity of the Labour Party – a decline which might have affected all classes equally. Indeed, research which has examined the links between class and political attitudes over time provides no evidence of a decline in the strength of the ties between class position and ideology.[21] Conversely, if absolute class voting were to revive, as it did in the 1992 general election increasing to a score of 56,[22] this might not indicate that social classes had been reborn but simply that the Labour Party had now become more popular in all classes alike.

Loglinear modelling, which enables one to look at the relationship between class and party *net* of any general changes in the popularity of the parties and also net of any general changes in the size of the social classes, would therefore appear to be a more appropriate statistical technique for investigating the relationship between class and vote. This technique is also more appropriate for dealing with a multiclass and multiparty system and does not require us to impose dichotomous treatments on the variables.

Previous research using loglinear models provides a somewhat different picture from that of the class dealignment school.[23] These models have shown that there have been large and statistically significant changes over time in the sizes of the classes and in the overall popularity of the parties, but that there continues to be a highly significant association between class and vote. This is not say that there have been no changes over time in the association – loglinear models which postulate a constant association between class and vote have not yielded a good fit to the data – but the key question is what form these changes have taken. The absence of a constant association is compatible with a variety of patterns of change – dealignment, realignment, or 'trendless fluctuation'. It is in fact the last interpretation of trendless fluctuation that has been preferred, although this interpretation has been based largely on inspection of residuals from the constant association model rather than on any formal modelling.

Applications of log linear models have not been immune to criticism however. An important weakness with early applications of log linear techniques on class voting data is their use of many degrees of freedom, thus weakening the power of tests of significance.[24] Certainly, they are relatively blunt-edged instruments with which to detect what might be quite small – but nevertheless, substantively important – changes in patterns of association through time. Our aim in this paper therefore is to further the methodological and substantive debate about class voting by introducing improved modelling techniques which enable us to estimate changes in the relationship between class and vote systematically, yet parsimoniously. Specifically, we employ a new statistical model for assessing changes in the overall strength of the class/party association. This model estimates changes in the log odds ratios between each successive pair of elections, and has been termed the uniform difference or 'UNIDIFF' model.[25]

Given its novelty in this area of research we describe the UNIDIFF model in more detail in the appendix. In brief, however, the model assumes that there is a general pattern to the association between party and class, although the overall strength of this association may vary from one election to another. On this basis, the model estimates a single parameter summarizing the strength of association between class and party for each election, and imposes the constraint that all odds ratios either uniformly increase *or* uniformly decrease as we move between elections. Thus as long as we obtain a good fit with the UNIDIFF model, the differences between the parameters for each pair of elections provide a useful measure of the extent to which the overall association between class and vote has strengthened or weakened. The great advantage of this measure is that it parsimoniously covers *all* the odds ratios and it does not constrain the trends to be linear. It thus gives a comprehensive summary of the movement in the class/party relation and allows a check on whether the relation has declined in a monotonic pattern, or has exhibited 'trendless fluctuation' and so on.

It can be seen then, that unlike the saturated loglinear model, which fits a large number of parameters for each election in a multiclass and multiparty system, the uniform difference model provides a single measure for each election. It consequently has the advantages of a single index like the Alford index, but without requiring either class or party to be dichotomized. This allows us to represent changes in the relations between all classes and all parties simultaneously, and to estimate the significance of these changes.

Our analysis proceeds by showing the varying and potentially misleading implications of the somewhat crude measures of association commonly used in research which has concluded that there has been a decline in class voting. We then present the loglinear analysis, giving particular emphasis to the results obtained with the UNIDIFF model.

Data

Our data come from the nine British Election Studies conducted since 1964.[26] The total size of the merged dataset containing all of the election surveys is 22842. After excluding non-voters and voters for minor parties, together with respondents for whom there is missing data on class or vote, the overall N becomes 16954.

We distinguish three party groupings – the Conservative Party, the Labour

Party, and the centre parties. The third category consists of the Liberals, joined in 1983 and 1987 by the SDP to form the Alliance, and replaced in 1992 by the Liberal Democrats from the merger of the two parties. Ideally one would further distinguish Plaid Cymru in Wales and the Scottish National Party in Scotland, but unfortunately there are too few cases in our sample to warrant separate treatment and we have excluded them from the analysis.

In our treatment of class we have used the seven-class version of the Goldthorpe schema. This is based upon occupation and employment status, and distinguishes the following classes:

I.   Higher service class (managers and administrators in large enterprises, plus full professionals)
II. Lower service class (managers and administrators in small enterprises, plus semi-professionals)
III. Routine non-manual class (clerical and secretarial occupations)
IV. Petty bourgeoisie (self-employed non-professional, including employers and farmers)
V.   Foremen and technicians
VI. Skilled working class
VII. Semi- and unskilled working class

In keeping with previous work in this area,[27] we operationalize class by allocating respondents to classes on the basis of their own occupation and employment status, or their most recent position if they were retired. If respondents were not economically active, their partners' present or last occupation was used.[28]

We should note that in the original surveys, occupations were coded according to the OPCS classification of occupations which was in force at the time. This classification changed in 1970, in 1980, and again in 1990, and strict comparability in the derived class schema cannot therefore be achieved. However, the 1983 British Election Study data were coded both to the 1970 and to the 1980 OPCS classifications and the two classifications give virtually identical estimates of the strength of the class/party association in 1983. Class/Party frequencies across all elections using the individual procedure are shown in Table 1.

TABLE 1
CLASS BY PARTY TABLE FOR BRITISH ELECTIONS 1964-92

CLASS

		Higher Service %	Lower Service %	Routine Non-manual %	Petty Bour-geoise %	Foreman and techni-cians %	Skilled working %	Semi and unskilled working %
1964	Con	65	61	59	74	38	25	26
	Lab	18	20	26	15	48	70	66
	Lib	17	19	15	12	15	5	8
		100 (100)	100 (168)	100 (196)	101 (95)	101 (120)	100 (257)	100 (423)
1966	Con	66	56	49	67	35	22	25
	Lab	19	29	41	19	62	73	70
	Lib	15	15	10	13	4	5	5
		100 (113)	100 (172)	100 (216)	99 (98)	101 (109)	100 (277)	100 (428)
1970	Con	66	61	51	69	39	33	32
	Lab	23	32	40	20	56	63	61
	Lib	12	8	9	11	6	4	7
		101 (111)	101 (185)	100 (187)	100 (103)	101 (109)	100 (232)	100 (376)
1974 Feb	Con	59	51	45	68	39	23	24
	Lab	17	26	30	19	40	59	61
	Lib	24	23	26	14	22	18	16
		100 (165)	100 (249)	101 (329)	101 (161)	101 (106)	100 (332)	101 (516)
1974 Oct	Con	57	47	44	70	35	20	22
	Lab	17	30	32	13	52	62	65
	Lib	26	23	24	17	13	18	14
		100 (213)	100 (184)	100 (307)	100 (139)	100 (114)	100 (304)	101 (481)
1979	Con	61	61	52	78	44	28	34
	Lab	25	19	32	13	44	58	53
	Lib	15	20	17	10	11	14	13
		101 (188)	100 (175)	101 (209)	101 (125)	99 (144)	100 (215)	100 (355)
1983	Con	60	53	53	71	44	33	29
	Lab	8	16	20	12	28	47	49
	Lib & SDP	32	31	28	17	28	20	22
		100 (296)	100 (497)	101 (547)	100 (227)	100 (183)	100 (404)	100 (723)
1987	Con	63	50	52	65	39	31	31
	Lab	11	20	26	16	36	48	48
	Lib & SDP	26	31	23	20	24	21	21
		100 (377)	101 (462)	101 (576)	101 (245)	99 (176)	100 (360)	100 (664)
1992	Con	66	50	54	66	41	37	28
	Lab	16	21	30	17	45	50	60
	Lib Dem	18	29	17	17	14	12	12
		100 (309)	100 (371)	101 (449)	100 (177)	100 (118)	99 (249)	100 (458)

Note: Liberal Party includes votes for Social Democrats

Analysis

First, we show the patterns of change between 1964 and 1992, obtained when using simple dichotomous indexes of class/party association.[29] As well as the Alford index, we present the odds ratios for salariat-Conservative/working class-Labour voting, and conventional estimates of absolute class voting. In addition, as there is no indisputable logic restricting the notion of a natural class/party alliance to the Conservative/salariat and Labour/working classes, we present estimates of changing levels of class voting using a classification that includes the centre parties. These are treated as the natural parties of the middle class, along with the Conservative Party. It should be noted that this logic is implicit in the Alford index. Finally, we present the results from an index favoured recently by at least one exponent of class dealignment: the odds of Conservative versus non-Conservative voting in the salariat multiplied by Labour versus non-Labour voting in the working class.[30]

TABLE 2:
TRENDS IN CLASS VOTING

	Alford Index	Relative class voting voting log odds ratio	Absolute class voting %	Modified absolute class voting %	'Crewe Index'
1964	43.9	2.2	64	73	3.5
1966	40.1	2.0	64	70	3.7
1970	29.8	1.4	60	64	2.6
1974 February	33.5	1.8	56	67	1.8
1974 October	37.7	1.9	57	68	1.9
1979	29.4	1.6	57	65	1.9
1983	30.2	1.9	52	67	1.2
1987	27.2	1.7	52	66	1.2
1992	32.5	1.7	56	69	1.8

Table 2 presents these estimates of class voting across the nine elections since 1964. As is well known, both the Alford index and the salariat/working class log odds ratios declined between 1964 and 1970. Nonetheless, they have not shown any further downward trend – even if fluctuating – since 1970, and they both show an increase between 1987 and 1992. The two-party/two-class version of the absolute class voting measure differs somewhat from this pattern, in that it shows a gradual decline throughout most of the period, only reversing in 1992. When the Liberal Democrats are treated as a natural party of the middle class, however, the decline in levels of class voting is slight. And by 1992 the proportion of the electorate voting for their natural class party had returned almost to that of the 1960s. On the basis of this index, one would not infer that a continuing decline was taking place. In contrast, when using Ivor Crewe's index (Con:non-Con x Lab:non-Lab), we find a pronounced downward trend, although again reversing in 1992.

Readers may of course take issue with the choice of these indexes. To some extent they are measuring different concepts, and as we have explained elsewhere there is no reason in principle why absolute and relative class voting should follow the same paths over time. However, the Alford index, the salariat:working class odds ratio and the Crewe index are all, as we understand them, attempting to measure the same basic concept of relative class voting. But all three are highly selective in the information they use and may therefore give misleading pictures of the trends. The uniform difference model, we argue, uses all the available information and provides a much more comprehensive and authoritative summary measure.

Estimating the UNIDIFF model

We begin by fitting the 'constant class voting' (CCV) loglinear model. This postulates that the sizes of the classes and the popularity of the parties have varied from election to election but fit the same class/party relationship (that is, the same odds ratios) in all elections. From Table 3 we can see that, the CCV model fits our data reasonably well: Deviance=138.88 on 96 df. Clearly, however, the CCV model does not yield an acceptable fit to the data on the usual 0.05 criterion, although it misclassifies only a small proportion (3.2 per cent) of the cases.

TABLE 3
MODEL FIT

Model Deviance (df)

CCV	138.88 (96)
Linear trends	115.94 (84)
UNIDIFF: trend	134.08 (95)
UNIDIFF: full	107.40 (88)

Within the loglinear framework a possible method for testing class dealignment is to fit linear trends to the class/party relationship. Proponents of the class dealignment thesis have not specified clearly what functional form they would expect dealignment to take, but their arguments frequently allude to 'glacial' processes of social change such as the growth of cross-class marriages.[31] These arguments suggest that dealignment will have a gradual and continuing character and that a linear trend model will be a reasonable representation. The linear trend model treats elections as ordinal and specifies that the change in odds ratios for each class/party combination is the same for all successive pairs of elections. Some odds ratios may increase through elections, others may decrease, depending on the estimated value of the trend parameter. The linear trend model fits somewhat better than the constant class voting model: Deviance=115.94 on 84 df. The improvement of 22.94 for the loss of 12 degrees of freedom just reaches significance at the 0.05 level.

The fit of the linear trend model is not substantively informative, however, because the model does not differentiate between moves towards randomness and moves away from it. Both can occur, and both will register as a trend, but this is not what is implied in the notion of class dealignment. Only trends towards randomness are consistent with the dealignment thesis.

A helpful strategy is to inspect the pattern of the fitted odds ratios derived from the linear trend model. For simplicity, we consider the fitted odds ratios for adjacent classes and adjacent parties (of which there are twelve). The changes in these ratios between 1964 and 1992 are shown in Table 4. As we can see, most move in the direction predicted by the class dealignment thesis, with the odds ratios approaching unity over time, although in some cases the move is very small and probably not significant, while two are clearly in the wrong direction, departing considerably further away from unity over time. The remaining two odds ratios cross over, reaching unity during the period but then continuing to move away from unity later on. Thus support for Labour as opposed to the Conservatives was initially stronger in the skilled working class than in the semi and unskilled working class, but by the end of period the position was reversed. This can be thought of as an example of class realignment, but not dealignment.

TABLE 4
THE RANGE OF FITTED ODDS RATIOS FOR THE LINEAR TREND MODEL

	Conservative-Labour	Labour-Liberal
Higher service- lower service	1.44 to 1.93	0.60 to 0.84
Lower service- routine non-manual	1.44 to 1.28	0.90 to 0.53
Routine non-manual- petty bourgeoisie	0.35 to 0.44	1.42 to 1.37
Petty bourgeoisie- foremen/technicians	6.34 to 3.96	0.29 to 0.52
Foremen/technicians skilled working	2.10 to 1.64	0.58 to 0.69
Skilled working- semi-/unskilled working	0.83 to 1.22	1.11 to 0.87

Odds ratios are given for pairs of adjacent parties and adjacent classes.
First figure: fitted odds ratio for the 1964 Election
Second figure: fitted odds ratio for the 1992 Election

Finally, we turn to the uniform difference model. Whereas the linear trend model fits a separate trend parameter for each of the class/party odds ratios, the uniform difference model fits a separate term for each election. It thus needs only 8 extra parameters compared with the 12 for the linear trend model. The UNIDIFF model significantly improves the fit to the data compared with the CCV model: Deviance=107.40 on 88 df, a reduction of 31.48 on 8 df (P=<.001).

The linear trend and uniform difference models are not nested and so we cannot make the standard comparison between them. However, it is possible to fit a linear trend to the UNIDIFF model and thus to make a formal comparison between the two uniform difference models. In the linear trend UNIDIFF model election year is treated as a single continuous variable rather than as eight discrete categories.[32] It thus saves seven degrees of freedom. While this yields a parsimonious representation of the data, the full UNIDIFF model which fits a separate parameter for each election gives a significant improvement in fit. The change in fit is 26.68 on 7 df (p< .001). We therefore prefer the full UNIDIFF model. The overall fit of the full UNIDIFF model is acceptable on the .05 criterion (p=0.09). Given the various possible sources of measurement error, such as the changes in the OPCS classification of occupations and changes in response rate, we would regard these levels of fit as quite acceptable.

As we noted earlier, the uniform difference model is also a particularly informative one. If it gives an acceptable fit, then the 8 interaction parameters can be used as a measure of the overall strength of the Class/Party association in each of the elections. As we have mentioned, one of the attractions of the Alford index to previous researchers was that it did give a simple summary index of the strength of class voting, albeit one that could be used only where class and party had both been dichotomized; the uniform difference model provides a potentially much more useful measure that is appropriate for multiparty systems and more complex class schemas.

We therefore check the 8 UNIDIFF parameters to see if they decline over time in the way that the class dealignment thesis predicts. These parameters are given in Table 5 and are plotted in Figure 1. As one would expect from previous research, the association in 1964 was higher than at any time afterwards and it then declined sharply in 1970. Since 1970, however, the pattern could be described as one of 'trendless fluctuation' around a rather lower level than had prevailed in the 1960s.

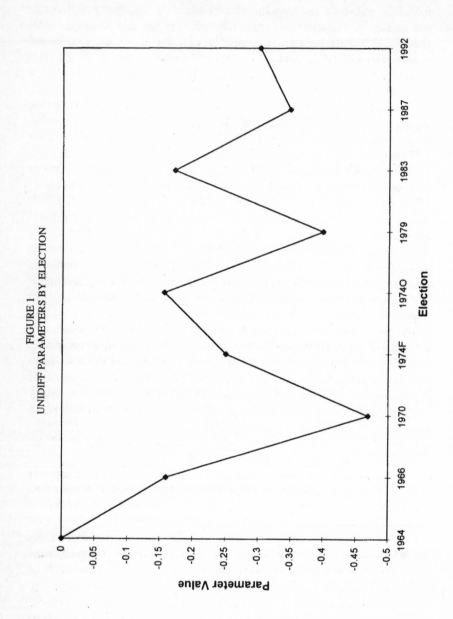

FIGURE 1
UNIDIFF PARAMETERS BY ELECTION

Inspection of the standard errors for the parameters shown in Table 5 (obtained with the Goldthorpe-Erikson procedure which may thus overstate significance – see appendix) indicates that only the associations in 1966, October 1974, and 1983 are *not* significantly lower than that in the highly class-polarized 1964 election.

TABLE 5
UNIDIFF PARAMETER ESTIMATES

Election	Estimate (standard error)
1964	0.0
1966	-0.16 (.11)
1970	-0.47 (.11)
1974 (Feb)	-0.25 (.11)
1974 (Oct)	-0.16 (.11)
1979	-0.40 (.11)
1983	-0.17 (.10)
1987	-0.35 (.10)
1992	-0.30 (.10)

Many possible hypotheses can be advanced to account for these changes, but few appear promising.[33] Our own interpretation of these fluctuations is that they derive from contingent political factors such as the incumbent government's record in satisfying the aspirations of its previous voters.[34] In this respect it is notable that the class/party association was weakest in 1970 and 1979 after two periods when Labour governments were widely felt to have failed to meet working-class aspirations.[35] The generally lower level of class voting in the later part of the period may also be related to the re-emergence of centre parties. These speculations await more detailed testing.

Conclusions

Our aim in this paper has been both methodological and substantive. We have elaborated and demonstrated the merits of the UNIDIFF model for estimating trends in class voting, and have also further tested the thesis of a weakening of the class/party association. As part of this remit we have examined the inferential problems resulting from the use of traditional dichotomous indices for estimating the class/party association. It was observed that the various indices produce widely differing estimates as a consequence of their choice of classes and parties for comparison. This finding clearly adds strength to our argument that the UNIDIFF model gives a preferable estimate of over time changes in the class/party relation, precisely because it encompasses information from all classes and all parties in its estimates. In this respect we have seen that the UNIDIFF model yields an acceptable fit to the data and its interaction terms provide a valuable measure of the election-to-election changes in the strength of the class/party association. These parameter estimates confirm that there have been considerable election-to-election fluctuations in the class/party relationship during the last thirty years, although the relationship has generally been somewhat weaker from 1970 onwards than it was in the 1960s.

We have not attempted in this paper to explain the election-to-election changes in the strength of the class/party association. Our aims have been more modest, and with only nine elections observed, formal hypothesis-testing about the sources of the fluctuations is unlikely to be illuminating. However, we hope to have demonstrated the relative advantage of the parameters in the uniform difference model as a way of summarizing the strength of the class/party association at each election. These models are better summary indicators of changing strengths of association between class and party than either Alford type measures – with their problem of, among others, the selection of which classes and parties to compare – or even the loglinear models we have used in earlier publications, with their rather unwieldy number of parameters and profligate use of degrees of freedom.

Finally, we observed that in the most recent election there were signs of an upturn in levels of class voting: between 1987 and 1992 there were small, non-significant increases in the class/party association. This adds more weight to the 'trendless fluctuation' thesis advanced in work using data from the 1960s to the 1980s, than to the class dealignment argument, which predicts a continuing reduction in the strength of the class/party association. Again, therefore, we must desist from concurring with the many commentators who have proclaimed the decline of class voting. The strength of association between class and vote in Britain has remained basically unmoved for over 20 years.

APPENDIX
THE UNIDIFF MODEL

The log-multiplicative layer effect or 'uniform difference' (UNIDIFF) model was independently developed by Xie, van der Heijden and Jansen, and Erikson and Goldthorpe in the context of comparative social mobility and is adapted here for the current application.[36] It is the most general (that is, unconstrained) model among a set of models in which the cross-table variation in the association of interest (here the Class/Party association) is constrained to be the log-multiplicative product of a common association parameter and a table-specific (here Election) component. All that is required is that each Class/Party table being compared has a common pattern of association; the categories of the variables involved are not assumed to be ordered. Most of these models are either special cases or slight generalizations of models proposed by Clogg.[37]

The model starts from the assumption that there is a general pattern to the net association between Party (P) and Class (C) (as defined by odds ratios) which persists over Elections (E), even though the overall strength of this association may vary from one election to another. This suggests a model of the form:

$$F_{ijk} = \tau\tau_i^P \tau_j^C \tau_k^E \tau_{ik}^{PE} \tau_{jk}^{CE} \exp(\omega_k \beta_{ij}^{PC})$$

$$(1)$$

$$i=1\ldots.I \text{ Parties}$$
$$j=1\ldots.J \text{ Classes}$$
$$k=1\ldots.K \text{ Elections}$$

where β^{pc} represents the general pattern of the PC association and ω_k the relative strength of association that is specific to a particular election, k. Thus in this model the PC and PCE interactions in the saturated model are replaced by the log-multiplicative product of two components: the overall PC association and a deviation parameter for the kth Election. Both Xie, and Erikson and Goldthorpe, describe an iterative maximum-likelihood procedure to calibrate this model, implemented in GLIM macros. This procedure alternately estimates the ω_k treating the β^{pc} as fixed and known and then treats the ω_k as fixed and estimates the β^{pc} until convergence is reached. The procedure will thus overestimate the precision of the estimates of the parameters of main interest, the ω_k. The standard errors could be estimated by the jacknife method[37]
The ratio of odds ratios for a pair of Parties: i,iÕ, a pair of Classes: j,jÕ and Elections k and k+1 is

$$\theta_{[ii':jj']k} = \exp(\beta_{ij}^{PC} + \beta_{i'j'}^{PC} - \beta_{i'j}^{PC} - \beta_{ij'}^{PC}) * \exp(\omega_k - \omega_{k+1})$$

$$(2)$$

Thus this model estimates a single strength-of-association parameter for each election, and imposes the constraint that all odds ratios either uniformly increase or uniformly decrease as we move between elections. With the fitted model, the differences between the ω parameters will show in which direction and to what extent the overall strength of the PC association differs across elections. If the difference between the ω parameter for a later election and an earlier election is negative, then all the fitted odds ratios in the later election are closer to 1 than are the corresponding odds ratios for the earlier election (that is, decreasing association), with the size of the change in association from one election to another being a function of the difference between their respective values. Similarly a positive difference between values indicates that all the fitted odds ratios are moving further away from 1 (that is, increasing association).

ACKNOWLEDGEMENTS

We wish to thank the directors of the British Election Studies who collected the original data, the ESRC Data Archive for making the data available, and John Goldthorpe, Paul Nieuwbeerta and Tom Payne for their assistance and comments. The present work was funded by the ESRC whose support we gratefully acknowledge (Award Y303253001).

NOTES

1. For contrasting examples from this diverse literature, see A. Przeworski, *Capitalism and Social Democracy* (Cambridge: Cambridge University Press, 1985); and E.G. Carmines, 'The Logic of Party Alignments', *Journal of Theoretical Politics*, Vol.3 (1991), pp.65–80.
2. See P. Dunleavy and C. Husbands, *British Democracy at the Crossroads* (London: Allen and Unwin, 1985); and H. Kitschelt, *The Transformation of European Social Democracy* (Cambridge: Cambridge University Press, 1994).
3. R. Inglehart, *Culture Shift* (Princeton: Princeton University Press, 1990); R.J. Dalton, *Citizen Politics in Western Democracies* (Chatham NJ: Chatham House, 1988).
4. Here of course we refer to Lipset and Rokkan's classic work: 'Cleavage Structures, Party Systems and Voter Alignments: an Introduction', in S.M. Lipset and S. Rokkan (eds)., *Party Systems and Voter Alignments: Cross-National Perspectives* (New York: Free Press, 1967).
5. The most general case for this is probably presented in M.N. Franklin, T.T. Mackie and H. Valen *et al.*, *Electoral Change: Responses to Evolving Social and Attitudinal Structures in Western Countries* (Cambridge: Cambridge University Press, 1992); see also R. Rose and I. McAllister, *Voters Begin to Choose: From Closed Class to Open Elections in Britain*, (London: Sage, 1986).
6. Dunleavy and Husbands, *British Democracy at The Crossroads*.
7. Thus Franklin *et al.* observe that 'almost all of the countries we have studied show a decline during our period in the ability of social cleavages to structure individual voting choice', p.385 (see Note 7).
8. R. Inglehart, *Culture Shift*; R.J. Dalton, *Citizen Politics in Western Democracies*; S.M. Lipset, *Political Man* (Baltimore: Johns Hopkins University Press, 1981), pp.509–21.
9. T. N. Clark and S. M. Lipset, 'Are Social Classes Dying?', *International Sociology*,Vol.6 (1991), pp.397–410; T. N. Clark, S. M. Lipset, and Rempel, M. 'The Declining Significance of Social Class', *International Sociology*, 8 (1993), pp.293–316; I. Crewe, 'Changing Votes and Unchanging Voters', *Electoral Studies*, Vol.11 (1992), pp.335–45. For more examples, see the review of recent work in this area by J. Manza, M. Hout and C. Brooks, 'Class Voting in Capitalist Democracies Since World War II: Dealignment, Realignment, or Trendless Fluctuation?' *Annual Review of Sociology*, 1995.
10. Clark and Lipset, 'Are Social Classes Dying?', p.397.
11. Ibid, p.408.
12. B. Sarlvik and I. Crewe, *Decade of Dealignment* (Cambridge: Cambridge University Press, 1983).
13. R. R. Alford, 'A Suggested Index of the Association of Social Class and Voting', *Public Opinion Quarterly*,Vol.26 (1962), pp.417–25. For a list of the numerous publications which have presented diagrams showing a decline in the Alford index in support of their contention that class has lost its influence on vote, see Manza, Hout and Brooks 'Class Voting in Capitalist Democracies Since World War II'.
14. I. Crewe, 'On the Death and Resurrection of Class Voting: some comments on How Britain Votes', *Political Studies, Vol.*34 (1986), pp.620–38, p.620.
15. M.N. Franklin, *The Decline of Class Voting in Britain* (Oxford: Clarendon Press, 1985); Franklin, *et al.*, *Electoral Change*.
16. J.H. Goldthorpe, *Social Mobility and Class Structure in Modern Britain* (Oxford: Clarendon Press, 1987).
17. For evidence of this, see G.A. Evans, 'Testing the Validity of the Goldthorpe Class Schema',

*European Sociological Review, Vol.*8 (1992), pp.211–32.

18. E. Scarbrough, The British Electorate twenty years on: electoral change and election surveys', *British Journal of Political Science,* Vol.17 (1987), pp.219–46, p.227.

19. These issues are being examined in more detail elsewhere. See A.F. Heath, 'Social Class Classifications: Does it Matter Which One We Use?' paper presented at the meeting of the Royal Statistical Society, Social Statistics Section, London, April 1995.

20. This problem also arises with apparently more sophisticated OLS regression methods employed by, for example, Franklin, *et al., Electoral Change,* and Rose and McAllister, *Voters Begin to Choose.* For more discussion of the limitations of OLS regression, see G. A. Evans, A. F. Heath and C. Payne, 'Modelling the Class/Party Relationship 1964–87', *Electoral Studies,* Vol.10 (1991), pp.99–117.

21. G.A. Evans, 'The decline of class divisions in Britain? Class and ideological preferences in the 1960s and the 1980s', *British Journal of Sociology,* Vol.44 (1993), pp.449–71.

22. A. F. Heath, R. M. Jowell and J. K. Curtice with B. T. Taylor, *Labour's Last Chance? The 1992 Election and Beyond* (Aldershot: Dartmouth, 1994).

23. A. F. Heath, R. Jowell and J. Curtice, *How Britain Votes* (Oxford: Pergamon, 1985); Evans, Heath and Payne, 'Modelling the Class/Party Relationship 1964–87'; A. F. Heath, R. Jowell, J. Curtice, G. A. Evans, J. Field and S. Witherspoon, *Understanding Political Change: The British Voter 1964–1987* (Oxford: Pergamon, 1991).

24. See C.C. Clogg and S.R. Eliason, Some common problems in log-linear analysis' in J.S. Long, ed. *Common Problems/Propper Solutions,* pp 226–57, (Newbury Park, CA: Sage).

25. See R. Erikson and J. H. Goldthorpe, *The Constant Flux: A Study of Class Mobility in Industrial Societies* (Oxford: Clarendon Press, 1992).

26. The surveys each contain a representative cross-section sample of the British electorate with response rates around 70%, ranging from 76% in the February 1974 survey to 61% in the 1979 survey. The studies have all excluded Northern Ireland. The 1964, 1970, February 1974, 1983, 1987 and 1992 samples were independent probability samples. The 1966, October 1974 and 1979 samples were not independent probability samples but contained panel elements drawn from the previous survey in the series. For further technical details see Heath, *et al. Understanding Political Change*; and Heath, Jowell and Curtice, *Labour's Last Chance?*

27. Heath, Jowell and Curtice, *How Britain Votes*; Evans, Heath and Payne, 'Modelling the class/party relationship, 1964–87.; Heath *et al Understanding Political Change.*

28. Elsewhere we have also examined class/party trends over the period from 1964–92 comparing the findings obtained using different methods of class allocation. Similar patterns of association and change through time were found for both the 'head-of-household' and 'individual' procedures. See A.F. Heath, G.A. Evans and C. Payne, 'Modelling the class–party relationship in Britain, 1964–92', *Journal of the Royal Statistical Society, A,* 158 (1995), pp.563–74.

29. When constructing indexes which dichotomize the class structure, we allocate the self-employed to the 'middle class' along with the Salariat and routine non-manual workers. This is contrasted with a 'working class' of foremen and technicians, and skilled, semi-skilled and unskilled manual workers.

30. Crewe, 'Changing Votes and Unchanging Voters', p.341. It should be noted that this is not how Crewe describes his index – he refers to the figures in his Table 2 as log odds ratios. But those figures could only have been obtained by the procedure we have described.

31. I. Crewe, 'The Electorate: Partisan Dealignment Ten Years On', in H. Berrington (ed.), *Change in British Politics* (London: Frank Cass, 1984).

32. P. Nieuwbeerta and N.D. De Graaf, 'Class Voting and the Influence of Varying Class Structures in 16 Western Countries: 1956–1990', in G.A. Evans ed. *The End of Class Politics?* (Oxford: Oxford University Press, forthcoming).

33. One possibility, for example, is that the greater the differences between the parties in their (class) ideologies, the stronger will the class/party association be. But if this were the case, we would have expected class voting to have been greater in the 1980s than in the 1960s. This was not the case. See Heath, *et al., Understanding Political Change.*

34. For more discussion of these arguments see Evans, Heath and Payne, 'Modelling the

     Class/Party Relationship 1964–87'.
35. Elsewhere we have shown that this decline was most pronounced in the working class, *ibid.* pp.109–10.
36. Y. Xie, 'The Log-Multiplicative Layer Effect Model for Comparing Mobility Tables', *American Sociological Review*, Vol.57 (1992), pp.482–94; P. G. M. van der Heijden and W. Jansen, 'A Class of Models for the Simultaneous Analysis of Square Contingency Tables', in L. Fahrmeir, B. Francis, R. Gilchrist and G. Tutz (eds.), *Advances in GLIM and Statistical Modelling: Proceedings of the GLIM 92 Conference and the 7th International Workshop on Statistical Modelling* (Berlin: Springer Verlag, 1992); Erikson and Goldthorpe, *The Constant Flux.*
37. C.C. Clogg, 'Some Models for the Analysis of Association in Multiway Cross-Classifications Having Ordered Categories', *Journal of the American Statistical Society*, Vol.77 (1982), pp.803–15. For a more detailed discussion see C. Payne, J. Payne and C. O'Muircheartaigh, 'Testing the Tightening Bond Hypothesis: An Application of New Models for Modelling Trends in Multiway Tables', *Journal of Statistical Planning and Inference*, (forthcoming).
38. See van der Heijden and Jansen, 'A Class of Models for the Simultaneous Analysis of Square Contingency Tables'.

Reference Section

Introduction

Despite four previous attempts we remain uncertain about what users of the Yearbook would like to see in the Reference Section. We are confident that the chronology of the year, details of parliamentary by-election results and the opinion poll data for the year are very useful to colleagues, providing a handy source for information that is not always easy to find. On this occasion we have also included authoritative details of the results of the elections to the European Parliament, held in June 1994. As for the remaining selection of material, however – the summaries of local election results, recent books and articles of interest, information about political parties and Politics journals – we can only hope that it is worthwhile collating it here. We have continued to follow the general principle that we should include only material that is not fairly readily accessible elsewhere and this has led us to drop details of the mass media and the section on government and parliament which appeared in previous issues.

David Broughton
David Denver

1. Chronology of Events 1994

JANUARY

5. Tim Yeo resigned as Minister for the Environment and Countryside after admitting being the father of an illegitimate child whose mother was a Conservative councillor.

6. It was disclosed that a number of media groups had expressed interest in acquiring a stake in Newspaper Publishing, publishers of the Independent and the Independent on Sunday.

8. Alan Duncan resigned as Parliamentary Private Secretary to Brian Mawhinney, the Minister for Health, following disclosure that he had gained financially from a transaction involving the purchase of a former council house belonging to a neighbour.

9. The Earl of Caithness resigned as Minister for Aviation and Shipping following the suicide the previous day of his wife, the Countess of Caithness.

12. Lord Howe of Aberavon, the former Foreign and Commonwealth Secretary, accused Lord Justice Scott, who was conducting an inquiry into arms-related sales to Iraq, of acting as 'detective, inquisitor, advocate and judge'.

13. A highly critical provisional report was published by the district auditor on the housing policies of the Conservative-controlled Westminster City Council, which was said to have used unlawful and unauthorized methods to persuade tenants to move from council property.

14. John Major settled his action for libel against the magazine, Scallywag, over allegations of a relationship with the caterer, Clare Latimer.

17. Appearing before the Scott inquiry into arms-related sales to Iraq, John Major maintained that he had taken no part in the formulation, consideration, amendment or interpretation of guidelines on arms exported to Iraq.

23. Brian Redhead, broadcaster and journalist, presenter of Radio Four's Today programme since 1975, died aged 64.

24. The Local Government Commission published its final proposals for the local government structure in the present areas of North Yorkshire, Humberside and Lincolnshire. These were broadly in line with its original recommendations of abolishing North Yorkshire and Humberside and establishing nine new unitary authorities in those areas.

25. Jimmy Boyce, the Labour MP for Rotherham, died aged 46.

27. The House of Commons Public Accounts Committee published a report which was strongly critical of the standards of probity, integrity and financial control in many parts of the public service.

31. Gerry Adams, the President of Sinn Fein, arrived in the United States which had granted him a two-day visa to attend a conference on Northern Ireland in New York.

FEBRUARY

1. Jo Richardson, the Labour MP for Barking, died aged 70.

4. British Coal confirmed its plans for the closure of five more pits, reducing its number of deep mines to 17.
The Chief Secretary to the Treasury, Michael Portillo, apologised after attacking standards of public life and education in countries other than Britain in a speech to students at Southampton University.

7. The body of Stephen Milligan, Conservative MP and PPS to Defence Procurement Minister Jonathan Aitken, was found in mysterious circumstances in London. His death at the age of 45 caused a by-election vacancy in his Eastleigh constituency.

9. Bryan Gould, Labour MP and former member of the Shadow Cabinet, announced that he would resign his seat of Dagenham in order to take up an academic post in his native New Zealand.
Sir Robin Butler, Cabinet Secretary, began two days of evidence to the Scott inquiry into arms-related sales to Iraq.

12. Hartley Booth resigned as PPS to Douglas Hogg (Minister of State at the

Foreign and Commonwealth Office) after admitting a relationship with a young female researcher, although he denied any sexual impropriety.

14. Eight bids were formally submitted for the licence to operate the National Lottery from November.

15. It was announced that the charge for National Health Service prescriptions would rise from £4.25 to £4.75 with effect from 1 April.

21. Two amendments to reintroduce the death penalty for murder were decisively rejected by the House of Commons. The House approved an amendment which reduced the age of consent for homosexual acts from 21 to 18 but rejected its further reduction to 16. All these decisions were taken on free votes during the committee stage of the Criminal Justice and Public Order Bill.

22. The General Synod of the Church of England approved the final canons required to allow for the ordination of women priests.

23. The Hong Kong Legislative Council approved a bill implementing parts of a plan put forward by the Governor, Chris Patten, for future constitutional developments. Fierce criticism from the Chinese authorities was one result.

26. The annual conference of Sinn Fein called for further clarification of the Downing Street declaration on Northern Ireland.

27. The Environment Secretary, John Gummer, a former leading member of the General Synod of the Church of England and a leading opponent of the ordination of women priests, was received into the Roman Catholic Church.

28. The Labour MP for Newham North-East, Ron Leighton, died aged 64.

MARCH

2. In evidence to the House of Commons select committee on foreign affairs, Douglas Hurd, the Foreign and Commonwealth Secretary, indicated that aid for Malaysia for the Pergau dam project and defence contracts had incorrectly become 'entangled' during a visit to that country by George Younger, then the Defence Secretary, in 1988. The two matters had been 'unlinked' soon after.

3. The House of Lords ruled that certain aspects of UK employment protection legislation relating to unfair dismissal were in conflict with European Union law in that it discriminated against part-time workers.

4. David Spedding was appointed to succeed Sir Colin McColl as head of MI6 in September.

8. William Waldegrave, Chancellor of the Duchy of Lancaster, said, in giving evidence to the House of Commons Treasury and Civil Service select committee, that in exceptional circumstances it was necessary for ministers to say something which was untrue in the House of Commons.

9. The IRA launched a mortar attack on Heathrow airport, although all four devices failed to explode.
    The House of Commons approved the establishment of a select committee on Northern Ireland affairs.

12. The first ordination of women priests (32 in all) in the Church of England took place in Bristol Cathedral.

13. Marshal of the RAF Sir Peter Harding resigned as the Chief of the Defence Staff after the News of the World published an account of his intimate relationship with Lady Buck.

19. An Army helicopter was brought down by an IRA mortar shell in Crossmaglen in Northern Ireland.

21. The Prime Minister and the Reverend Ian Paisley had a heated discussion on the prospects for a settlement in Northern Ireland.

27. The Foreign Ministers of the European Union countries agreed arrangements for a new 'blocking minority' within the EU Council of Minsters, to take account of the accession of four new countries to the Union at the beginning of 1995.

30. The IRA called a 72-hour ceasefire for early April.
    The House of Commons public accounts committee issued a critical report on the circumstances surrounding the provision of aid for the Pergau dam project in Malaysia.

    Lord Justice Scott completed the main public hearings of his inquiry into arms-related sales to Iraq.

APRIL

1. Railtrack assumed the ownership of British Rail's track, stations and signalling as the first stage in the privatization of the railway system. Eurotunnel confirmed that there would be a further delay in the opening of regular passenger services through the Channel Tunnel.

6. The controversial imposition of value added tax (VAT) on domestic fuel and power came into force at the rate of 8 per cent.

12. Bob Cryer, the Labour MP for Bradford South, died aged 59 in a car crash.

13. The Labour Party refused to endorse a report of the House of Commons select committee on home affairs on the issue of the funding of political parties.

    The Chancellor of the Exchequer, Kenneth Clarke, announced that in future he would publish the minutes of his monthly meetings with the Governor of the Bank of England to review monetary developments.

14. Sir James Kilfedder, the sole Popular Unionist MP, was elected chair of the new House of Commons select committee on Northern Ireland. Ann Clwyd MP began a sit-in underground at Tower Colliery, the last pit in South Wales, in an attempt to prevent its closure.

15. The order was signed bringing into effect the new boundaries of constituencies in England and Wales for elections to the European Parliament.

22. Richard Nixon, President of the United States 1969-1974, died aged 81.

23. Graham Leonard, the former Bishop of London, was re-ordained as a priest in the Roman Catholic Church.

26. Three police officers were charged with manslaughter over the events surrounding their attempts to deport Joy Gardiner in July 1993.

27. The Trades Union Congress decided to reserve three seats on its General Council for representatives of black workers.

MAY

5.　In the Rotherham by-election Labour retained the seat with a reduced share of the vote.

In the local government elections, the Liberal Democrats made gains of nearly 400 seats and Labour gained nearly 100 seats whilst the Conservatives lost over 400 seats and lost control of 18 councils. The British National Party lost its only seat.

6.　The Channel Tunnel was formally inaugurated when the Queen and President Mitterrand travelled through it on the first official train from France to the United Kingdom.

7.　Michael Brown resigned as an assistant government whip as allegations were due to be published in the News of the World concerning a sexual relationship between him, a civil servant and a male student.

12.　John Smith, leader of the Labour Party since July 1992, died suddenly of a heart attack aged 55. Campaigning by the parties for elections to the European Parliament was suspended until after his funeral on 20 May and his burial on Iona on 21 May. The party's deputy leader, Margaret Beckett, took over as acting leader.

16.　Bryan Gould formally resigned from the House of Commons, creating a by-election in his Dagenham constituency.

18.　The Labour Shadow cabinet announced that no declarations of candidacy for the party leadership should be made until after the elections to the European Parliament on 9 June.

19.　Baroness Thatcher stated that she did not intend to give evidence to the House of Commons select committee on foreign affairs over the Pergau dam issue.

21.　Ralph Miliband, formerly Professor of Politics at the University of Leeds, died aged 70.

23.　The three major parties published their manifestos for the elections to the European Parliament.

25.　It was announced that the Camelot consortium had been selected to run the National Lottery.

27. The Prime Minister, John Major, made an attack on the 'offensive problem' of begging on city streets for which there was 'no justification'.

31. At an election rally, John Major proposed that the European Union should proceed towards further integration on a 'multi-track, multi-speed, multi-layered' basis, with member states being free to do some things in their own way and at their own speed.

JUNE

1. Gordon Brown announced that he would not be a contender for the leadership of the Labour Party.

4. Lord Thorneycroft, former Chancellor of the Exchequer and Conservative Party Chairman, died aged 84.

5–6. The Queen and the leaders of the wartime allied nations including President Bill Clinton of the United States took part in commemorations marking the 50th anniversary of the D-Day landings in Normandy.

8. The Liberal Democrat candidate in the Newham North-East by-election, Alec Kellaway, announced on the eve of the election that he had defected to Labour and would take the Labour whip on the local council.

9. Elections were held to the European Parliament although the results were not declared until 12-13 June.

   In five parliamentary by-elections, the Liberal Democrats won the Eastleigh seat from the Conservatives, whilst Labour retained Bradford South, Barking, Dagenham and Newham North-East; in all five contests, the Conservative share of the vote dropped dramatically.

12–
13. The results of the elections to the European Parliament were declared. Labour won 62 of the 87 seats, the Conservatives 18, the Liberal Democrats two, the SNP two and the Democratic Unionist party, the SDLP and the Official Ulster Unionist Party one each.

15. Signal workers, members of the RMT union, held the first of a series of one-day strikes over pay.

16. Sir Norman Fowler announced that he was resigning as chairman of the Conservative Party after two years.

As nominations closed, it was announced that Tony Blair, John Prescott and Margaret Beckett would contest the leadership of the Labour Party. The latter two were also the only contenders for the deputy leadership of the party.

17. Michael Heseltine declared that he wished to remain President of the Board of Trade and not to be considered for the post of Conservative Party Chairman.

24. Heads of government of the member states of the European Union met on Corfu. John Major effectively vetoed the appointment of Belgian Prime Minister, Jean-Luc Dehaene, as the successor to Jacques Delors as President of the European Commission.

29. The Liberal Democrats confirmed that they would submit an election petition contesting the outcome of the European Parliament election in Devon and Plymouth East, which had been narrowly won by the Conservatives but which was contested by a 'Literal Democrat'.

30. Labour Party narrowly retained Monklands East in the by-election caused by the death of John Smith. There was a swing of 19 per cent to the SNP.

JULY

6. A White Paper was published setting out the government's decisions on the future of the BBC, whose Royal Charter would be renewed for a further 10 years from 1997.

7. It was confirmed that the Department of Trade and Industry was investigating alleged insider dealing in the shares of Anglia Television by Lord Archer, whose wife Mary was a non-executive director of that company.

10. Two Conservative MPs, Graham Riddick and David Tredinnick, were suspended from their posts as PPS's to ministers after revelations in the Sunday Times that they had apparently accepted payments for tabling questions in the House of Commons.

14. The Director of Public Prosecutions, Barbara Mills, stated that there

would be no prosecutions of British service personnel for alleged war crimes during the Falklands conflict in 1982.

15. The European Council unanimously approved the appointment of Luxembourg Prime Minister Jacques Santer to succeed Jacques Delors as President of the European Commission.

20. The Prime Minister carried out a major reshuffle of his Cabinet. Four members left the Cabinet; Jeremy Hanley was appointed Chairman of the Conservative Party and there were also widespread changes in posts below Cabinet level.

The House of Commons select committee on foreign affairs published a report strongly critical of the government's conduct in relation to the Pergau dam affair and its linkage to potential arms purchases by Malaysia.

21. Tony Blair was elected leader of the Labour Party with 57 per cent of the vote overall; John Prescott defeated Margaret Beckett for the deputy leadership also with about 57 per cent of the overall vote.

24. Sinn Fein rejected the Downing Street declaration as a basis for talks on the future of Northern Ireland.

28. Michael Heseltine, the President of the Board of Trade, announced that his department would take no further action against Lord Archer after the investigation of alleged insider dealing in the shares of Anglia Television prior to its takeover by MAI.

29. It was announced that Neil Kinnock had been nominated to succeed Bruce Millan as a member of the European Commission. Sir Leon Brittan was nominated for a second term of office.

30. The Guardian published parts of a leaked letter from Michael Portillo (Chief Secretary to the Treasury) to Michael Heseltine (President of the Board of Trade) which criticised the level of spending at the Department of Trade and Industry.

AUGUST

1. In a further step in the price war amongst the broadsheet daily newspapers, the Independent cut its cover price from 50p to 30p.

3.   The National Union of Rail, Maritime and Transport Workers (RMT) staged an eighth stoppage by its signal workers.

4.   A Gallup poll gave the Labour Party a record lead of 33 per cent over the Conservatives.

28. Conditional Sunday trading came legally into force under the provisions of the Sunday Trading Act 1994.

29. Gerry Adams, the President of Sinn Fein, indicated that a ceasefire by the IRA could be imminent.

31. The IRA formally called an open-ended 'complete cessation of military operations' but John Major asserted that Sinn Fein could not participate in talks on the future of Northern Ireland until the ceasefire had proved to be permanent.

SEPTEMBER

1.   It was confirmed that Larry Whitty, the Labour's general secretary since 1985, was to become the party's European co-ordinator.

5.   The 126th Trades Union Congress opened in Blackpool.

7.   In a speech in Leiden, John Major warned against the European Union developing in the direction of a 'two-tier Europe'.

11. Robert Maclennan was elected to succeed Charles Kennedy as President of the Liberal Democrats; two days later, party leader Paddy Ashdown announced his parliamentary front bench team.

16. The Prime Minister announced that the people of Northern Ireland would be allowed a referendum on the constitutional future of the province. He also announced the lifting of the six-year ban on the broadcasting of the voices of members of Sinn Fein.

17. Sir Karl Popper, former Professor of Logic and Scientific Method at the London School of Economics and Political Science, died aged 92.

18. The Liberal Democrats' annual conference opened in Brighton.

20. The Prime Minister began a three-day visit to South Africa- the first visit

by a UK Prime Minister since 1960.

21. The SNP's annual conference opened in Inverness.

28. The RMT union and Railtrack reached a settlement over the long-running pay dispute.

OCTOBER

4. At the Labour Party conference, the party leader, Tony Blair, outlined his wish to revise the party's constitution with an up-to-date statement of the party's objectives.

6. The Labour Party leadership was narrowly defeated at the party's annual conference when motions were passed to endorse Clause IV of the party's constitution and to abandon the Trident nuclear missile system.

11. The Conservative annual conference opened in Bournemouth.

12. The Conservative MP, John Blackburn, died aged 61, causing a by-election in his Dudley West constituency.

13. At the Conservative annual conference, Michael Howard, the Home Secretary, said he preferred that the introduction of identity cards should be on a voluntary rather than compulsory basis.

17. Tom Sawyer was confirmed as the successor to Larry Whitty as general secretary of the Labour Party.

19. In elections to the Labour Shadow Cabinet, two vacancies were filled by Harriet Harman and Margaret Beckett and Gavin Strang replaced Tom Clarke. The party leader announced the distribution of the shadow portfolios the following day.

20. Tim Smith resigned as an Under-Secretary of State at the Northern Ireland Office following revelations that he had failed to disclose payments from Mohamed al-Fayed in the register of Members' interests.

24. The Commission on Social Justice set up in December 1992 by the Labour Party presented its report which recommended far-reaching reform of the welfare and social security systems, allied with changes in taxation policies.

25. Neil Hamilton resigned as Under-Secretary of State for Corporate Affairs amid allegations of undeclared consultancy and payment arrangements. The Prime Minister announced the establishment of a standing committee under Lord Nolan to investigate conduct and standards in public life.

NOVEMBER

3. The Cabinet agreed not to include the privatization of the Post Office in the legislative programme of the next session of Parliament following strong criticism from some Conservative MPs.

9. The Appeal Court ruled that Michael Howard, the Home Secretary, had acted unlawfully in introducing a new criminal injuries compensation scheme in April 1994 without having first obtained parliamentary approval.

10. The High Court ruled that Douglas Hurd, the Foreign and Commonwealth Secretary, had acted unlawfully in approving aid totalling £234 million from the Overseas Development budget for the Pergau Dam in Malaysia.

11. The Liberal Democrats failed in their bid to overturn the result of the European Parliament election in Devon and Plymouth East.

14. The first National Lottery tickets went on sale, with the first draw taking place on 19 November.

The first commercial passenger train travelled through the Channel Tunnel.

15. It was announced that Sarah Hogg was to resign as the Head of the Prime Minister's Policy Unit.

16. The new session of Parliament opened with the Queen's Speech which contained 13 specific legislative proposals, including the European Communities (Finance Bill) to enable Britain to meet its commitments agreed at the European Council meeting held in Edinburgh in December 1992 which involved an increase in the contribution of the member states to the budget of the Community. Other Bills dealt with the promotion of greater competition in the gas industry, the creation of the jobseeker's allowance, reorganization of the structure of the National Health Service in England and Wales and various reforms to the Scottish criminal justice system.

17. Gerry Adams, the President of Sinn Fein, visited mainland Britain and held a press conference at the House of Commons.

23. Patrick Nicholls resigned as a vice-chairman of the Conservative Party in the wake of the publication of an article in which he was very critical of the role of France and Germany within the European Union given their history.

24. Sir Marcus Fox was re-elected as Chairman of the Conservative 1922 committee of backbenchers, defeating a challenge from Sir Nicholas Bonsor.

28. The government had a majority of 27 in the House of Commons when Labour moved an amendment on the second reading of the European Communities (Finance) Bill, which the Cabinet had stated would be seen as a vote of confidence; eight Conservative MPs abstained. They subsequently lost the Conservative whip and another Conservative MP resigned the Whip.

29. Kenneth Clarke, the Chancellor of the Exchequer, presented the annual budget for 1995-96, beginning in April 1995. The budget foresaw a reduction in the public sector borrowing requirement, with further spending cuts designed to eliminate the PSBR by 1998-1999 and 1999-2000.

30. The deadline for a possible leadership challenge to John Major as leader of the Conservative Party passed without any opposing nominations being lodged.

DECEMBER

6. At the end of a debate on the Budget, the government was defeated by eight votes on a procedural motion on the planned implementation in April 1995 of the second stage of the imposition of value added tax on domestic fuel and power.

   Lord Nolan outlined the initial work programme (issues and questions) for the standing committee of conduct in public life.

8. Following the government's defeat over the implementation of the second stage of imposing value added tax on domestic fuel and power, Kenneth Clarke, the Chancellor of the Exchequer, announced a package of measures to make good the revenue shortfall, mainly increased duties on alcohol, petrol and tobacco.

9. Talks on Northern Ireland were held in Belfast between government officials and representatives of Sinn Fein - the first such official contacts for 22 years.

10. Lord (Sir Keith) Joseph, former Secretary of State for Industry, former Secretary of State for Education and founder of the Centre for Policy Studies in 1974, died aged 76.

15. The government suffered a setback in the parliamentary by-election at Dudley West which Labour won from the Conservatives with a swing of 29 per cent, the 11th consecutive Conservative loss at a by-election since 1989.

19. A strongly critical report was published on the circumstances surrounding the attempted escape from Whitemoor Prison in September of six prisoners, five of them being IRA prisoners. A disciplinary inquiry into the matter was announced by Michael Howard, the Home Secretary.

21. Norman Blackwell was appointed to succeed Sarah Hogg as head of the Prime Minister's Policy Unit.

22. The European Union's Fisheries Ministers allowed Spain access to certain fishing grounds off South West England; William Waldegrave, the UK Fisheries Minister, abstained on the vote.

31. The New Year's Honours List was published. Honours were given to Elizabeth Smith, widow of John Smith the former Labour leader, and Sarah Hogg, former head of the Prime Minister's Policy Unit.

2. Parliamentary By-Elections 1994

(Note: By-elections are numbered consecutively from the general election of 1992.)

3. ROTHERHAM 5 May 1994 (Death of Mr J. Boyce)

Result

Candidate	Description	Votes
D. MacShane	Labour	14,912
D. Wildgoose	Liberal Democrat	7,958
N. Gibb	Conservative	2,649
Lord D. Sutch	Monster Raving Loony	1,114
K. Laycock	Natural Law Party	173

Labour hold: Majority 6,954

Turnout and Major Party Vote Shares (per cent)

	By-election	General Election	Change
Turnout	44.1	71.7	-27.6
Con	9.9	23.8	-13.9
Lab	55.6	64.0	-8.4
Lib Dem	29.7	12.3	+17.4

4. BARKING 9 June 1994 (Death of Ms J. Richardson)

Result

Candidate	Description	Votes
M. Hodge	Labour	13,704
G. White	Liberal Democrat	2,290
T. May	Conservative	1,976
G. Needs	National Front	551
G. Batten	UK Independence Party	406
H. Butensky	Natural Law Party	90

Labour hold: Majority 11,414

Turnout and Major Party Vote Shares (per cent)

	By-election	General Election	Change
Turnout	38.6	70.0	-31.4
Con	10.4	33.9	-23.5
Lab	72.1	51.6	+20.5
Lib Dem	12.0	14.5	-2.5

5. BRADFORD SOUTH 9 June 1994 (Death of Mr B. Cryer)

Result

Candidate	Description	Votes
G. Sutcliffe	Labour	17,014
H. Wright	Liberal Democrat	7,350
R. Farley	Conservative	5,475
D. Sutch	Monster Raving Looney	727
K. Laycock	Natural Law Party	187

Labour hold: Majority 9,664

Turnout and Major Party Vote Shares (per cent)

	By-election	General Election	Change
Turnout	44.0	75.6	-31.6
Con	17.8	38.4	-20.6
Lab	55.3	47.6	+7.7
Lib Dem	23.9	13.7	+10.2

6. DAGENHAM 9 June 1994 (Resignation of Mr B. Gould)

Result

Candidate	Description	Votes
J. Church	Labour	15,474
J. Fairrie	Conservative	2,130
P. Dunphy	Liberal Democrat	1,804
J. Tyndall	British National Party	1,511
P. Compobassi	UK Independence Party	457
M. Leighton	Natural Law Party	116

Labour hold: Majority 13,344

Turnout and Major Party Vote Shares (per cent)

	By-election	General Election	Change
Turnout	37.2	70.7	-33.5
Con	9.9	36.3	-26.4
Lab	72.0	52.3	+19.7
Lib Dem	8.4	11.5	-3.1

7. EASTLEIGH 9 June 1994 (Death of Mr S. Milligan)

Result

Candidate	Description	Votes
D. Chidgey	Liberal Democrat	24,473
M. Birks	Labour	15,234
S. Reid	Conservative	13,675
N. Farage	UK Independence Party	952
D. Sutch	Monster Raving Looney	783
P. Warburton	Natural Law Party	145

Liberal Democrat gain: Majority 9,239

Turnout and Major Party Vote Shares (per cent)

	By-election	General Election	Change
Turnout	58.9	82.9	-24.0
Con	24.7	51.3	-26.6
Lab	27.6	20.7	+6.9
Lib Dem	44.3	28.0	+16.3

8. NEWHAM NORTH EAST 9 June 1994 (Death of Mr R. Leighton)

Result

Candidate	Description	Votes
S. Timms	Labour	14,668
P. Hammond	Conservative	2,850
A. Kellaway	Liberal Democrat	821
A. Scholefield	UK Independence Party	509
J. Homeless	House Homeless People	342
R. Archer	Natural Law Party	228
V. Garman	Buy The Daily Sport	155

Labour hold: Majority 11,818

Turnout and Major Party Vote Shares (per cent)

	By-election	General Election	Change
Turnout	35.4	60.3	-24.9
Con	14.6	30.5	-15.9
Lab	74.9	58.3	+16.6
Lib Dem	4.2	11.2	-7.0

9. MONKLANDS EAST 30 June 1994 (Death of Mr J. Smith)

Result

Candidate	Description	Votes
H. Liddell	Labour	16,960
K. Ulrich	SNP	15,320
S. Gallagher	Liberal Democrat	878
S. Bell	Conservative	799
A. Bremner	Network Against Criminal Justice Bill	69
D. Paterson	Natural Law Party	58

Labour hold: Majority 1,640

Turnout and Major Party Vote Shares (per cent)

	By-election	General Election	Change
Turnout	70.2	75.1	-4.9
Con	2.3	16.1	-13.8
Lab	49.8	61.3	-11.5
Lib Dem	2.6	4.6	-2.0
SNP	44.9	18.0	+26.9

10. DUDLEY WEST 15 December 1994 (Death of Dr J. Blackburn)

Result

Candidate	Description	Votes
I. Pearson	Labour	28,400
G. Postles	Conservative	7,706
M. Hadley	Liberal Democrat	3,154
M. Floyd	UK Independence	590
A. Carmichael	National Front	561
M. Hyde	Liberal	548
M. Nattrass	New Britain	146
M. Nicholson	Freedom of Choice For Smokers	77
J. Oldbury	Natural Law Party	70
C. Palmer	21st Century Party	55

Labour gain: Majority 20,694

Turnout and Major Party Vote Shares (per cent)

	By-election	General Election	Change
Turnout	47.3	82.1	-34.8
Con	18.7	48.8	-30.1
Lab	68.8	40.7	+28.1
Lib Dem	7.6	10.5	-2.9

TABLE 2.1 Summary of By-election Results Apr 1992-Dec 1994

Constituency	Turnout Change	Change in Share of Vote			
		Con	Lab	Lib Dem	SNP
Newbury	-12.3	-29.0	-4.0	+27.8	
Christchurch	-6.4	-32.1	-9.4	+38.6	
Rotherham	-27.6	-13.9	-8.4	+17.4	
Barking	-31.4	-23.5	+20.5	-2.5	
Bradford South	-31.6	-20.6	+7.7	+10.2	
Dagenham	-33.5	-26.4	+19.7	-3.1	
Eastleigh	-24.0	-26.6	+6.9	+16.3	
Newham North East	-24.9	-15.9	+16.6	-7.0	
Monklands East	-4.9	-13.8	-11.5	-2.0	+26.9
Dudley West	-34.8	-30.1	+28.1	-2.9	

3. Public Opinion Polls 1994

TABLE 3.1 Voting Intentions in Major Polls 1994 (per cent)

Fieldwork	Company	Size	Sample Con	Lab	Dem	Lib Other
Jan						
7-8	ICM	1460	26	50	20	4
6-11	Gallup	1030	26	47	21	8
10-11	MORI	820	30	46	20	4
20-24	MORI	1936	28	48	20	4
26-31	Gallup	1085	26	46	23	6
Feb						
11-12	ICM	1434	26	51	20	4
22-28	Gallup	1060	25	49	21	6
24-28	MORI	1633	28	47	21	4
Mar						
11-12	ICM	1384	24	49	22	5
24-28	MORI	1898	27	49	20	4
31	NOP	1135	26	50	20	4
29-4/4	Gallup	1065	27	52	18	5
Apr						
6	MORI	1111	28	46	22	4
8-9	ICM	1407	26	48	22	4
21-25	MORI	1917	26	47	23	4
May						
6-7	ICM	1438	26	44	26	5
4-9	Gallup	115	55	46	25	5
13-14	MORI*	500	26	49	20	5
17	ICM	1019	26	48	23	4
19-23	MORI	1929	27	46	23	4
20-21	ICM	1420	25	49	23	3
25-30	Gallup	1042	21	54	22	4
Jun						
2-6	MORI	2669	23	50	22	5
16-20	MORI	1897	24	52	20	4
30-4/7	Gallup	1143	27	51	18	5
Jul						
8-9	ICM	1426	27	50	20	4
14-18	MORI	1899	23	51	21	5
27-1/8	Gallup	1161	23	57	15	6
Aug						
5-6	ICM	1431	23	55	17	5
18-22	MORI	1781	23	56	18	3
Sep						
1-5	Gallup	1045	22	57	17	5
9-10	ICM	1437	27	51	17	5
15-16	NOP	1117	28	50	17	5
22-26	MORI	1915	25	54	17	4
24-26	MORI	1065	25	52	18	5
28-3/10	Gallup	1115	26	54	17	4
Oct						
7-8	ICM	1464	26	58	13	3
20-24	MORI	1836	25	57	14	4
27-31	Gallup	1120	22	57	17	4
Nov						
4-5	ICM	1392	28	54	14	4
17-21	MORI	1833	24	55	17	4
30-5/12	Gallup	1061	22	61	14	4
Dec						
2-3	ICM	1037	27	53	16	5
15-19	MORI	1080	22	61	13	4

Notes: The figures shown are unadjusted voting intention percentages after the exclusion of respondents who did not indicate a party preference. Gallup results are normally reported to the nearest 0.5 but all such cases here have been rounded up.

* = telephone poll.

TABLE 3.2 Voting Intentions in Scotland 1994 (per cent)

	Con	Lab	Lib Dem	SNP
Jan	16	47	14	23
Feb	13	47	14	25
Mar	13	46	14	26
Apr	14	44	14	27
May	10	53	12	24
Jun	12	46	11	30
Jul	12	51	9	27
Aug	12	55	8	24
Sep	11	51	9	29
Oct	13	47	10	27
Nov	12	55	8	25

Note: System Three do not poll in December but have separate polls in early and late
January. The January figure shown is the average of the two January polls. Rows do
not total 100 because 'others' are not shown.

Source: System Three Scotland polls, published monthly in *The Herald* (Glasgow).

TABLE 3.3 Monthly Averages for Voting Intention 1994 (per cent)

	Con	Lab	Lib Dem		Con	Lab	Lib Dem
Jan	27	47	21	Jul	25	52	18
Feb	26	49	21	Aug	23	56	18
Mar	26	49	21	Sep	25	53	17
Apr	27	48	21	Oct	25	56	15
May	25	48	23	Nov	26	55	16
Jun	24	51	21	Dec	24	58	14

TABLE 3.4 Ratings of Party Leaders 1994

| | Major | | | Smith/Blair | | | Ashdown | | |
---	Pos	Neg	Net	Pos	Neg	Net	Pos	Neg	Net
Jan	22	72	-50	51	30	+21	57	24	+33
Feb	23	71	-48	53	30	+23	59	23	+36
Mar	23	71	-48	50	29	+21	55	24	+31
Apr	19	74	-55	49	31	+18	57	25	+32
May	19	74	-55				59	21	+38
Jun	19	74	-55		Blair		54	24	+30
Jul	20	73	-53	50	17	+33	57	23	+34
Aug	20	73	-53	58	14	+44	56	24	+32
Sep	21	72	-51	46	14	+32	53	27	+26
Oct	22	70	-48	51	15	+36	51	29	+22
Nov	21	71	-50	50	17	+33	50	28	+22
Dec	18	76	-58	55	17	+38	51	28	+23

Notes: The figures are based on responses to the questions 'Are you satisfied or dissatisfied with Mr Major as Prime Minister?'; 'Do you think that Mr Smith/Mr Blair is or is not proving a good leader of the Opposition?'; 'Do you think that Mr Ashdown is or is not proving a good leader of the Liberal Democratic Party?'.
The data are derived from the 'Gallup 9,000', which is an aggregation of all Gallup's polls in the month concerned.
The difference between 100 and the sum of positive and negative responses is the percentage of respondents who replied 'Don't know'.

Source: Gallup Political and Economic Index

TABLE 3.5 Best Person for Prime Minister 1994 (per cent)

	Major	Smith/Blair	Ashdown	Don't Know
Jan	18	34	20	24
Feb	19	34	21	26
Mar	19	31	19	27
Apr	15	32	21	28
May				
Jun		Blair		
Jul	15	32	21	32
Aug	16	42	15	28
Sep	17	39	15	29
Oct	17	41	14	28
Nov	16	40	13	31
Dec	14	44	13	29

Source: Gallup Political and Economic Index. The data are derived from the 'Gallup 9,000'.

TABLE 3.6 Approval/Disapproval of Government Record 1994 (per cent)

	Approve	Disapprove	Don't Know	Approve – Disapprove
Jan	14	77	9	-63
Feb	14	77	9	-63
Mar	14	77	10	-63
Apr	12	79	9	-67
May	11	80	9	-69
Jun	11	79	10	-68
Jul	11	78	11	-67
Aug	12	78	10	-66
Sep	12	77	11	-65
Oct	13	76	11	-63
Nov	11	78	11	-67
Dec	10	81	9	-71

Notes: These are answers to the question 'Do you approve or disapprove of the government's record to date?' The data are derived from the 'Gallup 9,000'.
Source: Gallup Political and Economic Index

TABLE 3.7 National and Personal Economic Evaluations 1994

	National Retrospective	National Prospective	Personal Retrospective	Personal Prospective
Jan	-21	0	-29	-12
Feb	-31	-6	-29	-20
Mar	-41	-17	-35	-25
Apr	-43	-22	-35	-30
May	-37	-10	-33	-22
Jun	-36	-10	-29	-16
Jul	-35	-6	-28	-17
Aug	-27	-1	-25	-8
Sep	-23	-3	-26	-12
Oct	-26	-7	-29	-11
Nov	-24	-4	-27	-8
Dec	-38	-20	-34	-22

Notes: The figures are based on answers to the following questions: 'How do you think the general economic situation in the country has changed over the last 12 months?'; 'How do you think the general economic situation in the country will develop over the next 12 months?'; 'How does the financial situation of your household now compare with what it was 12 months ago?'; 'How do you think the financial situation of your household will change over the next 12 months?'.
In each case entries are the percentage of respondents saying things have got/will get worse subtracted from the percentage saying things have got/will get better.
Source: Gallup Political and Economic Index.

4. Local Elections 1994

It would be fair to say that the structure of local government in Britain is currently in chaos. In Scotland and Wales the two-tier structure which has been in existence since 1974 will be replaced by unitary authorities (31 and 22 respectively) in 1996. Members of these new authorities were elected in 1995 and will not come up for re-election until 1999. In England, the London boroughs and metropolitan districts have not so far been subject to review but there have been numerous piecemeal changes in the shire counties as a consequence of the work of the Banham Commission and Government directives.

The 1994 local elections were, therefore, the last to be held under current arrangements. Following the established cycles, there were elections in Scottish Regions, London boroughs, metropolitan districts and shire districts with 'annual' elections. Full details of the results can be found in C. Rallings and M. Thrasher, Local Elections Handbook 1994 (Local Government Chronicle Elections Centre, University of Plymouth) and H. Bochel and D. Denver, Scottish Regional Elections 1994 (Election Studies, University of Dundee).

TABLE 4.1 Summary of 1994 Local Election Results

	Candidates	Seats Won	Gains/ Losses	% Share of Vote
Metropolitan Districts (36)				
Turnout 38.9%				
Con	755	76	-34	22.7
Lab	849	635	-6	51.4
Lib Dem	666	132	+56	22.8
Other	310	7	-16	3.2
London Boroughs (32)				
Turnout 46.0%				
Con	1835	519	-210	31.3
Lab	1917	1044	+152	1.6
Lib Dem	1633	327	+84	22.1
Other	449	27	-26	5.0
'Annual' Shire Districts (118)				
Turnout 42.6%				
Con	1598	263	-196	26.6
Lab	1665	859	-31	39.2
Lib Dem	1460	583	+246	29.7
Other	505	109	-19	4.5
England and Wales				
Turnout 43.4%				
Con	4188	858	-440	26.3
Lab	4431	2538	+115	44.2
Lib Dem	3760	1042	+386	25.3
Other	1263	143	-61	4.2
Scottish Regions (9)				
Turnout 45.6%				
Con	349	31		13.7
Lab	341	220		41.1
Lib Dem	260	60		12.2
SNP	371	73		26.8
Other	201	69		6.2

Note: Gains and losses cannot be calculated for Scottish Regions as the boundaries of electoral divisions were extensively redrawn.

Sources: C. Rallings and M. Thrasher; H. Bochel and D. Denver; D. Cowling, ITN.

TABLE 4.2 Monthly Party Vote Shares in Local Government By-elections 1994 (%)

	Con	Lab	Lib Dem	Oths	N of Wards
Jan	28.6	18.9	51.5	0.9	3
Feb	28.0	28.8	33.9	9.2	14
Mar	33.1	31.9	33.0	1.9	25
Apr	23.9	49.3	24.6	2.2	12
May	20.3	44.4	31.2	4.0	18
Jun	24.6	41.4	30.4	3.6	28
Jul	28.4	44.7	26.5	0.4	13
Aug	41.3	12.1	46.6	-	3
Sep	32.3	35.7	25.1	6.8	29
Oct	27.1	43.2	24.9	4.9	20
Nov	28.2	29.7	37.0	5.1	16
Dec	23.1	50.2	20.8	5.9	17

Note: These figures relate to the results of local government by-elections in wards and electoral divisions contested by all three major parties.

Source: David Cowling, ITN.

TABLE 4.3 Seats Won and Lost in Local Government By-elections 1994

	Con	Lab	Lib Dem	Others
Held	35	75	50	17
Lost	73	14	22	29
Gained	9	53	61	15
Net	-64	+39	+39	-14

Source: David Cowling, ITN.

LOCAL ELECTIONS 1994

TABLE 4.4 Quarterly Party Vote Shares in Local Government By-elections 1994 (%)

	Con	Lab	Lib Dem	Others	Number of wards
Q1	31.3	30.2	34.4	4.0	42
Q2	23.6	42.3	30.5	3.6	58
Q3	31.2	38.2	26.3	4.3	45
Q4	26.2	41.5	27.0	5.2	53

Note: These figures relate to the results of local government by-elections in wards and electoral divisions contested by all three major parties.
Source: David Cowling, ITN.

5. Results of Elections to the European Parliament 1994

The elections were held on June 9th 1994. The electorate is shown in brackets after the constituency name. Women cadidates are indicated by the prefix 'Ms.' and retiring Euro-MPs are asterisked.

1 Bedfordshire & Milton Keynes
(525,524) %

McNally E. Ms.	Lab	94,837	46.6
Currie E. Ms.	Con	61,628	30.3
Howes M. Ms.	Lib Dem	27,994	13.8
Sked A.	UK Ind	7,485	3.7
Francis A.	Green	6,804	3.3
Howes A.	New Brit	3,878	1.9
Sheaff L.	NLP	939	0.5

Turnout 38.7% Maj. 33,209 (16.3%)

2 Birmingham East (521,043)

Crawley C.	Ms.* Lab	90,291	58.2
Turner A.	Con	35,171	22.7
Cane C. Ms.	Lib Dem	19,455	12.6
Simpson P.	Green	6,268	4.0
Cook R.	Soc	1,969	1.3
Brierley M.	NLP	1,885	1.2

Turnout 29.8% Maj. 55,120 (35.6%)

3 Birmingham West (509108)

Tomlinson J.*	Lab	77,957	53.7
Harman D.	Con	38,607	26.6
McGeorge N.	Lib Dem	14,603	10.1
Juby B.	UK Ind	5,237	3.6
Abbott M.	Green	4,367	3.0
Carmichael A.	NF	3,727	2.6
Meads H.	NLP	789	0.5

Turnout 28.5% Maj. 39,350 (27.1%)

4 Bristol (503,669)

White I.*	Lab	90,790	44.1
Stockton Earl Of	Con	60,835	29.6
Barnard J.	Lib Dem	40,394	19.6
Boxall J.	Green	7,163	3.5
Whittingham T.	UK Ind	5,798	2.8
Dyball T.	NLP	876	0.4

Turnout 40.9% Maj. 29,955 (14.6%)

5 Buckinghamshire & Oxfordshire East
(487,692)

Elles J.*	Con	77,037	42.3
Enright D.	Lab	46,372	25.5
Bowles S. Ms.	Lib Dem	42,836	23.5
Roach L.	Green	8,433	4.6
Micklem A. Ms.	Lib	5,111	2.8
Clements G.	NLP	2,156	1.2

Turnout 37.3% Maj. 30,665 (16.9%)

6 Cambridgeshire
(495,383) %

Sturdy R.	Con	66,921	7.6
Johnson M. Ms.	Lab	62,979	35.4
Duff A.	Lib Dem	36,114	20.3
Wright M. Ms.	Green	5,756	3.2
Wiggin P.	Lib	4,051	2.3
Chalmers F.	NLP	2,077	1.2

Turnout 35.9% Maj. 3,942 (2.2%)

7 Cheshire East (502171)

Simpson B.*	Lab	87,586	53.7
Slater P.	Con	48,307	29.6
Harris P.	Lib Dem	20,552	12.6
Wild D.	Green	3,671	2.3
Dixon P.	MRLCP	1,600	1.0
Leadbetter P.	NLP	1,488	0.9

Turnout 32.5% Maj. 39,279 (24.1%)

8 Cheshire West & Wirral (538,571)

Harrison L.*	Lab	106,160	53.6
Senior D.	Con	58,984	29.8
Mottershaw I.	Lib Dem	20,746	10.5
Carson D.	BHR	6,167	3.1
Money M.	Green	5,096	2.6
Wilmot A.	NLP	929	0.5

Turnout 36.8% Maj. 47,176 (23.8%)

9 Cleveland & Richmond (499,580)

Bowe D.*	Lab	103,355	58.7
Goodwill R.	Con	45,787	26.0
Moore B.	Lib Dem	21,574	12.3
Parr G.	Green	4,375	2.5
Scott R.	NLP	1,068	0.6

Turnout 35.3% Maj. 57,568 (32.7)

10 Cornwall & Plymouth West (484,697)

Teverson R.	Lib Dem	91,113	41.9
Beazley C.*	Con	61,615	28.3
Kirk D. Ms.	Lab	42,907	19.7
Garnier P. Ms.	UK Ind	6,466	3.0
Holmes P.	Lib	6,414	3.0
Westbrook K. Ms.	Green	4,372	2.0
Jenkin L.	MK	3,315	1.5
Lyons F.	NLP	921	0.4
Fitzgerald M.	Subsid	606	0.3

Turnout 44.9% Maj. 29,498 (13.6%)

11 **Cotswolds** (497,588)

Plumb Lord*	Con	67,484	34.5
Kingham T. Ms.	Lab	63,216	32.4
Thomson J.	Lib Dem	44,269	22.7
Rendell M.	New Brit	11,044	5.7
McCanlis D.	Green	8,254	4.2
Brighouse H.	NLP	1,151	0.6

Turnout 39.3% Maj. 4,268 (2.2%)

12 **Coventry & Warwickshire North** (523,448)

Oddy C. Ms.*	Lab	89,500	52.6
Crabb J. Ms.	Con	45,599	26.8
Sewards G.	Lib Dem	17,453	10.3
Meacham R.	BIFT	9,432	5.5
Baptie P.	Green	4,36	0.6
Wheway R.	Lib	2,885	1.7
France R.	NLP	1,098	0.6

Turnout 32.5% Maj. 43,901 (25.8%)

13 **Cumbria & Lancashire North** (498,557)

Cunningham T.	Lab	97,599	48.0
Inglewood Lord.*	Con	74,611	36.7
Putnam R.	Lib Dem	24,233	11.9
Frost D.	Green	5,344	2.6
Docker I.	NLP	1,500	0.7

Turnout 40.8% Maj. 22,988 (11.3%)

14 **Devon & Plymouth East** (524,320)

Chichester G.	Con	74,953	31.7
Sanders A.	Lib Dem	74,253	31.4
Gilroy L. Ms.	Lab	47,596	20.1
Morrish D.	Lib	14,621	6.2
Edwards P.	Green	11,172	4.7
Huggett R.	Lit Dem	10,203	4.3
Everard J.	Ind	2,629	1.1
Pringle A.	NLP	908	0.4

Turnout 45.1% Maj. 700 (0.3%)

15 **Dorset & Devon East** (532,936)

Cassidy B.*	Con	81,551	37.2
Goldenberg P.	Lib Dem	79,287	36.2
Gardner A.	Lab	34,856	15.9
Floyd M.	UK Ind	10,548	4.8
Bradbury K. Ms.	Green	8,642	3.9
Mortimer I.	CNF	3,229	1.5
Griffiths M.	NLP	1,048	0.5

Turnout 41.2% Maj. 2,264 (1.0%)

16 **Durham** (532,051)

Hughes S.*	Lab	136,671	72.1
Bradbourn P.	Con	25,033	13.2
Martin N.	Lib Dem	20,935	11.1
Hope S.	Green	5,670	3.0
Adamson C.	NLP	1,198	0.6

Turnout 35.6% Maj. 111,638 (58.9)

17 **Essex North & Suffolk South** (497,098)

McIntosh A. Ms.*	Con	68,311	33.3
Pearson C.	Lab	64,678	31.5
Mole S.	Lib Dem	52,536	25.6
De Chair S.	Ind AES	12,409	6.0
Abbott J.	Green	6,641	3.2
Pullen N.	NLP	884	0.4

Turnout 41.3% Maj. 3,633 (1.8%)

18 **Essex South** (486,588)

Howitt R.	Lab	71,883	44.6
Stanbrook L.	Con	50,516	31.3
Williams G.	Lib Dem	26,132	16.2
Lynch B.	Lib	6,780	4.2
Rumens G.	Green	4,691	2.9
Heath M.	NLP	1,177	0.7

Turnout 33.1% Maj. 21,367 (13.3%)

19 **Essex West & Hertfordshire East** (504,095)

Kerr H.	Lab	66,379	36.2
Rawlings P. Ms.*	Con	63,312	34.5
James G. Ms.	Lib Dem	35,695	19.5
Smalley B.	Ind SB	10,277	5.6
Mawson F. Ms.	Green	5,632	3.1
Carter P.	SACMB	1,127	0.6
Davis L.	NLP	1,026	0.6

Turnout 36.4% Maj. 3,067 (1.7%)

20 **Glasgow** (463,364)

Miller B.	Lab	83,953	52.6
Chalmers T.	SNP	40,795	25.6
Sheridan T.	SML	12,113	7.6
Wilkinson R.	Con	10,888	6.8
Money J.	Lib Dem	7291	4.6
O'Brien P.	Green	2,252	1.4
Fleming J.	Soc	1,125	0.7
Wilkinson M.	NLP	868	0.5
Marsden C.	ICP	381	0.2

Turnout 34.5% Maj. 43,158 (27.0%)

21 **Greater Manchester Central** (481,779)

Newman E.*	Lab	74,935	53.4
Mason S. Ms.	Con	32,490	23.2
Begg J.	Lib Dem	22,988	16.4
Candeland B.	Green	4,952	3.5
Burke P.	Lib	3,862	2.8
Stanley P.	NLP	1,017	0.7

Turnout 20.1% Maj. 42,445 (30.3%)

22 **Greater Manchester East** (501,125)

Ford G.*	Lab	82,289	60.4
Pinniger J.	Con	26,303	19.3
Riley A.	Lib Dem	20,545	15.1
Clarke T.	Green	5,823	4.3
Stevens W.	NLP	1,183	0.9

Turnout 27.2% Maj. 55,986 (41.1%)

23 **Greater Manchester West** (512,618)

Titley G.*	Lab	94,129	61.8
Newns D.	Con	35,494	23.3
Harasiwka F.	Lib Dem	13,650	9.0
Jackson R.	Green	3,950	2.6
Harrison G.	McCarthy	3,693	2.4
Brotheridge T.	NLP	1,316	0.9

Turnout 29.7% Maj. 58,635 (38.5%)

24 **Hampshire North & Oxford** (525,982)

Mather G.	Con	72,209	35.8
Hawkins J. Ms.	Lib Dem	63,015	31.3

Tanner J.　　　Lab　　　48,525　24.1
Wilkinson D.　　UK Ind　　8,377　4.2
Woodin M.　　　Green　　7,310　3.6
Godfrey H.　　　NLP　　1,027　0.5
Boston R.　　　BTP　　1,018　0.5
Turnout 38.3%　Maj. 9,194 (4.6%)

25 Hereford & Shropshire (536,470)
Hallam D.　　　Lab　　　76,120　36.7
Prout C. Sir.*　Con　　　74,270　35.8
Gallagher J.　　Lib Dem　44,130　21.3
Norman F. Ms.　Green　　11,578　5.6
Mercer T.　　　NLP　　1,480　0.7
Turnout 38.7%　Maj. 1,850 (0.9%)

26 Hertfordshire (522,964)
Truscott P.　　Lab　　　81,821　39.1
Jenkinson P.　　Con　　　71,517　34.1
Griffiths D.　　Lib Dem　38,995　18.6
Howitt L. Ms.　Green　　7,741　3.7
Biggs M.　　　New Brit　6,555　3.1
McAuley J.　　NF　　1,755　0.8
Lucas D.　　　NLP　　734　0.4
Laine J.　　　21st Cen　369　0.2
Turnout 40.1%　Maj. 10,304 (4.9%)

27 Highlands & Islands (328,104)
Ewing W. Ms.*　SNP　　74,872　58.4
Macmillan M.　　Lab　　　19,956　15.6
Tennant M.　　Con　　　15,767　12.3
Morrison H.　　Lib Dem　12,919　10.1
Scott E. Ms.　　Green　　3,140　2.5
Carr M. UK　　Ind　　1,096　0.9
Gilmour M. Ms.　NLP　　522　0.4
Turnout 39.1%　Maj. 54,916 (42.8%)

28 Humberside (519,351)
Crampton P.*　Lab　　　87,295　51.9
Stewart D.　　Con　　　46,678　27.8
Wallis D. Ms.　Lib Dem　28,818　17.2
Mummery S. Ms.　Green　　4,170　2.5
Miszewska A. Ms.　NLP　　1,100　0.7
Turnout 32.4%　Maj. 40,617 (24.2%)

29 Itchen Test & Avon (550,406)
Kellett-Bowman E.*Con　81,456　35.4
Barron T.　　　Lib Dem　74,553　32.4
Read E.　　　Lab　　　52,416　22.8
Farage N.　　　UK Ind　12,423　5.4
Hulbert F. Ms.　Green　　7,998　3.5
Miller-Smith A.　NLP　　1,368　0.6
Turnout 41.8%　Maj. 6,903 (3.0%)

30 Kent East (499,662)
Watts M.　　　Lab　　　69,641　34.6
Jackson C.*　　Con　　　69,006　34.2
Macdonald J.　　Lib Dem　44,549　22.1
Bullen C.　　　UK Ind　9,414　4.7
Dawe S.　　　Green　　7,196　3.6
Beckley C.　　NLP　　1,746　0.9
Turnout 40.3%　Maj. 635 (0.3%)

31 Kent West (505,374)
Skinner P.　　　Lab　　　77,346　41.0
Patterson B.*　Con　　　60,569　32.1
Daly J.　　　Lib Dem　33,869　17.9
Mackinlay C.　　UK Ind　9,750　5.2
Kemp P. Ms.　　Green　　5,651　3.0
Bowler J.　　　NLP　　1,598　0.9
Turnout 37.3%　Maj. 16,777 (8.9%)

32 Lancashire Central (504,514)
Hendrick M.　　Lab　　　73,420　42.4
Welsh M.*　　Con　　　61,229　35.4
Ross-Mills J. Ms.　Lib Dem　25,778　14.9
Hill D.　　　BHR　　6,751　3.9
Maile C.　　　Green　　4,169　2.4
Ayliffe J. Ms.　NLP　　1,727　1.0
Turnout 33.2%　Maj. 12,191 (7.0%)

33 Lancashire South (514,840)
Hindley M.*　　Lab　　　92,598　54.3
Topham R.　　Con　　　51,194　30.0
Ault J.　　　Lib Dem　17,008　10.0
Gaffney J.　　　Green　　4,774　2.8
Rokas E. Ms.　Ind　　3,439　2.0
Renwick J.　　NLP　　1,605　0.9
Turnout 33.1%　Maj. 41,404 (24.3%)

34 Leeds (521,989)
McGowan M.*　Lab　　　89,160　56.9
Carmichael N.　Con　　　36,078　23.0
Harvey J., Ms.　Lib Dem　17,575　11.2
Meadowcroft M.　Lib　　6,617　4.2
Nash C. Ms.　　Green　　6,283　4.0
Hayward S. Ms.　NLP　　1,018　0.7
Turnout 30.0%　Maj. 53,082 (33.9%)

35 Leicester (515,343)
Waddington S. Ms. Lab　87,048　4.9
Marshall A.　　Con　　　66,764　34.4
Jones M.　　　Lib Dem　28,890　14.9
Forse G.　　　Green　　8,941　4.6
Saunders P. Ms.　NLP　　2,283　1.2
Turnout 37.6%　Maj. 20,284 (10.5%)

36 Lincolnshire & Humberside South (539,981)
Hardstaff V. Ms.　Lab　　83,172　42.4
Newton Dunn W.*Con　69,427　35.4
Melton K.　　　Lib Dem　27,241　13.9
Robinson R. Ms.　Green　　8,563　4.4
Wheeler E.　　Lib　　3,434　1.8
Selby I.　　　NAC　　2,973　1.5
Kelly H.　　　NLP　　1,429　0.7
Turnout 36.3%　Maj. 13,745 (7.0%)

37 London Central (494,610)
Newens S.*　　Lab　　　75,711　47.0
Elliott A.　　　Con　　　50,652　31.4
Ludford S. Ms.　Lib Dem　20,176　12.5
Kortvelyessy N. Ms.　Green　7,043　4.4
Le Fanu H.　　UK Ind　4,157　2.6
Slapper C.　　Soc　　1,593　1.0
Hamza S. Ms.　NLP　　1,215　0.8
Weiss G.　　　Rainbow　547　0.3

Turnout 32.6% Maj. 25,059 (15.6%)

38 London East (511,523)

Tongue C. Ms.*	Lab	98,759	57.8
Taylor V. Ms.	Con	41,370	24.2
Montgomery K.	Lib Dem	15,546	9.1
Batten G.	UK Ind	5,974	3.5
Baguley J.	Green	4,337	2.5
Tillett O.	TWP	3,484	2.0
Kahn N.	NLP	1,272	0.7

Turnout 33.4% Maj. 57,389 (33.6%)

39 London North (541,269)

Green P. Ms.*	Lab	102,059	55.5
Keegan M.	Con	53,711	29.2
Mann I.	Lib Dem	15,739	8.6
Jago H. Ms.	Green	5,666	3.1
Booth I.	UK Ind	5,099	2.8
Fabrizi G.	EPP	880	0.5
Hinde J.	NLP	856	0.5

Turnout 34.0% Maj. 48,348 (26.3%)

40 London North East (486,016)

Lomas A.*	Lab	80,226	62.1
Gordon S.	Con	23,179	17.9
Appiah K.	Lib Dem	10,242	7.9
Lambert J. Ms.	Green	8,386	6.5
Murat E.	Lib	2,573	2.0
Compobassi P.	UK Ind	2,015	1.6
Archer R.	NLP	1,111	0.9
Fischer M.	CPGB	869	0.7
Hyland A.	ICP	679	0.5

Turnout 26.6% Maj. 57,047 (44.1%)

41 London North West (481,272)

Evans R.	Lab	80,192	47.4
Bethell Lord.*	Con	62,750	37.1
Leighter H. Ms.	Lib Dem	18,998	11.2
Johnson D.	Green	4,743	2.8
Murphy A. Ms.	CPGB	858	0.5
Sullivan T. Ms.	NLP	807	0.5
Palmer C.	21st Cen	740	0.4

Turnout 35.1% Maj. 17,442 (10.3%)

42 London South & Surrey East (486,358)

Moorhouse J.*	Con	64,813	38.8
Rolles G. Ms.	Lab	56,074	33.5
Reinisch M.	Lib Dem	32,059	19.2
Cornford J.	Green	7,046	4.2
Major J.	MRL	3,339	2.0
Reeve A.	RCP	2,983	1.8
Levy P.	NLP	887	0.5

Turnout 34.4% Maj. 8,739 (5.2%)

43 London South East (493,178)

Spiers S.	Lab	71,505	41.0
Price P.*	Con	63,483	36.4
Fryer J.	Lib Dem	25,271	14.5
Mouland I.	Green	6,399	3.7
Almond R.	Lib	3,881	2.2
Lowne K.	NF	2,926	1.7
Small J.	NLP	1,025	0.6

Turnout 35.4% Maj. 8,022 (4.6%)

44 London South Inner (510,609)

Balfe R.*	Lab	85,079	61.0
Boff A.	Con	25,859	18.6
Graves A.	Lib Dem	20,708	14.9
Collins S.	Green	6,570	4.7
Leighton M.	NLP	1,179	0.9

Turnout 27.3% Maj. 59,220 (42.5%)

45 London South West (479,246)

Pollack A. Ms.*	Lab	81,850	49.7
Treleaven P.	Con	50,875	30.9
Blanchard G.	Lib Dem	18,697	11.4
Walsh T.	Green	5,460	3.3
Scholefield A.	UK Ind	4,912	3.0
Hopewell C.	RCP	1,840	1.1
Simson M.	NLP	625	0.4
Quanjar J.	SEP	377	0.2

Turnout 34.4% Maj. 30,975 (18.8%)

46 London West (505,791)

Elliott M.*	Lab	94,562	51.9
Guy R.	Con	52,287	28.7
Mallinson W.	Lib Dem	21,561	11.8
Bradley J.	Green	6,134	3.4
Roberts G.	UK Ind	4,583	2.5
Binding W.	NF	1,963	1.1
Johnson R.	NLP	1,105	0.6

Turnout 36.0% Maj. 42,275 (23.2%)

47 Lothians (522,363)

Martin D.*	Lab	90,531	44.9
Brown K.	SNP	53,324	26.5
McNally P.	Con	33,526	16.6
Campbell H. Ms.	Lib Dem	17,883	8.9
Harper R.	Green	5,149	2.6
McGregor J.	Soc	637	0.3
Siebert M.	NLP	500	0.3

Turnout 38.7% Maj. 37,207 (18.5%)

48 Merseyside East & Wigan (518,196)

Wynn T.*	Lab	91,986	72.0
Manson C.	Con	17,899	14.0
Clucas F. Ms.	Lib Dem	8,874	6.9
Melia J.	Lib	4,765	3.7
Brown L.	Green	3,280	2.6
Hatchard G.	NLP	1,009	0.8

Turnout 24.7% Maj. 74,087 (58.0%)

49 Merseyside West (515,909)

Stewart K.*	Lab	78,819	58.4
Varley C.	Con	27,008	20.0
Bamber D.	Lib Dem	19,097	14.1
Radford S.	Lib	4,714	3.5
Lever L. Ms.	Green	4,573	3.4
Collins J.	NLP	852	0.6

Turnout 26.2% Maj. 51,811 (38.4%)

50 Midlands West (533,742)

Murphy S.*	Lab	99,242	59.5
Simpson M.	Con	44,419	26.6
Baldauf-Good G.	Lib Dem	12,195	7.3
Hyde M.	Lib	5,050	3.0
Mattingly C.	Green	4,390	2.6

Oldbury J.	NLP	1,641	1.0

Turnout 31.3% Maj. 54,823 (32.8%)

51 Norfolk (513,553)

Needle C.	Lab	102,760	45.2
Howell P.*	Con	76,424	33.6
Burall P.	Lib Dem	39,107	17.2
Holmes A.	Green	7,938	3.5
Parsons B.	NLP	1,075	0.5

Turnout 44.3% Maj. 26,336 (11.6%)

52 Northamptonshire & Blaby (524,916)

Billingham A. Ms.	Lab	95,317	46.1
Simpson A.*	Con	69,232	33.5
Scudder K.	Lib Dem	27,616	13.4
Bryant A. Ms.	Green	9,121	4.4
Whittaker I.	Ind	4,397	2.1
Spivack B.	NLP	972	0.5

Turnout 39.4% Maj. 26,085 (12.6%)

53 Northumbria (516,680)

Adam G.	Lab	103,087	59.3
Flack J.	Con	36,929	21.2
Opik L.	Lib Dem	20,195	11.6
Lott D.	UK Ind	7,210	4.2
Hartshorne J.	Green	5,714	3.3
Walch L.	NLP	740	0.4

Turnout 33.7% Maj. 66,158 (38.1%)

54 Nottingham & Leicestershire North West (507,915)

Read M. Ms.*	Lab	95,344	49.8
Brandon-Bravo M.	Con	55,676	29.1
Wood A.	Lib Dem	23,836	12.5
Blount S. Ms.	Green	7,035	3.7
Downes J.	UK Ind	5,849	3.1
Walton P.	Ind OE	2,710	1.4
Christou J. Ms.	NLP	927	0.5

Turnout 33.7% Maj. 39,668 (20.7%)

55 Nottinghamshire North & Chesterfield (490,330)

Coates K.*	Lab	114,353	63.1
Hazell D.	Con	38,093	21.0
Pearce S. Ms.	Lib Dem	21,936	12.1
Jones G.	Green	5,159	2.9
Lincoln S. Ms.	NLP	1,632	0.9

Turnout 37.0% Maj. 76,260 (42.1%)

56 Peak District (511,357)

McCarthy A. Ms.	Lab	105,853	53.1
Fletcher R.	Con	56,546	28.3
Barber S. Ms.	Lib Dem	29,979	15.0
Shipley M.	Green	5,598	2.8
Collins D.	NLP	1,533	0.8

Turnout 39.0% Maj. 49,307 (24.7%)

57 Scotland Mid & Fife (546,060)

Falconer A.*	Lab	95,667	45.8
Douglas D.	SNP	64,254	30.8
Page P.	Con	28,192	13.5
Lyall H. Ms.	Lib Dem	17,192	8.2
Johnston M.	Green	3,015	1.4

Pringle T.	NLP	532	0.3

Turnout 38.3% Maj. 31,413 (15.0%)

58 Scotland North East (573,799)

Macartney A.	SNP	92,890	42.8
McCubbin H.*	Lab	61,665	28.4
Harris R.	Con	40,372	18.6
Horner S.	Lib Dem	18,008	8.3
Farnsworth K.	Green	2,569	1.2
Ward M. Ms.	CPGB	689	0.3
Mair L.	NEEPS	584	0.3
Paterson D.	NLP	371	0.2

Turnout 37.7% Maj. 31,225 (14.4%)

59 Scotland South (500,643)

Smith A.*	Lab	90,750	45.2
Hutton A.	Con	45,595	22.7
Creech C. Ms.	SNP	45,032	22.4
Millar D.	Lib Dem	13,363	6.7
Hein J.	Lib	3,249	1.6
Hendry L. Ms.	Green	2,429	1.2
Gay G.	NLP	539	0.3

Turnout 40.1% Maj. 45,155 (22.5%)

60 Sheffield (476,530)

Barton R.*	Lab	76,397	58.3
Anginotti S. Ms.	Lib Dem	26,109	19.9
Twitchen K. Ms.	Con	22,374	17.1
New B.	Green	4,742	3.6
England M.	Comm	834	0.6
Hurford R.	NLP	577	0.4

Turnout 27.5% Maj. 50,288 (38.4%)

61 Somerset & Devon North (515,696)

Watson G.	Lib Dem	106,218	43.6
Daly M. Ms.*	Con	83,678	34.3
Pilgrim J.	Lab	34,540	14.2
Taylor D.	Green	10,870	4.5
Livings G.	New Brit	7,165	2.9
Lucas M.	NLP	1,200	0.5

Turnout 47.1% Maj. 22,540 (9.3%)

62 South West Downs (486,793)

Provan J.	Con	83,813	43.7
Walsh J.	Lib Dem	62,746	32.7
Armstrong L. Ms.	Lab	32,344	16.8
Paine E.	Green	7,703	4.0
Weights B.	Lib	3,630	1.9
Kember P.	NLP	1,794	0.9

Turnout 39.5% Maj. 21,067 (11.0%)

63 South Wales Central (477,182)

David W.*	Lab	115,396	61.4
Verity L. Ms.	Con	29,314	15.6
Llywelyn G.	PC	18,857	10.0
Dixon J.	Lib Dem	18,417	9.8
Von Ruhland C.	Green	4,002	2.1
Griffiths R.	CPGB	1,073	0.6
Duguay G.	NLP	889	0.5

Turnout 39.4% Maj. 86,082 (45.8%)

64 South Wales East (454,794)

Kinnock G. Ms.	Lab	144,907	74.0

Blomfield-			
Smith R. Ms.	Con	24,660	12.6
Woolgrove C.	Lib Dem	9,963	5.1
Mann C.	PC	9,550	4.9
Coghill R.	Green	4,509	2.3
Williams S. Ms.	Welsh Soc	1,270	0.7
Brussatis R.	NLP	1,027	0.5

Turnout 43.1% Maj. 120,247 (61.4%)

65 South Wales West (395,131)

Morris D.*	Lab	104,263	66.1
Buckland R.	Con	19,293	12.2
Bushell J.	Lib Dem	15,499	9.8
Adams C. Ms.	PC	12,364	7.8
Evans J. Ms.	Green	4,114	2.6
Evans H. Ms.	NLP	1,112	0.7
Beany C.	Beanus	1,106	0.7

Turnout 39.9% Maj. 84,970 (53.9%)

66 Staffordshire East & Derby (518,799)

Whitehead P.	Lab	102,393	55.6
Evans J. Ms.	Con	50,197	27.3
Brass D. Ms.	Lib Dem	17,469	9.5
Crompton I.	UK Ind	6,993	3.8
Clarke R.	Green	4,272	2.3
Jones R.	NF	2,098	1.1
Grice D. Ms.	NLP	793	0.4

Turnout 31.6% Maj. 52,196 (28.3%)

67 Staffordshire West & Congleton (502,395)

Tappin M.	Lab	84,337	53.1
Brown A.	Con	44,060	27.8
Stevens J.	Lib Dem	24,430	15.4
Hoppe D.	Green	4,533	2.9
Lines D.	NLP	1,403	0.9

Turnout 31.6% Maj. 40,277 (25.4%)

68 Strathclyde East (492,618)

Collins K.*	Lab	106,476	58.0
Hamilton I.	SNP	54,136	29.5
Cooklin B.	Con	13,915	7.6
Stewart B.	Lib Dem	6,383	3.5
Whitelaw A.	Green	1,874	1.0
Gilmour D.	NLP	787	0.4

Turnout 37.3% Maj. 52,340 (28.5%)

69 Strathclyde West (489,129)

McMahon H.*	Lab	86,957	44.4
Campbell C.	SNP	61,934	31.6
Godfrey J.	Con	28,414	14.5
Herbison D.	Lib Dem	14,772	7.5
Allan K. Ms.	Green	2,886	1.5
Gilmour S. Ms.	NLP	918	0.5

Turnout 40.1% Maj. 25,023 (12.8%)

70 Suffolk & Norfolk South West (477,688)

Thomas D.	Lab	74,304	40.5
Turner A.*	Con	61,769	33.7
Atkins R.	Lib Dem	37,975	20.7
Slade T.	Green	7,760	4.2
Kaplan E.	NLP	1,530	0.8

Turnout 38.4% Maj. 12,535 (6.8%)

71 Surrey (514,130)

Spencer T.*	Con	83,405	43.3
Thomas S. Ms.	Lib Dem	56,387	29.2
Wolf F. Ms.	Lab	30,894	16.0
Porter S. Ms.	UK Ind	7,717	4.0
Charlton H.	Green	7,198	3.7
Walker J.	Ind BIE	4,627	2.4
Thomas J. Ms.	NLP	2,638	1.4

Turnout 37.5% Maj. 27,018 (14.0%)

72 Sussex East & Kent South (513,550)

Stewart-Clark J. Sir.*Con		83,141	38.6
Bellotti D.	Lib Dem	76,929	35.8
Palmer N.	Lab	35,273	16.4
Burgess A.	UK Ind	9,058	4.2
Addison R. Ms.	Green	7,439	3.5
Williamson T. Ms.	Lib	2,558	1.2
Cragg P.	NLP	765	0.4

Turnout 41.9% Maj. 6,212 (2.9%)

73 Sussex South & Crawley (492,784)

Donelly B.	Con	62,860	33.9
Edmond Smith J. Ms. Lab		61,114	33.0
Williams J.	Lib Dem	41,410	22.3
Beever P. Ms.	Green	9,348	5.0
Horner D.	Ind Scept	7,106	3.8
Furness N.	AFC	2,618	1.4
Hankey A.	NLP	901	0.5

Turnout 37.6% Maj. 1,746 (0.9%)

74 Thames Valley (543,685)

Stevens J.*	Con	70,485	37.3
Howarth J.	Lab	69,727	36.9
Bathurst N.	Lib Dem	33,187	17.5
Unsworth P.	Green	6,120	3.2
Clark J.	Lib	5,381	2.8
Owen P.	MRL	2,859	1.5
Grenville M.	NLP	758	0.8

Turnout 34.8% Maj. 758 (0.4%)

75 Tyne & Wear (516,436)

Donnelly A.*	Lab	107,604	74.4
Liddell-Grainger I. Con		19,224	13.3
Maughan P.	Lib Dem	8,706	6.0
Edwards G.	Green	4,375	3.0
Lundgren W. Ms.	Lib	4,164	2.9
Fisken A.	NLP	650	0.5

Turnout 28.0% Maj. 88,380 (61.1%)

76 Wales Mid & West (401,529)

Morgan E. Ms.	Lab	78,092	40.5
Phillips M.	PC	48,858	25.4
Bone P.	Con	31,606	16.4
Hughes J. Ms.	Lib Dem	23,719	12.3
Rowlands D.	UK Ind	5,536	2.9
Busby C.	Green	3,938	2.0
Griffiths-Jones T.	NLP	988	0.5

Turnout 48.0% Maj. 29,234 (15.2%)

77 Wales North (475,829)

Wilson J.*	Lab	88,091	40.8
Wigley D.	PC	72,849	33.8
Hughes G.	Con	33,450	15.5

Parry R. Ms.	Lib Dem	14,828	6.9
Adams P.	Green	2,850	1.3
Hughes D.	NLP	2,065	1.0
Cooksey M.	Ind	1,623	0.8

Turnout 45.3% Maj. 15,242 (7.1%)

78 Wight & Hampshire South (488,398)

Perry R.	Con	63,306	34.9
Hancock M.	Lib Dem	58,205	32.1
Fry S. Ms.	Lab	40,442	22.3
Browne J.	Ind	12,140	6.7
Fuller P.	Green	6,697	3.7
Treend W.	NLP	722	0.4

Turnout 37.2% Maj. 5,101 (2.8%)

79 Wiltshire North & Bath (496,591)

Jackson C. Ms.*	Con	71,872	34.9
Matthew J. Ms.	Lib Dem	63,085	30.6
Norris J. Ms.	Lab	50,489	24.5
Cullen P.	Lib	6,760	3.3
Davidson M.	Green	5,974	2.9
Hedges T.	UK Ind	5,843	2.8
Cooke D.	NLP	1148	0.6
Day J.	CPP	725	0.4

Turnout 41.5% Maj. 8,787 (4.3%)

80 Worcestershire & Warwickshire South (551,162)

Corrie J.	Con	73,573	35.2
Gschaider G. Ms.	Lab	72,369	34.6
Larner P.	Lib Dem	44,168	21.1
Alty J. Ms.	Green	9,273	4.4
Hards C.	Nat Ind	8,447	4.0
Brewster J.	NLP	1,510	0.7

Turnout 38.0% Maj. 1,204 (0.6%)

81 Yorkshire North (475,686)

McMillan-Scott E.*	Con	70,036	38.0
Regan B.	Lab	62,964	4.2
Pitts M.	Lib Dem	43,171	23.5
Richardson D.	Green	7,036	3.8
Withers S.	NLP	891	0.5

Turnout 38.7% Maj. 7,072 (3.8%)

82 Yorkshire South (523,401)

West N.*	Lab	109,004	72.7
Howard J.	Con	20,685	13.8

Roderick C. Ms.	Lib Dem	11,798	7.9
Davies P.	UK Ind	3,948	2.6
Waters J.	Green	3,775	2.5
Broome N.	NLP	681	0.5

Turnout 28.6% Maj. 88,319 (58.9%)

83 Yorkshire South West (547,469)

Megahy T.*	Lab	94,025	59.2
Adamson C. Ms.	Con	34,463	21.7
Ridgway D.	Lib Dem	21,595	13.6
Cooper A.	Green	7,163	4.5
Mead G.	NLP	1,674	1.1

Turnout 29.0% Maj. 59,562 (37.5%)

84 Yorkshire West (490,745)

Seal B.*	Lab	90,652	53.4
Booth R.	Con	42,455	25.0
Bidwell C.	Lib Dem	20,452	12.1
Pearson R.	New Brit	8,027	4.7
Harris C.	Green	7,154	4.2
Whitley D.	NLP	894	0.5

Turnout 34.6% Maj. 48,197 (28.4%)

85 Northern Ireland (1,150,304)

Paisley I.*	DUP	163,246	29.2
Hume J.*	SDLP	161,992	28.9
Nicholson J.*	UUUP	133,459	23.8
Clark-Glass M. Ms.	Alliance	23,157	4.1
Hartley T.	SF	21,273	3.8
McGuinnes D. Ms.	SF	17,195	3.0
Molloy F.	SF	16,747	3.0
Ross H.	Ulst Ind	7,858	1.4
Boal M. Ms.	Con	5,583	1.0
Lowry J.	WP	2,543	0.5
Cusack N.	Ind Lab	2,464	0.4
Anderson J.	NLP	1,418	0.3
Campion J. Ms.	Peace	1,088	0.2
Kerr D.	Ind Ulst	571	0.1
Thompson S. Ms.	NLP	454	0.1
Kennedy M.	NLP	419	0.1
Mooney R.	NI Ind	400	0.1

Turnout 48.7%

(Note: these are first preference votes. Three candidates were elected under STV.)

Summary Statistics

England			Scotland		
Electorate	36,170,925		Electorate	3,916,080	
Turnout	35.5%		Turnout	38.2%	
Conservative	3,913,547	30.5	Conservative	216,669	14.5
Labour	5,179,403	40.3	Labour	635,955	42.5
Liberal Democrat	2,367,650	18.4	Liberal Democrat	107,811	7.2
Green	451,834	3.5	SNP	487,237	32.6
Other	934,313	7.3	Green	23,314	1.6
			Other	24,911	1.7

Wales			Great Britain		
Electorate	2,204,465		Electorate	42,291,470	
Turnout	43.1%		Turnout	36.2%	
Conservative	138,323	14.6	Conservative	4,268,539	27.9
Labour	530,749	55.9	Labour	6,753,881	44.2
Liberal Democrat	82,426	8.7	Liberal Democrat	2,557,887	16.7
Plaid Cymru	162,478	17.1	Plaid Cymru	162,478	1.1
Green	19,413	2.0	SNP	487,237	3.2
Other	16,689	1.8	Green	494,561	3.2
			Other	568,139	3.7

Party Labels and Candidate Descriptions

21st Cen	21st Century Party	MK	Mebyon Kernow
AFC	Anti-Federalist Conservative	MRL	Monster Raving Loony
Alliance	Alliance Party	MRLCP	Monster Raving Loony Christian
Beanus	Eurobean From the Planet Beanus		Party
BHR	British Home Rule	NAC	Network Against CSA
BIFT	British Independence & Free Trade	Nat Ind	National Independence
BTP	Boston Tea Party	NEEPS	North East Ethnic Party
CNF	Conservative Non-Federal	New Brit	New Britain
Comm	Communist	NF	National Front
Con	Conservative	NI Ind	Independence for N. Ireland
CPGB	Communist Party of Great Britain	NLP	Natural Law Party
CPP	Christian Peoples Party	PC	Plaid Cymru
DUP	Democratic Unionist Party	Peace	Peace Coalition
EPP	European Peoples Party	Rainbow	Rainbow Connection Party
Green	Green	RCP	Restoration of Capital Punishment
ICP	International Communist Party	SACMM	Sportsman Anti Common Market
Ind	Independent		Bureaucracy
Ind AES	Independent Anti Euro Super-State	SDLP	Social Democratic and Labour Party
Ind BIE	Independent Britain in Europe	SEP	Spirit of Europe Party
Ind Lab	Independent Labour	SF	Sinn Fein
Ind OE	Independent Out of Europe	SML	Scottish Militant Labour
Ind SB	Independent for a Sovereign	SNP	Scottish National Party
	Britain	Soc	Socialist
Ind Scept	Independent Euro Sceptic	Subsid	Subsidiarity
Ind Ulst	Independent Ulster	TWP	Third Way Party
Lab	Labour	UK Ind	UK Independence Party
Lib	Liberal	Ulst Ind	Independence for Ulster
Lib Dem	Liberal Democrat	UUUP	United Ulster Unionist Party
Lit Dem	Literal Democrat	Welsh Soc	Welsh Socialist
McCarthy	McCarthy	WP	Workers Party

6. Recent Books and Articles of Interest

BRITISH ELECTIONS

Books

Denver, D., Elections and Voting Behaviour in Britain (second edition), Harvester Wheatsheaf, 1994.

Heath, A., R. Jowell, and J. Curtice with Bridget Taylor (eds.), Labour's Last Chance? The 1992 Election and Beyond, Dartmouth, 1994.

Linton, M., Money and Votes, Institute for Public Policy Research, 1994

Journal Articles

Field, W. H., 'Electoral Volatility and the Structure of Competition: A Reassessment of Voting Patterns in Britain, 1959-92', West European Politics, 17:4, October 1994, pp. 149-165.

Franklin, M., R. Niemi and G. Whitten, 'The Two Faces of Tactical Voting', British Journal of Political Science, 24:4, October 1994, pp. 549-57.

Nadeau, R., R. Niemi and T. Amato,' Expectations and Preferences in British General Elections', American Political Science Review, 88:2, June 1994, pp.371-383.

Norris, P. and I. Crewe, 'Did the British Marginals Vanish? Proportionality and Exaggeration in the British Electoral System', Electoral Studies, 13:3, September 1994, pp. 201-221.

Nadeau, R. and M. Mendelson, 'Short-Term Popularity Boosts Following Leadership Change in Great Britain', Electoral Studies, 13:3, September 1994, pp. 222-228.

Pattie, C., E. Fieldhouse and R. Johnston, 'The Price of Conscience: The Electoral Correlates and Consequences of Free Votes and Rebellions in the British House of Commons, 1987-92', British Journal of Political Science, 24:3, July 1994, pp. 359-80.

Rallings, C., and M. Thrasher, 'The Parliamentary Boundary Commissions: Rules, Interpretations and Politics', Parliamentary Affairs, 47:3, July 1994, pp. 387-404.

Sharp, S. A. 'A Statistical Study of Selective Candidate Withdrawal in a British General Election', Electoral Studies, 13:2, June 1994, pp. 122-131.

Tether, P., 'The Overseas Vote in British Politics 1982-1992', Parliamentary Affairs, 47:1, January 1994, pp. 73-93.

BRITISH PARTIES

Books

Margetts, H. and G. Smyth (eds.) Turning Japanese? Britain with a Permanent Party of Government, Lawrence and Wishart, 1994.

Norris, P. and J Lovenduski, Political Recruitment, Cambridge University Press, 1994

Robins, L., H. Blackmore and R. Pyper, Britain's Changing Party System, Leicester University Press, 1994.

Shaw, E., The Labour Party Since 1979: Crisis and Transformation, Routledge, 1994.

Whiteley, P., P. Seyd and J. Richardson, True Blues: The Politics of Conservative Party Membership, Clarendon Press, 1994.

Journal Articles

Alderman, K., and N. Carter, 'The Labour Party and the Trade Unions: Loosening the Ties?', Parliamentary Affairs, 47:3, July 1994, pp. 321-37.

Baker, D., A. Gamble and S. Ludlam, 'The Parliamentary Siege of Maastricht 1993: Conservative Divisions and British Ratification', Parliamentary Affairs, 47:1, January 1994, pp. 37-60.

Barbrook, A. T., 'Atlantic Crossing: Campaign Finance in Britain and the USA', Parliamentary Affairs, 47:3, July 1994, pp. 434-45.

Brand, J., J. Mitchell and P. Surridge, 'Social Constituency and Ideological Profile: Scottish Nationalism in the 1990s', Political Studies, 42:4, December 1994, pp. 616-29.

Denver, D. and H. Bochel, 'Merger or Bust: Whatever Happened to Members of the SDP?', British Journal of Political Science, 24:3, July 1994, pp. 403-17.

Fisher, J., 'Political Donations to the Conservative Party', Parliamentary Affairs, 47:1, January 1994, pp. 61-72.

Fisher, J., 'Why Do Companies make Donations to Political Parties?', Political Studies, 42:4, December 1994, pp. 690-99.

Hay, C., 'Labour's Thatcherite Revisionism: Playing the Politics of "Catch-Up"', Political Studies, 42:4, December 1994, pp. 700-7.

Lovenduski, J and P. Norris, 'Labour and the Unions: After the Brighton Conference', Government and Opposition, 29:2, Spring 1994, pp. 201-217.

Pattie, C., P. Whiteley, R. Johnston and P. Seyd, 'Measuring Local Campaign Effects: Labour Party Constituency Campaigning at the 1987 General Election', Political Studies, 42:3, September 1994, pp. 469-79.

Whiteley, P., P. Seyd, J. Richardson and P. Bissell, 'Explaining Party Activism: The Case of the British Conservative Party', British Journal of Political Science, 24:1, January 1994, pp. 79-94.

Whiteley, P., P. Seyd. J. Richardson and P. Bissell, 'Thatcherism and the Conservative Party', Political Studies, 42:2, June 1994, pp. 185-203.

PUBLIC OPINION

Books

Jowell, R. et al. British Social Attitudes: The 10th Report, Dartmouth, 1994.

OTHER

Butler, D., A. Adonis and T. Travers, Failure in British Government: The Politics of the Poll Tax, Oxford University Press, 1994.

Butler, D. and G. Butler (eds.), British Political Facts 1900-94, St. Martin's Press, 1994 (7th edition).

Cockett, R., Thinking the Unthinkable: Think-Tanks and the Economic Counter-Revolution 1931-1983, Harper-Collins, 1994.

Franklin, R., Packaging Politics: Political Communications in Britain's Media Democracy, Edward Arnold, 1994.

Negrine, R., Politics and the Mass Media in Britain, Routledge, 1994 (2nd edition).

Parliamentary Affairs, 47:4, October 1994. British Government and Politics Since 1945: Changes in Perspective.

Richardson, J., 'Doing Less by Doing More: British Government 1979-1983', West European Politics, 17:3, July 1994, pp. 178-197.

Searing, D., Westminster's World: Understanding Political Roles, Harvard University Press, 1994.

7. Political Parties

THE CONSERVATIVE PARTY

Main Addresses

Conservative and Unionist Central
Office
32 Smith Square
Westminster
London SW1P 3HH
Tel: 0171-222-9000
Fax: 0171-222-1135

Scottish Conservative and Unionist
Central Office
Suite 1/1
14 Links Place
Edinburgh EH6 7EZ
Tel: 0131-555-2900
Fax: 0131-555-2869

Other Addresses

Conservative Research Department
32 Smith Square
Westminster
London SW1P 3HH
Tel: 0171-222-9000
Fax: 0171-233-2065
Director: Andrew Lansley (until Oct.
1995)
Deputy Directors: Alistair Cooke,
Julian Lewis

Conservative Political Centre
32 Smith Square
Westminster
London SW1P 3HH
Tel: 0171-222-9000
Fax: 0171-233-2065
Director: Alistair Cooke

National Union of Conservative and
Unionist Associations
32 Smith Square
Westminster
London SW1P 3HH
Tel: 0171-222-9000
Fax: 0171-222-1135

Small Business Bureau Limited
Curzon House
Church Road
Windlesham
Surrey GU20 6BH
Tel: 01276-453020
Fax: 01276-451602
Managing Director: Alan Cleverly

One Nation Forum
32 Smith Square
Westminster
London SW1P 3HH
Tel: 0171-222-9000
Fax: 0171-222-1135
Chairman: Sir Geoffrey Pattie
Secretary: Tom Peet

National Union Advisory Committees
Conservative Women's National
Committee
Chairman: Joyce Anelay
Secretary: Mary Shaw

Young Conservatives' National
Advisory Committee
Chairman: Adrian Lee

Conservative Trade Unionists' National
Committee
Chairman: Arthur Newell

National Local Government Advisory
Committee
Chairman: Elgar Jenkins
Secretary: David Trowbridge

Association of Conservative Clubs
Chairman: Sir Marcus Fox
Secretary: Ken Hargreaves

Officers

Party Chairman	Brian Mawhinney
Deputy Chairmen	Michael Trend
Vice Chairmen	Dame Angela Rumbold (Candidates)
	Graham Bright (Campaigns)
	Charles Hendry (Communications)
	Eric Pickles (Local government)
	Baroness Seccombe (Women)
Chairman of the Scottish Party	Sir Michael Hirst

Board of Treasurers
Lord Hambro (Chairman)
Sir Philip Harris (Deputy Chairman)
Sir Malcolm Chaplin
William Highes
David Davies
Sir Nigel Mobbs

Board of Management Brian Mawhinney
Dame Angela Rumbold
Paul Judge (Director-General, Conservative Central Office)
Sir Malcolm Chaplin (Party Treasurer)
Sir Basil Feldman (Chairman of the National Union)
Sir Marcus Fox (Chairman of the 1922 Committee)
Tom Spencer (Leader of British Section of the European People's Party)
Lord Sheppard (Chairman, Grand Metropolitan plc)
Sir Peter Bowness (Leader of Conservative Group on the Association of Metropolitan Authorities)
David Kelly (President of the National Union)
Dame Hazel Byford (Senior Vice-President of the National Union)
Tony Garrett (Chief Agent and Secretary to the Board)

Staff

Director-General	Paul Judge
Directors:	
Research	Andrew Lansley (until Oct. 1995)
Communications	Hugh Culver
Campaigning	Tony Garrett
Finance/Administration	Martin Saunders
Treasurer's	Jeffrey Speed
Deputy Directors:	
Research Department	Alistair Cooke, Julian Lewis
Departmental Heads	
Local Government	David Trowbridge
Speakers	Penny Brook
International Office	Richard Normington
Conservatives Abroad	David Smith
News	Vanessa Ford
Training	Geoffrey Harper
Election unit	John Earl
Legal	Paul Gribble

Regional Directors

		Telephone
London and Eastern	Tim Cowell	0171-2229000
Yorkshire & North East	Peter Smith	01532-450731
North West	Ron Bell	0161-7971231
Midlands	Rachael Dyche	01455-239556
Southern	David Simpson	01932-866477
Western	Bill Henderson	01392-58231
Wales	Martin Perry	01222-616031
Scotland	Roger Pratt	0131-5552900

THE LABOUR PARTY

Address
The Labour Party
John Smith House
150 Walworth Road
London SE17 1JT
Tel: 0171-701-1234
Fax: 0171-234-3300

Regional Secretaries

Northern & Yorkshire	Andrew Sharp	01924-291221
North West	Eileen Murfin	01925-574913
Central	Roy Maddox	0115-9462195
West Midlands	Fiona Gordon	0121-553-6601
South East	George Catchpole	01473-255668
Greater London	Terry Ashton	0171-490-4904
South West	Graham Manuel	0117-9298018
Wales	Anita Gale	01222-398567
Scotland	Jack McConnell	0141-332-8946

Officers and Staff

Leader	Tony Blair
Deputy Leader	John Prescott
General Secretary	Tom Sawyer
European Coordinator	Larry Whitty
Chief Party Spokesperson	David Hill
Election Campaigning	Joy Johnson
Organization and Development	Peter Coleman
Policy	Roland Wales
Finance	Paul Blagborough
Parliamentary Labour Party Secretary	Alan Haworth
Labour Party News	Virginia Gibbons
Computers	Roger Hough
Women's Officer	Deborah Lincoln
Youth Officer	Tom Watson
Senior Development Officer	Nick Smith

National Executive Committee 1994-1995

Chair	Gordon Colling
Vice-Chair	Diane Jeuda
Treasurer	Tom Burlison (GMB)
Ex Officio Members	Tony Blair, John Prescott

Division 1 - Trade Unions

Vernon Hince	(RMT)
Gordon Colling	(GPMU)
Tom Sawyer	(Unison)
Dan Duffy	(TGWU)
Nigel Harris	(AEU)
Richard Rosser	(TSSA)
David Ward	(NCU - ENG)
Bill Connor	(USDAW)
Derek Hodgson	(UCW)
Diana Holland	(TGWU)
Margaret Wall	(MSF)
Maggie Jones	(Unison)

Division 2 - Socialist, Co-operative and Other Organizations

John Evans	(National Union of Labour and Social Clubs)

Division 3 - Constituency Labour Parties

Diane Abbott	(Hackney N. & Stoke Newington)
David Blunkett	(Sheffield Brightside)
Gordon Brown	(Dunfermline East)
Robin Cook	(Livingston)
Harriet Harman	(Peckham)
Dennis Skinner	(Bolsover)
Jack Straw	(Blackburn)

Division 4 - Women Members

Margaret Beckett	(Derby South CLP)
Brenda Etchells	(AEU)
Diana Jeuda	(USDAW)
Joan Lestor	(Eccles CLP)
Clare Short	(Birmingham Ladywood CLP)

Youth Representative
Catherine Taylor

Result of Elections to National Executive Committee 1994-5
Names asterisked were elected. Figures for 1993 in the trade union section are shown in brackets if applicable. The basis of voting in the CLP and women's sections was altered in 1994.

Treasurer
*Tom Burlison   Unopposed

Trade Unions

*Dan Duffy	4,002,000	(4,594,000)
*Vernon Hince	3,985,000	(4,484,000)
*Gordon Colling	3,929,000	(4,184,000)
*Diana Holland	3,922,000	
*Bill Connor	3,896,000	(4,588,000)
*Margaret Wall	3,889,000	
*Derek Hodgson	3,858,000	(4,417,000)
*Nigel Harris	3,827,000	(4,123,000)
*Richard Rosser	3,209,000	(3,966,000)
*David Ward	3,088,000	(4,439,000)
*Tom Sawyer	3,079,000	(4,527,000)
*Maggie Jones	2,319,000	
Helen McGrath	1,717,000	
Arthur Scargill	1,068,000	
Charles Kelly	956,000	
Dennis Nash	92,000	

Socialist, Co-operative and Other Organizations

*John Evans	25,000	(44,000)
Joanna Tait	9,000	
Marianne Hood	3,000	

Constituency Labour Parties

*Robin Cook	83,923	Tam Dalyell	28,433
*David Blunkett	80,150	Alice Mahon	26,668
*Gordon Brown	76,753	Chris Smith	24,964
*Harriet Harman	67,355	Jeremy Corbyn	16,418
*Dennis Skinner	59,237	Phyllis Starkey	15,522
*Jack Straw	50,850	Alan Simpson	8,724
*Diane Abbott	36,539	Clive Soley	7,721
Ken Livingstone	47,960	George Stevenson	5,313
Marjorie Mowlam	35,045	John Spellar	5,261
Dawn Primarolo	33,377	Terry King	5,177
Peter Hain	29,573		

Women Members   (%)

		*Clare Short	16.72
* Margaret Beckett	18.77	*Brenda Etchells	14.05
*Joan Lestor	17.79	Hilary Armstrong	10.03
*Diana Jeuda	16.88	Maggie Cosin	2.2

Labour Leadership Election (July 1994)

	MPs/ MEPs %	Party Members %	TU Members %	Total %
Leadership				
Tony Blair	60.5	58.2	52.3	57.0
John Prescott	19.6	24.4	28.4	24.1
Margaret Beckett	19.9	17.4	19.3	18.9
Deputy Leadership				
John Prescott	53.7	59.4	56.6	56.5
Margaret Beckett	46.3	40.6	43.4	43.5

THE LIBERAL DEMOCRATS

Addresses

The Liberal Democrats
Party Headquarters
4 Cowley Street
London SW1P 3NB
Tel: 0171-222-7999
Fax: 0171-799-2170

Scottish Liberal Democrats
4 Clifton Terrace
Edinburgh EH12 5DR
Tel: 0131-337-2314
Fax: 0131-337-3556

Welsh Liberal Democrats
57 St Mary Street
Cardiff CF1 1FE
Tel: 01222-382210
Fax: 01222-222864

Associated Organizations

Association of Liberal Democrat
Councillors
President: Tim Razzall
Chair: Bill Le Bretton
Tel: 01422-843785
Fax: 01422-843036

Association of Liberal Democrat Trade
Unionists
President: Tudor Gates
Chair: Andrew Hudson
Tel: 0181-451-1138

Youth and Student Liberal Democrats
National Chair: Philip Jones
Tel: 0171-222-7999 ext. 587

Women Liberal Democrats
President: Hilary Campbell
Chair: Lindsay Granshaw
Tel: 0171-222-7999 ext. 408

Liberal International (British Group)
President: Sir David Steel

Federation of European Liberal
Democrat and Reform Parties
97 Rue Belliard
1047 Brussels
Belgium
Tel: (00)-322-284-2207
Fax: (00)-322-231-1907
President: Willy de Clerq
Secretary-General: Christian Ehlers

Regional Contacts

Chilterns	Dave Hodgson	01908-503001
Devon and Cornwall	Terry Tonkin	01803-842246
East Midlands	Richard Lustig	0116-2543833
Eastern	Nina Stimson	01223-460795
Hampshire and Isle of Wight	Gerald Vernon-Jackson	01256-478799
London	Jonathon Davies	0171-2220134
Northern	Philip Appleby	01388-601341
North West	Viv Bingham	0161-2365799
South East	Dave Manning	01273-202300
West Midlands	Jim Gosling	01384-872296
Western	Gill Pardy	01983-70983
Yorkshire and Humberside	Andrew Meadowcroft	01709-816601

Party Officers

Party Leader	Paddy Ashdown
President	Robert Maclennan
Vice-Presidents	Andrew Duff (England)
	Marilyne MacLaren (Scotland)
	Rev. Roger Roberts (Wales)
Chair of Finance	Tim Clement-Jones
Treasurer	Tim Razzall

Scottish Party

Leader	Jim Wallace
President	Roy Thomson
Convenor	Marilyne Maclaren
Chief Executive	Andy Myles

Welsh Party

Leader	Alex Carlile
President	Martin Thomas
Administrator	Judi Lewis

Federal Party Staff

General Secretary	Graham Elson
Press Officer	Elizabeth Johnson
Campaigns and Elections Director	Chris Rennard
Campaign Officers	Paul Rainger, Candy Piercy, Melab Owain, Derek Barrie, Willie Rennie, David Loxton, Paul Schofield
Candidates Officers	Sandra Dunk, Garry White
Policy Director	Neil Stockley
Policy Officers	David Cloves, Iain King, Wyn Evans, Candida Goulden
International Officer	Kishwer Khan
Finance Controller	Ken Loughlin
Head of Membership Services	Keith House
Membership Finance Co-Ordinator	Helen Sharman
Conference Organizer	Penny McCormack
Agents' Officer	Paul Bensilum
Liberal Democrat News Editor	David Boyle

Periodicals

Liberal Democrat News	Weekly party newspaper
Liberator	Eight times a year, independent forum for debate

OTHER PARTIES

Scottish National Party (SNP)
6 North Charlotte Street
Edinburgh EH2 4JH
Tel: 0131-226-3661
Fax: 0131-226-7373
President Winifred Ewing
National Convenor Alex Salmond
Parliamentary Leader Margaret Ewing
National Secretary Alasdair Morgan
Director of Organisation Alison Hunter
Communications and Research Keith Pringle

Plaid Cymru (PC)
51 Cathedral Road
Cardiff CF1 9HD
Tel: 01222-231944
Fax: 01222-222506
President Dafydd Wigley
General Secretary Karl Davies

Green Party
10 Station Parade
Balham High Road
London SW12 9AZ
Tel: 0181-673-0045
Fax: 0181-675-4434

The Liberal Party
Gayfere House
22 Gayfere Street
London SW1P 3HP
Tel: 0171-233-2124
Fax: 01704-539315

Democratic Left
6 Cynthia Street
London N1 9JF
Tel: 0171-278-4443
Fax: 0171-278-4425
Federal Secretary Nina Temple

Northern Ireland

Ulster Unionist Council
3 Glengall Street
Belfast BT12 5AE
Tel: 01232-324601
Fax: 01232-246738
Leader James Molyneaux
Party Chairman Jim Nicholson
Party Secretary Jim Wilson

Ulster Democratic Unionist Party
91 Dundela Avenue
Belfast BT4 3BU
Tel: 01232-471155
Fax: 01232-471797
Leader Ian Paisley
Deputy Leader Peter Robinson
Party Chairman James McClure
Secretary Nigel Dodds
Press Officer Samuel Wilson

Social Democratic and Labour Party
(SDLP)
Cranmore House
611c Lisburn Road
Belfast BT9 7GT
Tel: 01232-668100
Fax: 01232-669009
Leader John Hume
Deputy Leader Seamus Mallon
Party Chairman Mark Durkan
Party Administrator Gerry Cosgrove

Sinn Fein
44 Cearnog Pharnell (Parnell Square)
Dublin 1
Republic of Ireland
Tel: (00) 872-6100/872-8932
Fax: (00) 873-3411
Belfast Office
51-55 Falls Road
Belfast BT12
Tel: (01232) 230261
Uachtaran Gerry Adams
Leas-Uachtaran Pat Doherty
Ard Runai Lucilita Bhreatnach
Cathaoirleach Tom Hartley
Oifigeach Phoibliochta Rita O'Hare

Alliance Party
88 University Street
Belfast BT7 1HE
Tel: 01232-324274
Fax: 01232-333147
Leader John Alderdice
Party Chairman Dr Philip McGarry
General Secretary David Ford
President Jim Hendron

8 Politics Journals

American Journal of Political Science
Journals Division
University of Wisconsin Press
114 North Murray Street
Madison, Wisconsin
WI 53715, USA
Editor: Kenneth J. Meier (University of
Wisconsin, Milwaukee)

American Political Science Review
American Political Science Association
1527 New Hampshire Avenue N.W.
Washington D.C. 20036, USA
Managing Editor:
G. Bingham Powell, Jr. (University of
Rochester)

Australian Journal of Political Science
Department of Political Science
University of Melbourne
Victoria 3067
Australia
Editors:
John Dryzek and Brian Galligan

British Journal of Political Science
Cambridge University Press
The Edinburgh Building
Shaftesbury Road
Cambridge CB2 2RU, UK
Editors: David Sanders and Albert
Weale (University of Essex)

Canadian Journal of Political Science
Canadian Political Science Association
Suite 205
1 Stewart Street
Ottawa
Ontario K1N 6H7, Canada
Co-editors: Richard Vernon (University
of Western Ontario) and Guy Laforest
(Laval University, Quebec)
Administrative Editor:
John McMenemy (Wilfrid Laurier
University)

Comparative Political Studies
Sage Publications Limited
6 Bonhill Street
London EC2A 4PU, UK
Editor: James A. Caporaso (University
of Washington)

Comparative Politics
Subscription Fulfillment Office
Boyd Printing Co. Inc.
49 Sheridan Avenue, PO Box 1413
Albany NY 12201-1413, USA
Editor-in-Chief: Dankwart A. Rustow
(City University of New York)

Democratization
Frank Cass and Co. Limited
Newbury House
890-900 Eastern Avenue
Newbury Park
Ilford, Essex, IG2 7HH, UK
Editors: Peter Burnell and Ian Campbell
(University of Warwick)

Electoral Studies
Elsevier Science Limited
Applied Social Science Division
The Boulevard
Langford Lane
Kidlington
Oxford OX5 1GB, UK
Editors: Bo Sarlvik (University of
Goteborg, Sweden), Iain McLean
(Nuffield College, Oxford) and Harold
Clarke (University of North Texas)

Environmental Politics
Frank Cass and Co. Limited
Newbury House
890-900 Eastern Avenue
Newbury Park
Ilford, Essex, IG2 7HH, UK
Editors: Stephen C. Young (University
of Manchester) and Michael Waller
(University of Keele)

European Journal of Political Research
Kluwer Academic Publishers Group
PO Box 322
3300 AH Dordrecht
The Netherlands
Editors: Michael Laver (Trinity
College, Dublin, Ireland) and Peter Mair
(University of Leiden, the Netherlands)
Annual Review Editor: John Coakley
(University College, Dublin, Ireland)
Political Data Yearbook Editors: Ruud
Koole and Peter Mair (University of
Leiden, the Netherlands)

German Politics
Frank Cass and Co. Limited
Newbury House
890-900 Eastern Avenue
Newbury Park
Ilford, Essex
IG2 7HH, UK
Editors: Eva Kolinsky (University of
Keele), Stephen Padgett (University of
Liverpool), William Paterson
(University of Birmingham) and Gordon
Smith (London School of Economics
and Political Science)

Government and Opposition
London School of Economics and
Political Science
Houghton Street
London WC2A 2AE, UK
Editors: Ghita Ionescu, Isabel de
Madariaga, Ernest Gellner and Geraint
Parry

*International Journal of Public Opinion
Research*
Journals Subscriptions Department
Oxford University Press
Walton Street
Oxford OX2 6DP, UK
Editors: Seymour Martin Lipset
(Stanford University), Elisabeth Noelle-
Neumann (Institut fur Demoskopie,
Allensbach) and Robert Worcester
(MORI)

International Political Science Review
Elsevier Science Limited
Applied Social Science Division
The Boulevard
Langford Lane
Kidlington
Oxford OX5 1GB, UK
Editors: Nazli Chouri (Massachussetts
Institute of Technology, USA), John
Meisel (Queen's University, Kingston,
Canada) and Jean Laponce (University
of British Columbia, Vancouver,
Canada)

Journal of Common Market Studies
Blackwell Publishers
108 Cowley Road
Oxford OX4 1JF, UK
Editors: Simon Bulmer (University of
Manchester) and Drew Scott (University
of Edinburgh)

*Journal of Commonwealth and
Comparative Politics*
Frank Cass and Co. Limited
Newbury House
890-900 Eastern Avenue
Newbury Park
Ilford, Essex
IG2 7HH, UK
Editors: David Potter (Open University)
and Arnold Hughes (University of
Birmingham)

Journal of European Public Policy
Routledge Journals
ITPS Limited
Cheriton House
North Way
Andover SP10 5BE
Editors: Jeremy Richardson (University
of Essex) and Robert Lindley
(University of Warwick)

Journal of Legislative Studies
Frank Cass
Newbury House
890-900 Eastern Avenue
Newbury Park
Ilford, Essex
IG2 7HH, UK
Editor:
Philip Norton (University of Hull)

Journal of Politics
Journals Department
University of Texas Press
2100 Comal
Austin, Texas 78722-2550, USA
Editors: Jon R. Bond and Edward B.
Portis (Texas A and M University)

Journal of Regional and Federal Studies
Frank Cass and Co. Limited
Newbury House
890-900 Eastern Avenue
Newbury Park
Ilford, Essex
IG2 7HH, UK
Editors: Sean Loughlin (University of
Wales, Cardiff), Paul Hainsworth
(University of Ulster, Jordanstown),
Michael Keating (University of Western
Ontario, Canada) and Charlie Jeffery
(University of Birmingham)

Journal of Theoretical Politics
Sage Publications Limited
6 Bonhill Street
London EC2A 4PU, UK
Editors: Richard Kimber (University of
Keele), Jan-Erik Lane (University of
Oslo) and Elinor Ostrom (Indiana
University)

Legislative Studies Quarterly
Comparative Legislative Research Center
349 Schaeffer Hall
University of Iowa
Iowa City, Iowa 52242, USA
Editors: Wayne L. Francis (University
of Florida), Gerhard Loewenberg
(University of Iowa) and John R.
Hibbing (University of Nebraska)

Parliamentary Affairs
Journals Subscription Department
Oxford University Press
Walton Street
Oxford OX2 6DP, UK
Editor: F.F. Ridley (University of
Liverpool)

Party Politics
Sage Publications Limited
6 Bonhill Street
London EC2A 4PU, UK
Editors: David M. Farrell, Ian Holliday
(University of Manchester) and Kenneth
Janda (Northwestern University)

Political Behavior
Plenum Publishing Corporation
233 Spring Street
New York NY 10013, USA
Editor: Richard A. Brody (Stanford
University)

Political Geography
Elsevier Science Limited
Applied Social Science Division
The Boulevard
Langford Lane
Kidlington
Oxford OX5 1GB, UK
Editor: Peter J. Taylor (Department of
Geography, University of Newcastle-
upon-Tyne)

Political Quarterly
Blackwell Publishers
108 Cowley Road
Oxford OX4 1JF, UK
Editors: Colin Crouch and David
Marquand

Political Research Quarterly
252 Orson Spencer Hall
University of Utah
Salt Lake City
Utah 84112, USA
Editor: Walter J. Stone (University of
Colorado at Boulder)

Political Science
Business Manager
Informations and Publications Section
Victoria University
P.O. Box 600
Wellington
New Zealand
Editors: Paul Harris and Stephen
Levine (Victoria University of
Wellington, New Zealand)

Political Science Quarterly
Academy of Political Science
475 Riverside Drive
Suite 1274
New York NY 10115-1274, USA
Editor: Demetrios Caraley (Barnard
College, Columbia University)

Political Studies
Journals Department
Blackwell Publishers
108 Cowley Road
Oxford   OX4 1JF, UK
Editor: Michael Moran (University of
Manchester)

Politics
Journals Department
Blackwell Publishers
108 Cowley Road
Oxford   OX4 1JF, UK
Editors: Gary Browning (Oxford
Brookes University) and Ben Rosamond
(University of Warwick)

Politics Review
Philip Allan Publishers,
Market Place,
Deddington,
Oxfordshire OX15 0SE
Editor: John Benyon (University of
Leicester)

Public Choice
Kluwer Academic Publishers Group
P. O. Box 322
3300 AH Dordrecht
The Netherlands
Editors: Charles K. Rowley and Robert
D. Tollison (George Mason University,
Virginia, USA)

Public Opinion Quarterly
Journals Fulfillment Department
University of Chicago Press
PO Box 37005
Chicago, Illinois
IL 60637, USA
Editor: Stanley Presser

Res Publica
Politologisch Institut Vzw
E. van Evenstraat 2B
B-3000 Leuven, Belgium
Editor: Kris Deschouwer (Vrije
Universiteit Brussel)

Revue Française de Science Politique
Presses de la Fondation Nationale des
Sciences Politiques
44 Rue du Four
75006 Paris, France
Directeur: Jean-Luc Parodi

Scandinavian Political Studies
Scandinavian University Press,
PO Box 2959,
Toyen,
N-0608 Oslo, Norway
Editors: Sten Berglund and Goran
Djupsund (Abo Academy)

Talking Politics
Politics Association,
Studio 16,
Mex Business Park,
Hamilton Road,
Longsight
Manchester M13 0PD
Editor: Lynton Robins (De Montford
University, Leicester)

West European Politics
Frank Cass and Co. Limited
Newbury House
890-900 Eastern Avenue
Newbury Park
Ilford, Essex
IG2 7HH, UK
Editors: Gordon Smith (London School
of Economics and Political Science) and
Vincent Wright (Nuffield College,
Oxford)

World Politics
The Johns Hopkins University Press
Journals Publishing Division
2715 N. Charles Street
Baltimore MD 21218-4319, USA
Editorial Board Chairman: John
Waterbury